KU-187-731

Coláiste Oideachais Mhuire Gan Smal
Luimneach

METHUEN · ENGLISH · TEXTS

GENERAL EDITOR · JOHN DRAKAKIS

ANDREW MARVELL

Selected Poetry and Prose

METHUEN · ENGLISH · TEXTS
GENERAL EDITOR · JOHN DRAKAKIS

JOHN CLARE: *Selected Poetry and Prose* ed. Merryn and Raymond Williams
JOSEPH CONRAD: *Selected Literary Criticism and The Shadow-Line* ed. Allan Ingram
JOHN DONNE: *Selected Poetry and Prose* ed. T. W. and R. J. Craik
ANDREW MARVELL: *Selected Poetry and Prose* ed. Robert Wilcher

Forthcoming

William Blake	*Selected Poetry and Prose* ed. David Punter
Emily Brontë	*Wuthering Heights* ed. Heather Glen
Charles Dickens	*Hard Times* ed. Terry Eagleton
George Eliot	*The Mill on The Floss* ed. Sally Shuttleworth
Henry Fielding	*Joseph Andrews* ed. Stephen Copley
Ben Jonson	*The Alchemist* ed. Peter Bement
Christopher Marlowe	*Dr Faustus* ed. John Drakakis
Wilfred Owen	*Selected Poetry and Prose* ed. Jennifer Breen
Alexander Pope	*Selected Poetry and Prose* ed. Robin Sowerby
Mary Shelley	*Frankenstein* ed. Patrick Lyons
Percy Bysshe Shelley	*Selected Poetry and Prose* ed. Alasdair Macrae
Edmund Spenser	*The Faerie Queene Book 1 and Selected Poems* ed. Elizabeth Watson
Alfred, Lord Tennyson	*Selected Poetry and Prose* ed. Peter King
William Wordsworth	*Selected Poetry* ed. Philip Hobsbaum
W. B. Yeats	*Selected Poetry and Prose* ed. Graham Martin

ANDREW MARVELL

Selected Poetry and Prose

Edited by Robert Wilcher

METHUEN · LONDON AND NEW YORK

First published in 1986 by
Methuen & Co. Ltd
11 New Fetter Lane,
London EC4P 4EE

Published in the USA by
Methuen & Co.
in association with Methuen, Inc.
29 West 35th Street,
New York NY 10001

Typeset in Great Britain by
Scarborough Typesetting Services
and printed by
Richard Clay, The Chaucer Press
Bungay, Suffolk

British Library Cataloguing in Publication Data

Marvell, Andrew
Selected poetry and prose. – (Methuen English texts)
I. Title II. Wilcher, Robert
828'.409 PR3546.A6

ISBN 0 416 40230 5

Library of Congress Cataloging in Publication Data

Marvell, Andrew, 1621–1678.
Selected poetry and prose.
(Methuen English texts)
Bibliography: p.
I. Wilcher, Robert, 1942– . II. Title.
III. Series.
PR3546.A6 1986 821'.4
86–12578

ISBN 0 416 40230 5

To my mother

Contents

Acknowledgements

In preparing this selection from Marvell's works, I have been principally indebted to the researches of that distinguished line of scholars whose editions are listed at the end of the Introduction. I owe a more personal debt of gratitude to Mrs E. E. Duncan-Jones for her valuable advice on the notes to the extracts from Marvell's prose, to Dr B. S. Benedikz of the Rare Book Room in the University of Birmingham Library for assistance with a number of ecclesiastical conundrums, and to John Drakakis for his encouragement and practical counsel.

R.W.
Birmingham
November 1985

Introduction

THE TIMES AND THE MAN

Andrew Marvell was twenty-one years old when the royal standard was raised at Nottingham on 22 August 1642 and the armed conflict between Charles I and Parliament began. He had been dead only a few days when, in the autumn of 1678, England was shaken by Titus Oates's spurious revelation of a Roman Catholic conspiracy to assassinate Charles II and place his brother James on the throne. The intervening decades had witnessed fundamental and far-reaching changes in the political, religious and intellectual fabric of English life, and among the many rewards of studying the writings Marvell left behind are the insights they afford into the experience of living through a turbulent and decisive period of history. For although his career fell into two distinct phases, during the first of which – according to his own account – he had 'not the remotest relation to public matters',[1] there could be no escaping the moral and psychological pressures exerted by an age of revolution and counter-revolution in church and state. In such an age, personal and political allegiances may pull in opposite directions, comfortably theoretical debates may crystallize into unavoidable and harshly practical choices, and choices made in response to a particular set of circumstances may be overtaken and challenged by the rapid advance of events and ideas into uncharted territory. And since some of Marvell's poems locate themselves at precise historical moments, and many of them gain in significance if they are read in the context of unpredictable and disorientating change, his own life and work can be profitably approached by way of the drama that was playing itself out on the great stage of public affairs while he was still a young man and a private citizen.

When the members of the Short and Long Parliaments assembled in 1640, they were largely united in their desire for ecclesiastical reform and in their grievances against Charles I's conduct of the country's financial and political business during the eleven years since the last parliament had been dissolved in 1629. William Laud, who as Bishop of London and Archbishop of Canterbury had seemed to many to be steering the English church back towards the doctrines and practices of Roman Catholicism, was removed to the Tower to await his fate; the Earl of Strafford, Charles's chief political adviser, was impeached and executed in the spring of 1641; bills were passed providing for regular parliaments in future and setting constraints upon the king's power to raise money without parliamentary grant. But this early unanimity was soon put under strain by the more radical programme which was being urged by the Puritan majority in the Commons. Many who wanted the Laudian influence in the Church of England reversed and the power of the bishops curbed were not prepared to countenance such extreme measures as the replacement of the episcopacy itself by committees of laymen and the rewriting of the Book of Common Prayer advocated in the Root and Branch Bill; and the serious threat to the royal prerogative evident in the more revolutionary items in the Grand Remonstrance drawn up by John Pym and his allies drove moderates like Lord Falkland and Edward Hyde (the future Earl of Clarendon) into opposition. These growing disagreements were eventually to be fought out on the battlefields of the Civil War.

Further divisions opened up within the ranks of the reformers themselves as the situation continued to unfold over the next few years. Champions of religious toleration, like the poet John Milton who had contributed vigorously to the pamphleteering campaign against what he had called 'the pomp of Prelatism'[2] in the early 1640s, discovered that the transition from an episcopal to a Presbyterian system of church government had simply substituted one brand of authoritarianism for another – or as Milton phrased it in a bitter epigram of 1646, '*New Presbyter* is but *Old Priest* writ large'.[3] By 1647, when the royalist forces had been defeated and the king was in the hands of Parliament, the victorious New Model Army found itself at odds with a House of Commons in which Presbyterians were in the ascendancy. Many of the high-ranking officers, among them Oliver Cromwell and his son-in-law Henry Ireton, were Independents who supported the ideal of freedom of conscience in religious matters, but it became clear in the course of the momentous debates held in Putney Parish Church at the end of October that on wider issues of policy they had little sympathy with the radical faction in the army. In particular, spokesmen for the Leveller movement, which had been pressing for widespread democratic and egalitarian reforms, threw down a challenge to traditional assumptions concerning economic and political privilege. After listening to Ireton's stubborn defence of the principle that only those with 'a permanent fixed interest in this kingdom' had a right to be represented in its government, Colonel Thomas Rainborough was moved to an exasperated conclusion: 'Sir, I see that it is impossible to have liberty but all property must be taken away.'[4] During the outbreak of armed hostilities in the Second Civil War of 1648, the unforeseen consequences of the reforming zeal that had inspired the early days of the Long Parliament were bitterly lamented in a Leveller pamphlet: 'To be short, all the quarrel we have at this day in the Kingdom, is no other than a quarrel of Interests, and Parties, a pulling down of one Tyrant, to set up another, and instead of Liberty, heaping upon ourselves a greater slavery than that we fought against.'[5]

Many who had gone along with each new development in the process of stripping the monarchy of its traditional powers were reluctant to take the final step that Cromwell had come to acknowledge as politically inevitable by the end of 1648. On 5 December, the House of Commons was purged of those members who were in favour of an accommodation with the king; on 1 January 1649, the Lords refused to support a proposal to set up a High Court of Justice to try Charles; and on 4 January, the remaining members of the Long Parliament – the Rump – declared that they alone were the supreme power in England, and the trial went ahead. Charles I was executed on 30 January. Thomas Lord Fairfax, the commander-in-chief of the parliamentary forces, held aloof from this climactic series of events, and although he acted with Oliver Cromwell to suppress a Leveller mutiny in the army in May 1649, he drew the line at undertaking a pre-emptive strike against Scotland in the following year and resigned his command. The Rump Parliament became increasingly corrupt and unpopular, and in 1653 Fairfax's successor, Cromwell, dismissed it and replaced it with an assembly of godly men nominated by himself and his fellow officers. When this proved ineffectual and refractory, a new constitution was drawn up which vested ultimate political authority in the person of Cromwell as the Lord Protector. In spite of his subsequent efforts to rule through elected parliaments, the country was effectively under a military dictatorship until he died in 1658.

Very little is known about Andrew Marvell's activities and affiliations during the revolutionary period. External facts are few and far between and the attitudes expressed in poems that can be dated to the 1640s and early 1650s are open to conflicting interpretations. Born at Winestead in Yorkshire on 31 March 1621, he had spent his childhood in Hull, where his father was Master of the Charterhouse and a lecturer in Holy Trinity Church from 1624 till his death by drowning in 1641. He was a student at Trinity College, Cambridge, between 1633 and 1641, when he left without completing his MA degree. Some time between the summer of 1642 and the autumn of 1647, he spent four years travelling through Holland, France, Italy and Spain. In the late 1640s he was back in London, and poems written at this time – among them the commendatory verses on Richard Lovelace's *Lucasta* – have been taken to indicate that he was mixing in royalist circles. His ideological position in 1650 is clouded by the apparently contradictory tendencies of his ode on Cromwell's return from Ireland and his satire on the death of Tom May. Serious political involvement with the royal cause seems unlikely, however, since by early 1651 he had been engaged by the former general of the parliamentary armies, Lord Fairfax, to teach languages to his daughter Mary. Marvell remained with the Fairfaxes at Nun Appleton in Yorkshire until the beginning of 1653, when he applied unsuccessfully for a government post and was offered instead the position of private tutor to William Dutton, a protégé of Oliver Cromwell. In this capacity, he lived for some time at Eton in the house of the Reverend John Oxenbridge (see the letter written to Cromwell from there on pp. 174–5), and later accompanied his young charge to the Protestant academy at Saumur in France. During these years he addressed a long panegyric to his eminent employer, 'The first anniversary of the government under His Highness the Lord Protector', which was presumably finished in time for the occasion it celebrated in December 1654, and composed some verses 'On the victory obtained by Blake over the Spaniards' during the summer of 1657, in which he also contrived to express admiration for Cromwell. In September, perhaps in recognition of these marks of his loyalty to the Commonwealth, he was appointed Latin secretary in the office of John Thurloe, who was secretary to the Council of State. The private phase of Marvell's life as student, traveller and tutor was over and he had entered the service of his country.

His career as a civil servant was cut short by the restoration of the monarchy in May 1660, but by then he was representing his native city of Hull in the House of Commons, having been elected first in January 1659 to the Parliament of Richard Cromwell, to whom the Protectorship had passed after the death of his father, and again in April 1660 to the Convention Parliament which recalled Charles II from exile. He was elected for a third time to the Cavalier Parliament in May 1661, in which he continued to sit as Member for Hull until his death on 16 August 1678.

That Marvell was a conscientious constituency MP can be gathered from the long series of letters he sent to the Hull Corporation about proceedings in the House and other matters of political and commercial interest in the capital. Beginning in November 1660 with news of legislation to disband the standing army and remove the garrison from Hull, these regular reports (nearly 300 in all) continued until a month or so before he died, when he communicated the result of a debate that took place on 6 July 1678 concerning the duty levied on the importation and exportation of wines. Throughout his time at Westminster, he also corresponded with the Trinity House Corporation, the chief authority of the port of Hull, about such maritime business as the erection of a lighthouse at Spurn Head. Politically, he began his parliamentary career as a supporter of the restored monarch's attempt to foster reconciliation among antagonistic religious factions, acting as teller for the ayes when the House voted on a bill that would have implemented Charles II's promise of indulgence to those who found themselves unable to conform to the re-established Church of England. The bill was defeated, and subsequently a series of measures were passed which prevented Nonconformists from holding public office and led to the expulsion of some 2000 dissenting clergy from their benefices.

Marvell was abroad on a diplomatic mission to Russia and Scandinavia between July 1663 and January 1665, acting as secretary to the Earl of Carlisle. He returned to find England engaged in a naval conflict with Holland over trading rivalry, and he later took a vigorous part in the parliamentary and literary campaign against the administration's mismanagement of the war, which culminated in the dismissal of the Lord Chancellor, the Earl of Clarendon, in the autumn of 1667. From his activities in the House of Commons and from the verse satires that began to circulate at this time (though not everything attributed to his pen was authentic), it is evident that Marvell had been drawn into the embryonic opposition that was taking shape in Parliament; and in the course of the ensuing decade he was to establish himself in the public mind as a champion of democratic and religious freedoms.

During March 1668, he contributed to the thwarting of a move to renew the Conventicles Act, which forbade any communal worship not in accordance with the practice of the Church of England; and two years later, he was apprising his nephew of another 'terrible Bill against Conventicles', which seemed to him to be 'the quintessence of arbitrary malice', but which he feared 'must probably pass, being the price of money'.[6] More than once, he expressed a sense of hopelessness and personal impotence when he surveyed the political scene. In the spring of 1670, he confided the opinion that 'the King was never since his coming in, nay, all things considered, no king since the Conquest, so absolutely powerful at home, as he is at present. Nor any parliament, or places, so certainly and constantly supplied with men of the same temper'; and he added despondently, 'In such a conjuncture, dear Will, what probability is there of my doing anything to the purpose?'[7] Writing to a friend in the East in August of the next year, he introduced an account of recent manoeuvres at Westminster and in Europe with the remark, 'I address myself, which is all I am good for, to be your Gazettier', and went on to complain that 'we truckle to France in all things, and to the prejudice of our alliance and honour'.[8] Whatever hopes may have been engendered by the overthrow of Clarendon and the formation of a triple alliance uniting the Protestant powers of England, Holland and Sweden in 1668 had been subverted by Charles II's clandestine negotiations with Louis XIV in 1670 and the concerted Anglo-French attack on the Dutch by land and sea in 1672. During the war that followed, it seems likely that Marvell was associated with a fifth-column organization operating out of The Hague, which aimed at detaching England from its new confederacy with the Catholic French.[9]

At about the same time, he was stung into literary activity by an Anglican divine, Samuel Parker, who had been promoting intolerance against Nonconformists in a number of inflammatory treatises. *The Rehearsal Transpros'd*, which appeared anonymously in 1672, drew a scurrilous *Reproof* from Parker, and as Marvell prepared to answer it in the form of a 'second part', he explained to a like-minded colleague in Parliament that he felt himself compelled against his natural inclination to enter the arena of public controversy: 'I am (if I may say it with reverence) drawn in, I hope by a good Providence, to intermeddle in a noble and high argument which therefore by how much it is above my capacity I shall use the more industry not to disparage it.'[10] In spite of his diffidence, it was Marvell's venture into prose polemic and satire that earned him his contemporary reputation as 'the liveliest droll of the age, who writ in a burlesque strain, but with so peculiar and entertaining a conduct, that from the king down to the tradesman his book was read with great pleasure'.[11] A 'mock speech from the throne' and several verse satires on the king and his chief minister, the Earl of Danby, dating from the mid-1670s, have been ascribed to him, and in 1676 he returned to the defence of religious toleration against the Anglican hierarchy in a pamphlet entitled *Mr Smirke: Or, the Divine in Mode*. On 27 March 1677, he made the last of his rare contributions to parliamentary debate in a long speech against a measure that he believed would strengthen the already excessive authority of the bishops; and at the end of the year, he published the last of his major prose works, *An Account of the Growth of Popery and Arbitrary Government in England*, in which he documented with painstaking and damning detail the sorry course of events since the Dutch War of 1665 and set out his fears for the future of a nation which seemed indifferent to the dangers, both at home and abroad, threatening its traditional liberties. A reward was offered for information about the author and printer of this relentless exposure of corruption and ineptitude among Charles II's ministers and in a body of MPs that had been elected as far back as 1661. Marvell was to take a mischievous pleasure in the stir caused by his final intervention in public affairs in a letter he wrote to his nephew on 10 June 1678 (reprinted on pp. 178–9). And when he died two months later from the effects of a chill caught during a visit to Hull, the rumour – albeit groundless – that he had been poisoned by the Jesuits bore witness to the significant place which he had come to occupy in the political scene of post-Restoration England.

When he was buried on 18 August in St Giles-in-the-Fields, the expenses of the funeral were met by the Hull Corporation.

POSTHUMOUS REPUTATION

Three years after his death, a volume of *Miscellaneous Poems* was published by his former landlady and housekeeper, Mary Palmer, who claimed to have been secretly married to him and affirmed in a note 'To the reader' that 'all these poems, as also the other things in this book contained, are printed according to the exact copies of my late dear husband, under his own hand-writing, being found since his death among his other papers.' Her claim has not been endorsed by modern scholarship,[12] but she does deserve credit for transmitting to posterity the collection of verse on which Andrew Marvell's modern reputation as one of the outstanding lyric poets of the seventeenth century has been founded. In fact, that reputation took a long time to develop, and the changing fashions in Marvell criticism serve to illustrate the dependence of literary taste on the wider political and cultural contexts in which individual readings are undertaken.

The bulk of the poems first made public in 1681 seem to have escaped contemporary notice, and, apart from a handful of lyrics included in Tonson's *Miscellany* of 1716, were not reprinted until 1726. The verse satires, by contrast, were widely circulated in manuscript during his lifetime, and for many years continued to figure prominently in popular anthologies. It was as a writer of prose, however, and especially as the author of the two parts of *The Rehearsal Transpros'd* – described in 1687 as 'the wittiest books that have appeared in this age'[13] – that he was chiefly celebrated in his own century. And during the next, although admiration for both the polemical prose and the satires was maintained, his achievements as a writer took second place to the symbolic value of what William Mason was to call 'Marvell's patriot fame'.[14] Indeed, when Thomas Cooke reissued the poetry in 1726, his avowed purpose was to keep alive the memory of a man who was 'a pattern for all free-born Englishmen'. And his next editor, Captain Edward Thompson, admitted that the publication of the first collected *Works* in 1776 was chiefly motivated by 'the pleasing hopes of adding a number of strenuous and sincere friends to our Constitution' in an age when 'arbitrary power' was 'daily putting a check to every notion of rational and manly liberty'.

Times and tastes were altering, however, and soon after the turn of the century a new note begins to make itself heard. In 1806, the Reverend William Lisle Bowles discovered 'Upon the hill and grove at Bilbrough' and 'Upon Appleton House' among the antecedents of Pope's 'Windsor Forest', and paused to admire 'some of the descriptive touches' and the 'little circumstances of rural nature', which could only have been observed 'with the eye and feeling of a true poet'.[15] Charles Lamb, in his turn, paid tribute to the 'witty delicacy' of 'the garden-loving poet', and as the nineteenth century wore on, the prose fell into neglect and the political poems and satires into disfavour. A Victorian version of Marvell as a forerunner of Romanticism gradually evolved. Hartley Coleridge praised the 'heartfelt tenderness' and 'childish simplicity of feeling' in those poems 'which he wrote for himself', disparaged 'those he made to order, for Fairfax or Cromwell', and refused to accept the authenticity of 'a quantity of obscene and scurrilous trash' that had been 'scraped together, out of the state poems' and attributed to Marvell by Thompson.[16] By 1885, Marvell's 'personal sympathy with nature' was being compared to Wordsworth's 'commerce with the inanimate world'; by 1892, he had been found to possess a passion for nature, 'exactly as we moderns mean nature, the great spiritual influence which deepens and widens life for us'; and by 1901, he had been dubbed 'the laureate of grass, and of greenery'.[17] At the same time, his connection with the Metaphysical poets of the earlier seventeenth century was being recognized, usually in the form of reservations about 'that over-activity of fancy' (Hartley Coleridge) which was responsible for what Bowles had called his 'conceits and false thoughts'.

But a change of climate was on the way, and the revival of interest in the poetry of wit and paradox and ratiocination – heralded by Grierson's edition of Donne in 1912 – provided an auspicious context for a revaluation of Marvell's stature as a writer. It was Grierson who, in 1921, ranked him alongside Donne and Dryden for those very qualities that many Victorians had resisted: 'passionate, paradoxical argument, touched with humour and learned imagery'.[18] In the same year, T. S. Eliot published an essay which both stimulated and set the pattern for a good deal of what was to follow. Defining Metaphysical wit as 'a tough reasonableness beneath the slight lyric grace' and detecting in 'To his coy mistress' an 'alliance of levity and seriousness (by which the seriousness is intensified)', Eliot pronounced that Marvell's best verse was 'the product of European, that is to say Latin, culture' and associated him with a tradition of 'sophisticated literature' which stretched from Catullus, Propertius and Ovid to Gautier, Baudelaire and Laforgue. The man who was intent on re-establishing contact with this tradition in his own verse had good reason to emphasize the achievement of one of the last English poets to draw strength from it before a 'dissociation of sensibility' overtook the national culture, divorcing intellect from emotion to the detriment of later literature.[19] A further impetus was soon given to the serious reassessment of the nature and value of

Marvell's poetry by the appearance of H. M. Margoliouth's standard edition of the *Poems and Letters* in 1927 and Pierre Legouis's monumental study, *André Marvell: Poète, Puritain, Patriote*, published in Paris, in 1928.

In the half-century since the foundations of modern Marvell scholarship and criticism were laid by these pioneering activities of the 1920s, individual poems and the entire corpus have been subjected to various and often antagonistic methods of interpretation. New Critical readers, who eschew biography, social context and literary history for a detailed analysis of each poem as an autonomous entity, have teased satisfying ironies and ambiguities out of the texts. Those favouring a more historical approach have combed them for literary allusions and have been led with J. B. Leishman to the conclusion that Marvell is the sort of writer who 'is almost always acting upon hints and suggestions provided by earlier poets' and who 'invites the reader to join him in a kind of highly sophisticated game'.[20] Others have proceeded with greater solemnity to uncover their debts to biblical typology, Pauline theology or Renaissance Neoplatonism and have treated them as arcane allegories of spiritual experiences or of philosophical or occult systems. Others again have been busy identifying the genres to which they belong or from which they deviate in witty violation of literary expectations.

More recently, renewed attention has been given to the political dimension of Marvell's thought. The ideological positions and rhetorical strategies adopted in his public and polemical works have been examined in the light of both historical scholarship and contemporary concern with the relation between the individual and the state. Nor has this interest been confined to the Cromwell poems, the prose and the satires, but has infiltrated readings of the lyric poetry that was once ignored or celebrated for its 'childish simplicity'. The 'laureate of grass, and of greenery' is once again emerging as the 'strenuous asserter of the constitution, laws and liberties of England' that he was proudly proclaimed to be in the epitaph composed by his favourite nephew, William Popple, and engraved on the monument erected to his memory in St Giles's church in 1764.

Most of Marvell's verse was not published until after his death, in the *Miscellaneous Poems* of 1681. The leaves containing the three major Cromwell poems have been cancelled in most extant copies, presumably for political reasons, but they survive (except for the last 140 lines of 'A poem upon the death of O.C.') in a copy in the British Library (C. 59. i. 8). The Cromwell poems were evidently not available to Thomas Cooke for the first collected edition of Marvell's poetry in 1726. When Captain Edward Thompson compiled a collected edition of the verse and prose in 1776, however, he had access to a manuscript volume in the possession of descendants of William Popple. This volume, now in the Bodleian Library in Oxford (catalogued as Eng. poet. d. 49), is a 1681 folio, with corrections to the printed poems and manuscript additions which include the complete texts of the three cancelled poems, 'The last instructions to a painter' and a number of other post-Restoration satires.

Unless otherwise indicated in the Notes, the texts of all the poems in the present selection are based on the annotated and expanded copy of the *Miscellaneous Poems*. The texts of the letters and extracts from Marvell's prose works are derived from the earliest printed versions. Omissions in the extracts are indicated by ellipses in square brackets. Spelling has been modernized and punctuation revised where it has been deemed helpful for the contemporary reader. In the interests of economy, textual variants and emendations adopted from previous editions have not been recorded. Attention is drawn in the Notes, however, to a small number of editorial decisions which substantially affect the meaning. The principal editions of Marvell's work are listed below:

Thomas Cooke, *The Works of Andrew Marvell*, 2 vols, 1726.

Edward Thompson, *The Works of Andrew Marvell*, 4 vols, 1776.

A. B. Grosart, *The Complete Works of Andrew Marvell*, Fuller Worthies' Library, 4 vols, Blackburn, 1872–5.

G. A. Aitken, *The Poems and Satires of Andrew Marvell*, The Muses' Library, 2 vols, London, Routledge & Kegan Paul, 1892.

Edward Wright, *The Poems and Some Satires of Andrew Marvell*, Methuen's Little Library, London, 1904.

H. M. Margoliouth, *The Poems and Letters of Andrew Marvell*, 2 vols, Oxford, Clarendon Press, 1927, 2nd edn 1952, 3rd edn revised by Pierre Legouis with the collaboration of E. E. Duncan-Jones, 1971.

Hugh Macdonald, *The Poems of Andrew Marvell*, The Muses' Library, London, Routledge & Kegan Paul, 1952.

Dennis Davison, *Andrew Marvell: Selected Poetry and Prose*, Life, Literature and Thought Library, London, Harrap, 1952.

Frank Kermode, *Selected Poetry of Andrew Marvell*, Signet Classics, New York, 1967.

George deF. Lord, *Andrew Marvell: Complete Poetry*, Modern Library College Editions, New York, Random House, 1968, reissued in Everyman's Library, London, Dent, 1984.

D. I. B. Smith, *The Rehearsal Transpros'd and The Rehearsal Transpros'd: The Second Part*, Oxford, Clarendon Press, 1971.

Elizabeth Story Donno, *Andrew Marvell: The Complete Poems*, Harmondsworth, Penguin, 1972.

NOTES TO THE INTRODUCTION

1 *The Rehearsal Transpros'd: The Second Part* (1673).

2 *Of Reformation touching Church-Discipline in England* (1641).

3 'On the new forcers of conscience under the Long Parliament'.

4 'The Putney debates', in *Puritanism and Liberty*, ed. A. S. P. Woodhouse, 2nd edn, London, Dent, 1974, p. 71.

5 William Walwyn, *The Bloody Project, or New Design in the Present War Discovered* (1648).

6 Letter to William Popple, dated 21 March 1670.

7 ibid.

8 Letter to a friend in Persia, dated 9 August 1671.

9 See K. H. D. Haley, *William of Orange and the English Opposition, 1672–4*, Oxford, Clarendon Press, 1953, pp. 52–66.

10 Letter to Sir Edward Harley, dated 3 May 1673.

11 Gilbert Burnet, *History of My Own Time* (before 1715), ed. Osmund Airy, Oxford, Clarendon Press, 1897, vol. 1, pp. 467–8.

12 See Fred S. Tupper, 'Mary Palmer, alias Mrs Andrew Marvell', *PMLA*, 53 (1938), 367–92.

13 *A Supplement to Burnet's History of My Own Time*, ed. H. C. Foxcroft, Oxford, Clarendon Press, 1902, p. 216.

14 William Mason, 'An ode to Independency' (1756).

15 William Lisle Bowles, *The Works of Alexander Pope*, London, Johnson, 1806, vol. 1, pp. 122–4.

16 Hartley Coleridge, *The Worthies of Yorkshire and Lancashire*, Leeds, Bingley, 1832.

17 Edmund Gosse, *From Shakespeare to Pope*, Cambridge, Cambridge University Press, 1885, p. 219; E. K. Chambers, *The Academy*, 42 (1892), 230; H. C. Beeching, *The National Review*, 37 (1901), 753.

18 Sir Herbert Grierson, Introduction to *Metaphysical Lyrics and Poems of the Seventeenth Century*, Oxford, Clarendon Press, 1921, p. xxxvii.

19 T. S. Eliot, 'Andrew Marvell' and 'The Metaphysical poets' (1921), both reprinted in *Selected Essays*, 3rd edn, London, Faber & Faber, 1951.

20 *The Art of Marvell's Poetry*, London, Hutchinson, 1966, pp. 29 and 56.

ANDREW MARVELL

Selected Poetry and Prose

A DIALOGUE BETWEEN THE SOUL AND BODY

SOUL: O, who shall from this Dungeon raise
A soul enslaved so many ways?
With bolts of bones, that fettered stands
In feet, and manacled in hands.
Here blinded with an eye; and there
Deaf with the drumming of an ear.
A soul hung up, as 'twere, in chains
Of nerves, and arteries, and veins.
Tortured, besides each other part,
In a vain head, and double heart.

BODY: O, who shall me deliver whole,
From bonds of this tyrannic soul?
Which, stretched upright, impales me so,
That mine own precipice I go;
And warms and moves this needless frame
(A fever could but do the same);
And, wanting where its spite to try,
Has made me live to let me die.
A body that could never rest,
Since this ill spirit it possessed.

SOUL: What magic could me thus confine
Within another's grief to pine?
Where whatsoever it complain,
I feel, that cannot feel, the pain.
And all my care itself employs,
That to preserve, which me destroys:
Constrained not only to endure
Diseases, but, what's worse, the cure;
And ready oft the port to gain,
Am shipwrecked into health again.

BODY: But physic yet could never reach
The maladies thou me dost teach:
Whom first the cramp of hope does tear,

* Numbers in square brackets refer to pages on which notes may be found.

And then the palsy shakes of fear;
The pestilence of love does heat,
Or hatred's hidden ulcer eat;
Joy's cheerful madness does perplex,
Or sorrow's other madness vex;
Which knowledge forces me to know,
And memory will not forgo.
What but a soul could have the wit
To build me up for sin so fit?
So architects do square and hew
Green trees that in the forest grew.

ON A DROP OF DEW

See how the orient dew,
Shed from the Bosom of the Morn
Into the blowing roses,
Yet careless of its mansion new;
For the clear region where 'twas born
Round in itself incloses;
And in its little globe's extent,
Frames as it can its native element.
How it the purple flower does slight,
Scarce touching where it lies,
But gazing back upon the skies,
Shines with a mournful light;
Like its own tear,
Because so long divided from the sphere.
Restless it rolls and unsecure,
Trembling lest it grow impure,
Till the warm sun pity its pain,
And to the skies exhale it back again.
So the soul, that drop, that ray
Of the clear fountain of eternal day,
Could it within the human flower be seen,
Remembering still its former height,
Shuns the sweet leaves and blossoms green;

And, recollecting its own light,
Does, in its pure and circling thoughts, express
The greater heaven in an heaven less.
In how coy a figure wound,
Every way it turns away:
So the world excluding round,
Yet receiving in the day.
Dark beneath, but bright above:
Here disdaining, there in love.
How loose and easy hence to go,
How girt and ready to ascend;
Moving but on a point below,
It all about does upward bend.
Such did the manna's sacred dew distill;
White, and entire, though congealed and chill.
Congealed on earth: but does, dissolving, run
Into the glories of th' almighty sun.

EYES AND TEARS

1

How wisely Nature did decree,
With the same eyes to weep and see!
That, having viewed the object vain,
We might be ready to complain.

2

Thus since the self-deluding sight
In a false angle takes each height,
These tears, which better measure all,
Like wat'ry lines and plummets fall.

3

Two tears, which Sorrow long did weigh
Within the scales of either eye,
And then paid out in equal poise,
Are the true price of all my joys.

4

What in the world most fair appears,
Yea even laughter, turns to tears:
And all the jewels which we prize,
Melt in these pendants of the eyes.

5

I have through every garden been,
Amongst the red, the white, the green;
And yet, from all the flowers I saw,
No honey but these tears could draw.

6

So the all-seeing sun each day
Distills the world with chemic ray;
But finds the essence only showers,
Which straight in pity back he pours.

7

Yet happy they whom grief doth bless,
That weep the more, and see the less:
And, to preserve their sight more true,
Bathe still their eyes in their own dew.

8

*So Magdalen, in tears more wise
Dissolved those captivating eyes,
Whose liquid chains could flowing meet
To fetter her Redeemer's feet.

9

Not full sails hasting loaden home,
Nor the chaste lady's pregnant womb,
Nor Cynthia teeming shows so fair,
As two eyes swoll'n with weeping are.

10

The sparkling glance that shoots desire,
Drenched in these waves, does lose its fire.
Yea oft the Thund'rer pity takes
And here the hissing lightning slakes.

11

The incense was to Heaven dear,
Not as a perfume, but a tear.
And stars show lovely in the night,
But as they seem the tears of light.

12

Ope then, mine eyes, your double sluice,
And practise so your noblest use.
For others too can see, or sleep;
But only human eyes can weep.

13

Now like two clouds dissolving, drop,
And at each tear in distance stop:
Now like two fountains trickle down;
Now like two floods o'erturn and drown.

14

Thus let your streams o'erflow your springs,
Till eyes and tears be the same things:
And each the other's difference bears;
These weeping eyes, those seeing tears.

**Magdala, lascivos sic quum dimisit amantes,*
Fervidaque in castas lumina solvit aquas;
Haesit in irriguo lachrymarum compede Christus,
Et tenuit sacros uda Catena pedes.

A DIALOGUE, BETWEEN THE RESOLVED SOUL AND CREATED PLEASURE

Courage, my Soul, now learn to wield
The weight of thine immortal shield.
Close on thy head thy helmet bright.
Balance thy sword against the fight.
See where an army, strong as fair,
With silken banners spreads the air.
Now, if thou be'st that thing divine,
In this day's combat let it shine:
And show that Nature wants an art
To conquer one resolved heart.

PLEASURE: Welcome the creation's guest,
Lord of earth, and heaven's heir.
Lay aside that warlike crest,
And of Nature's banquet share:
Where the souls of fruits and flowers
Stand prepared to heighten yours.

SOUL: I sup above, and cannot stay
To bait so long upon the way.

PLEASURE: On these downy pillows lie,
Whose soft plumes will thither fly:
On these roses strewed so plain
Lest one leaf thy side should strain.

SOUL: My gentler rest is on a thought,
Conscious of doing what I ought.

PLEASURE: If thou be'st with perfumes pleased,
Such as oft the gods appeased,
Thou in fragrant clouds shalt show
Like another god below.

SOUL: A soul that knows not to presume
Is heaven's and its own perfume.

PLEASURE: Everything does seem to vie
Which should first attract thine eye:
But since none deserves that grace,
In this crystal view *thy* face.

SOUL: When the Creator's skill is prized,
The rest is all but earth disguised.

PLEASURE: Hark how music then prepares
For thy stay these charming airs;
Which the posting winds recall,
And suspend the river's fall.

SOUL: Had I but any time to lose,
On this I would it all dispose.
Cease, Tempter. None can chain a mind
Whom this sweet chordage cannot bind.

CHORUS: *Earth cannot show so brave a sight*
As when a single soul does fence
The batteries of alluring sense,
And heaven views it with delight.
  Then persevere: for still new charges sound;
  And if thou overcom'st thou shalt be crowned.

PLEASURE: All this fair, and soft, and sweet,
  Which scatteringly doth shine,
Shall within one beauty meet,
  And she be only thine.

SOUL: If things of sight such heavens be,
What heavens are those we cannot see!

PLEASURE: Wheresoe'er thy foot shall go
  The minted gold shall lie;
Till thou purchase all below,
  And want new worlds to buy.

SOUL: Were't not a price who'd value gold?
And that's worth nought that can be sold.

PLEASURE: Wilt thou all the glory have
That war or peace commend?
Half the world shall be thy slave,
The other half thy friend.

SOUL: What friends, if to my self untrue!
What slaves, unless I captive you!

PLEASURE: Thou shalt know each hidden cause;
And see the future time:
Try what depth the centre draws;
And then to heaven climb.

SOUL: None thither mounts by the degree
Of knowledge, but humility.

CHORUS: *Triumph, triumph, victorious Soul;*
The world has not one pleasure more:
The rest does lie beyond the pole,
And is thine everlasting store.

THE CORONET

When for the thorns with which I long, too long,
With many a piercing wound,
My Saviour's head have crowned,
I seek with garlands to redress that wrong:
Through every garden, every mead,
I gather flowers (my fruits are only flowers),
Dismantling all the fragrant towers
That once adorned my shepherdess's head.
And now when I have summed up all my store,
Thinking (so I myself deceive)
So rich a chaplet thence to weave
As never yet the King of Glory wore:
Alas, I find the Serpent old
That, twining in his speckled breast,
About the flowers disguised does fold,
With wreaths of fame and interest.

Ah, foolish man, that would'st debase with them,
And mortal glory, heaven's diadem!
But thou who only could'st the Serpent tame,
Either his slipp'ry knots at once untie,
And disentangle all his winding snare;
Or shatter too with him my curious frame,
And let these wither, so that he may die,
Though set with skill and chosen out with care.
That they, while Thou on both their spoils dost tread,
May crown thy feet, that could not crown thy head.

THE DEFINITION OF LOVE

1

My love is of a birth as rare
As 'tis for object strange and high:
It was begotten by Despair
Upon Impossibility.

2

Magnanimous Despair alone
Could show me so divine a thing,
Where feeble Hope could ne'er have flown,
But vainly flapped its tinsel wing.

3

And yet I quickly might arrive
Where my extended soul is fixed,
But Fate does iron wedges drive,
And always crowds itself betwixt.

4

For Fate with jealous eye does see
Two perfect loves; nor lets them close:
Their union would her ruin be,
And her tyrannic power depose.

5

And therefore her decrees of steel
Us as the distant poles have placed,
(Though love's whole world on us doth wheel)
Not by themselves to be embraced:

6

Unless the giddy heaven fall,
And earth some new convulsion tear;
And, us to join, the world should all
Be cramped into a planisphere.

7

As lines so loves oblique may well
Themselves in every angle greet:
But ours so truly parallel,
Though infinite, can never meet.

8

Therefore the love which us doth bind,
But Fate so enviously debars,
Is the conjunction of the mind,
And opposition of the stars.

THE NYMPH COMPLAINING FOR THE DEATH OF HER FAWN

The wanton troopers riding by
Have shot my fawn and it will die.
Ungentle men! They cannot thrive
To kill thee. Thou ne'er didst alive
Them any harm: alas, nor could
Thy death yet do them any good.
I'm sure I never wished them ill;
Nor do I for all this; nor will:
But, if my simple prayers may yet
Prevail with heaven to forget
Thy murder, I will join my tears

Rather than fail. But, O my fears!
It cannot die so. Heaven's King
Keeps register of everything:
And nothing may we use in vain.
Ev'n beasts must be with justice slain;
Else men are made their deodands.
Though they should wash their guilty hands
In this warm life-blood, which doth part
From thine, and wound me to the heart,
Yet could they not be clean: their stain
Is dyed in such a purple grain.
There is not such another in
The world, to offer for their sin.
  Unconstant Sylvio, when yet
I had not found him counterfeit,
One morning (I remember well),
Tied in this silver chain and bell,
Gave it to me: nay, and I know
What he said then; I'm sure I do.
Said he, 'Look how your huntsman here
Hath taught a fawn to hunt his *dear*.'
But Sylvio soon had me beguiled.
This waxed tame, while he grew wild,
And quite regardless of my smart,
Left me his fawn, but took his heart.
  Thenceforth I set myself to play
My solitary time away
With this: and very well content,
Could so mine idle life have spent.
For it was full of sport; and light
Of foot, and heart; and did invite
Me to its game: it seemed to bless
Itself in me. How could I less
Than love it? O I cannot be
Unkind, t' a beast that loveth me.
  Had it lived long, I do not know
Whether it too might have done so

As Sylvio did: his gifts might be
Perhaps as false or more than he.
But I am sure, for ought that I
Could in so short a time espy,
Thy love was far more better than
The love of false and cruel men.
  With sweetest milk, and sugar, first
I it at mine own fingers nursed.
And as it grew, so every day
It waxed more white and sweet than they.
It had so sweet a breath! And oft
I blushed to see its foot more soft,
And white (shall I say than my hand?),
Nay, any lady's of the land.
  It is a wond'rous thing, how fleet
'Twas on those little silver feet.
With what a pretty skipping grace,
It oft would challenge me the race:
And when 't had left me far away,
'Twould stay, and run again, and stay.
For it was nimbler much than hinds;
And trod, as on the four winds.
  I have a garden of my own,
But so with roses overgrown,
And lilies, that you would it guess
To be a little wilderness.
And all the spring time of the year
It only loved to be there.
Among the beds of lilies, I
Have sought it oft, where it should lie;
Yet could not, till itself would rise,
Find it, although before mine eyes.
For, in the flaxen lilies' shade,
It like a bank of lilies laid.
Upon the roses it would feed,
Until its lips ev'n seemed to bleed:
And then to me 'twould boldly trip,

And print those roses on my lip.
But all its chief delight was still
On roses thus itself to fill:
And its pure virgin limbs to fold
In whitest sheets of lilies cold.
Had it lived long, it would have been
Lilies without, roses within.
  O help! O help! I see it faint:
And die as calmly as a saint.
See how it weeps. The tears do come
Sad, slowly dropping like a gum.
So weeps the wounded balsam; so
The holy frankincense doth flow.
The brotherless Heliades
Melt in such amber tears as these.
  I in a golden vial will
Keep these two crystal tears; and fill
It till it do o'erflow with mine;
Then place it in Diana's shrine.
  Now my sweet fawn is vanished to
Whither the swans and turtles go:
In fair Elysium to endure,
With milk-white lambs, and ermines pure.
O do not run too fast: for I
Will but bespeak thy grave, and die.
  First my unhappy statue shall
Be cut in marble; and withal,
Let it be weeping too – but there
Th' engraver sure his art may spare;
For I so truly thee bemoan,
That I shall weep though I be stone:
Until my tears, still dropping, wear
My breast, themselves engraving there.
There at my feet shalt thou be laid,
Of purest alabaster made:
For I would have thine image be
White as I can, though not as thee.

CLORINDA AND DAMON

C: Damon, come drive thy flocks this way.
D: No, 'tis too late they went astray.
C: I have a grassy scutcheon spied,
Where Flora blazons all her pride.
The grass I aim to feast thy sheep:
The flowers I for thy temples keep.
D: Grass withers; and the flowers too fade.
C: Seize the short joys then, ere they vade.
Seest thou that unfrequented cave?
D: That den?
C: Love's shrine.
D: But virtue's grave.
C: In whose cool bosom we may lie
Safe from the sun.
D: Not heaven's eye.
C: Near this, a fountain's liquid bell
Tinkles within the concave shell.
D: Might a soul bathe there and be clean,
Or slake its drought?
C: What is't you mean?
D: These once had been enticing things,
Clorinda, pastures, caves, and springs.
C: And what late change?
D: The other day
Pan met me.
C: What did great Pan say?
D: Words that transcend poor shepherds' skill;
But he e'er since my songs does fill:
And his name swells my slender oat.
C: Sweet must Pan sound in Damon's note.
D: Clorinda's voice might make it sweet.
C: Who would not in Pan's praises meet?

Chorus

Of Pan the flowery pastures sing,
Caves echo, and the fountains ring.
Sing then while he doth us inspire;
For all the world is our Pan's choir.

THE MOWER AGAINST GARDENS

Luxurious man, to bring his vice in use,
  Did after him the world seduce:
And from the fields the flowers and plants allure,
  Where Nature was most plain and pure.
He first enclosed within the garden's square
  A dead and standing pool of air:
And a more luscious earth for them did knead,
  Which stupefied them while it fed.
The pink grew then as double as his mind;
  The nutriment did change the kind.
With strange perfumes he did the roses taint;
  And flowers themselves were taught to paint.
The tulip, white, did for complexion seek;
  And learned to interline its cheek:
Its onion root they then so high did hold,
  That one was for a meadow sold.
Another world was searched, through oceans new,
  To find the *Marvel of Peru*.
And yet these rarities might be allowed
  To man, that sovereign thing and proud,
Had he not dealt between the bark and tree,
  Forbidden mixtures there to see.
No plant now knew the stock from which it came;
  He grafts upon the wild the tame:
That the uncertain and adult'rate fruit
  Might put the palate in dispute.
His green seraglio has its eunuchs too,
  Lest any tyrant him outdo.

And in the cherry he does Nature vex,
  To procreate without a sex.
'Tis all enforced: the fountain and the grot;
  While the sweet fields do lie forgot:
Where willing Nature does to all dispense
  A wild and fragrant innocence:
And fauns and fairies do the meadows till,
  More by their presence than their skill.
Their statues, polished by some ancient hand,
  May to adorn the gardens stand:
But howsoe'er the figures do excel,
  The gods themselves with us do dwell.

DAMON THE MOWER

1

Hark how the Mower Damon sung,
With love of Juliana stung!
While everything did seem to paint
The scene more fit for his complaint.
Like her fair eyes the day was fair;
But scorching like his am'rous care.
Sharp like his scythe his sorrow was,
And withered like his hopes the grass.

2

'Oh what unusual heats are here,
Which thus our sunburned meadows sear!
The grasshopper its pipe gives o'er;
The hamstringed frogs can dance no more.
But in the brook the green frog wades;
And grasshoppers seek out the shades.
Only the snake, that kept within,
Now glitters in its second skin.

3

'This heat the sun could never raise,
Nor Dog Star so inflames the days.

It from an higher beauty grow'th,
Which burns the fields and mower both:
Which mads the dog, and makes the sun
Hotter than his own Phaëton.
Not July causeth these extremes,
But Juliana's scorching beams.

4

'Tell me where I may pass the fires
Of the hot day, or hot desires.
To what cool cave shall I descend,
Or to what gelid fountain bend?
Alas! I look for ease in vain,
When remedies themselves complain.
No moisture but my tears do rest,
Nor cold but in her icy breast.

5

'How long wilt thou, fair shepherdess,
Esteem me, and my presents less?
To thee the harmless snake I bring,
Disarmed of its teeth and sting.
To thee chameleons changing hue,
And oak leaves tipped with honey dew.
Yet thou ungrateful hast not sought
Nor what they are, nor who them brought.

6

'I am the Mower Damon, known
Through all the meadows I have mown.
On me the morn her dew distills
Before her darling daffodils.
And, if at noon my toil me heat,
The sun himself licks off my sweat.
While, going home, the evening sweet
In cowslip-water bathes my feet.

7

'What, though the piping shepherd stock
The plains with an unnumbered flock,
This scythe of mine discovers wide
More ground than all his sheep do hide.
With this the golden fleece I shear
Of all these closes every year.
And though in wool more poor than they,
Yet am I richer far in hay.

8

'Nor am I so deformed to sight,
If in my scythe I looked right;
In which I see my picture done,
As in a crescent moon the sun.
The deathless fairies take me oft
To lead them in their dances soft;
And, when I tune myself to sing,
About me they contract their ring.

9

'How happy might I still have mowed,
Had not Love here his thistles sowed!
But now I all the day complain,
Joining my labour to my pain;
And with my scythe cut down the grass,
Yet still my grief is where it was:
But, when the iron blunter grows,
Sighing I whet my scythe and woes.'

10

While thus he threw his elbow round,
Depopulating all the ground,
And, with his whistling scythe, does cut
Each stroke between the earth and root,
The edged steel by careless chance
Did into his own ankle glance;

And there among the grass fell down,
By his own scythe, the Mower mown.

11

'Alas!' said he, 'these hurts are slight
To those that die by Love's despite.
With shepherd's-purse, and clown's-all-heal,
The blood I staunch, and wound I seal.
Only for him no cure is found,
Whom Juliana's eyes do wound.
'Tis death alone that this must do:
For Death thou art a Mower too.'

THE MOWER TO THE GLOW-WORMS

1

Ye living lamps, by whose dear light
The Nightingale does sit so late,
And studying all the summer night,
Her matchless songs does meditate;

2

Ye country comets, that portend
No war, nor prince's funeral,
Shining unto no higher end
Than to presage the grass's fall;

3

Ye glow-worms, whose officious flame
To wand'ring mowers shows the way,
That in the night have lost their aim,
And after foolish fires do stray;

4

Your courteous lights in vain you waste,
Since Juliana here is come,
For she my mind hath so displaced
That I shall never find my home.

THE MOWER'S SONG

1

My mind was once the true survey
Of all these meadows fresh and gay;
And in the greenness of the grass
Did see its hopes as in a glass;
When Juliana came, and she
What I do to the grass, does to my thoughts and me.

2

But these, while I with sorrow pine,
Grew more luxuriant still and fine;
That not one blade of grass you spied,
But had a flower on either side;
When Juliana came, and she
What I do to the grass, does to my thoughts and me.

3

Unthankful meadows, could you so
A fellowship so true forgo,
And in your gaudy May-games meet,
While I lay trodden under feet?
When Juliana came, and she
What I do to the grass, does to my thoughts and me.

4

But what you in compassion ought,
Shall now by my revenge be wrought:
And flowers, and grass, and I and all,

Will in one common ruin fall.
For Juliana comes, and she
What I do to the grass, does to my thoughts and me.

5

And thus, ye meadows, which have been
Companions of my thoughts more green,
Shall now the heraldry become
With which I will adorn my tomb;
For Juliana comes, and she
What I do to the grass, does to my thoughts and me.

THE GALLERY

1

Clora, come view my soul, and tell
Whether I have contrived it well.
Now all its several lodgings lie
Composed into one gallery;
And the great arras-hangings, made
Of various faces, by are laid;
That, for all furniture, you'll find
Only your picture in my mind.

2

Here thou art painted in the dress
Of an inhuman murderess;
Examining upon our hearts
Thy fertile shop of cruel arts:
Engines more keen than ever yet
Adorned tyrant's cabinet;
Of which the most tormenting are
Black eyes, red lips, and curled hair.

3

But, on the other side, th' art drawn
Like to Aurora in the dawn;

When in the East she slumb'ring lies,
And stretches out her milky thighs;
While all the morning choir does sing,
And manna falls, and roses spring;
And, at thy feet, the wooing doves
Sit perfecting their harmless loves.

4

Like an enchantress here thou show'st,
Vexing thy restless lover's ghost;
And, by a light obscure, dost rave
Over his entrails, in the cave;
Divining thence, with horrid care,
How long thou shalt continue fair;
And (when informed) them throw'st away,
To be the greedy vulture's prey.

5

But, against that, thou sit'st afloat
Like Venus in her pearly boat.
The halcyons, calming all that's nigh,
Betwixt the air and water fly.
Or, if some rolling wave appears,
A mass of ambergris it bears.
Nor blows more wind than what may well
Convoy the perfume to the smell.

6

These pictures and a thousand more,
Of thee, my gallery do store;
In all the forms thou can'st invent
Either to please me, or torment:
For thou alone to people me,
Art grown a numerous colony;
And a collection choicer far
Than or Whitehall's, or Mantua's were.

7

But, of these pictures and the rest,
That at the entrance likes me best:
Where the same posture, and the look
Remains, with which I first was took.
A tender shepherdess, whose hair
Hangs loosely playing in the air,
Transplanting flowers from the green hill,
To crown her head, and bosom fill.

MOURNING

1

You, that decipher out the fate
Of human offsprings from the skies,
What mean these infants which of late
Spring from the stars of Chlora's eyes?

2

Her eyes confused, and doubled o'er,
With tears suspended ere they flow,
Seem bending upwards, to restore
To heaven, whence it came, their woe.

3

When, moulding of the wat'ry spheres,
Slow drops untie themselves away;
As if she, with those precious tears,
Would strow the ground where Strephon lay.

4

Yet some affirm, pretending art,
Her eyes have so her bosom drowned,
Only to soften near her heart
A place to fix another wound.

5

And, while vain pomp does her restrain
Within her solitary bower,
She courts herself in am'rous rain;
Herself both Danaë and the shower.

6

Nay others, bolder, hence esteem
Joy now so much her master grown,
That whatsoever does but seem
Like grief, is from her windows thrown.

7

Nor that she pays, while she survives,
To her dead love this tribute due;
But casts abroad these donatives,
At the installing of a new.

8

How wide they dream! The Indian slaves
That sink for pearl through seas profound
Would find her tears yet deeper waves
And not of one the bottom sound.

9

I yet my silent judgement keep,
Disputing not what they believe:
But sure as oft as women weep,
It is to be supposed they grieve.

TO HIS COY MISTRESS

Had we but world enough, and time,
This coyness, Lady, were no crime.
We would sit down, and think which way
To walk, and pass our long love's day.
Thou by the Indian Ganges' side

Should'st rubies find: I by the tide
Of Humber would complain. I would
Love you ten years before the flood:
And you should, if you please, refuse
Till the conversion of the Jews.
My vegetable love should grow
Vaster than empires, and more slow.
An hundred years should go to praise
Thine eyes, and on thy forehead gaze.
Two hundred to adore each breast:
But thirty thousand to the rest.
An age at least to every part,
And the last age should show your heart.
For, Lady, you deserve this state;
Nor would I love at lower rate.
  But at my back I always hear
Time's winged chariot hurrying near:
And yonder all before us lie
Deserts of vast eternity.
Thy beauty shall no more be found;
Nor, in thy marble vault, shall sound
My echoing song: then worms shall try
That long preserved virginity:
And your quaint honour turn to dust;
And into ashes all my lust.
The grave's a fine and private place,
But none, I think, do there embrace.
  Now therefore, while the youthful glew
Sits on thy skin like morning dew,
And while thy willing soul transpires
At every pore with instant fires,
Now let us sport us while we may;
And now, like am'rous birds of prey,
Rather at once our time devour,
Than languish in his slow-chapped power.
Let us roll all our strength, and all
Our sweetness, up into one ball:

And tear our pleasures with rough strife,
Thorough the iron gates of life.
Thus, though we cannot make our sun
Stand still, yet we will make him run.

THE UNFORTUNATE LOVER

1

Alas, how pleasant are their days
With whom the infant Love yet plays!
Sorted by pairs, they still are seen
By fountains cool, and shadows green.
But soon these flames do lose their light,
Like meteors of a summer's night:
Nor can they to that region climb,
To make impression upon time.

2

'Twas in a shipwreck, when the seas
Ruled, and the winds did what they please,
That my poor Lover floating lay,
And, ere brought forth, was cast away:
Till at the last the master-wave
Upon the rock his mother drave;
And there she split against the stone,
In a Caesarian section.

3

The sea him lent those bitter tears
Which at his eyes he always wears:
And from the winds the sighs he bore,
Which through his surging breast do roar.
No day he saw but that which breaks,
Through frighted clouds in forked streaks.
While round the rattling thunder hurled,
As at the funeral of the world.

4

While Nature to his birth presents
This masque of quarrelling elements,
A num'rous fleet of corm'rants black,
That sailed insulting o'er the wrack,
Received into their cruel care
Th' unfortunate and abject heir:
Guardians most fit to entertain
The orphan of the hurricane.

5

They fed him up with hopes and air,
Which soon digested to despair.
And as one corm'rant fed him, still
Another on his heart did bill.
Thus while they famish him, and feast,
He both consumed, and increased:
And languished with doubtful breath,
Th' amphibium of life and death.

6

And now, when angry heaven would
Behold a spectacle of blood,
Fortune and he are called to play
At sharp before it all the day:
And tyrant Love his breast does ply
With all his winged artillery.
Whilst he, betwixt the flames and waves,
Like Ajax, the mad tempest braves.

7

See how he nak'd and fierce does stand,
Cuffing the thunder with one hand;
While with the other he does lock,
And grapple, with the stubborn rock:
From which he with each wave rebounds,
Torn into flames, and ragg'd with wounds.

And all he says, a lover dressed
In his own blood does relish best.

8

This is the only banneret
That ever Love created yet:
Who though, by the malignant stars,
Forced to live in storms and wars;
Yet dying leaves a perfume here,
And music within every ear:
And he in story only rules,
In a field sable a lover gules.

THE PICTURE OF LITTLE T.C. IN A PROSPECT OF FLOWERS

1

See with what simplicity
This nymph begins her golden days!
In the green grass she loves to lie,
And there with her fair aspect tames
The wilder flowers, and gives them names:
But only with the roses plays;
    And them does tell
What colour best becomes them, and what smell.

2

Who can foretell for what high cause
This darling of the gods was born!
Yet this is she whose chaster laws
The wanton Love shall one day fear,
And, under her command severe,
See his bow broke and ensigns torn.
    Happy, who can
Appease this virtuous enemy of man!

3

O then let me in time compound,
And parley with those conquering eyes;
Ere they have tried their force to wound,
Ere, with their glancing wheels, they drive
In triumph over hearts that strive,
And them that yield but more despise.
Let me be laid,
Where I may see thy glories from some shade.

4

Meantime, whilst every verdant thing
Itself does at thy beauty charm,
Reform the errors of the spring;
Make that the tulips may have share
Of sweetness, seeing they are fair;
And roses of their thorns disarm:
But most procure
That violets may a longer age endure.

5

But O young beauty of the woods,
Whom Nature courts with fruits and flowers,
Gather the flowers, but spare the buds;
Lest Flora angry at thy crime,
To kill her infants in their prime,
Do quickly make the example yours;
And, ere we see,
Nip in the blossom all our hopes and thee.

YOUNG LOVE

1

Come little infant, love me now,
While thine unsuspected years
Clear thine aged father's brow
From cold jealousy and fears.

2

Pretty surely 'twere to see
  By young love old time beguiled:
While our sportings are as free
  As the nurse's with the child.

3

Common beauties stay fifteen;
  Such as yours should swifter move;
Whose fair blossoms are too green
  Yet for lust, but not for love.

4

Love as much the snowy lamb
  Or the wanton kid does prize,
As the lusty bull or ram,
  For his morning sacrifice.

5

Now then love me: time may take
  Thee before thy time away:
Of this need we'll virtue make,
  And learn love before we may.

6

So we win of doubtful Fate;
  And, if good she to us meant,
We that good shall antedate,
  Or, if ill, that ill prevent.

7

Thus as kingdoms, frustrating
  Other titles to their crown,
In the cradle crown their king,
  So all foreign claims to drown,

8

So, to make all rivals vain,
  Now I crown thee with my love:
Crown me with thy love again,
  And we both shall monarchs prove.

THE GARDEN

1

How vainly men themselves amaze
To win the palm, the oak, or bays;
And their uncessant labours see
Crowned from some single herb or tree,
Whose short and narrow verged shade
Does prudently their toils upbraid;
While all flowers and all trees do close
To weave the garlands of repose.

2

Fair Quiet, have I found thee here,
And Innocence, thy sister dear!
Mistaken long, I sought you then
In busy companies of men.
Your sacred plants, if here below,
Only among the plants will grow.
Society is all but rude,
To this delicious solitude.

3

No white nor red was ever seen
So am'rous as this lovely green.
Fond lovers, cruel as their flame,
Cut in these trees their mistress' name.
Little, alas, they know, or heed,
How far these beauties hers exceed!
Fair trees! wheres'e'er your barks I wound,
No name shall but your own be found.

4

When we have run our passion's heat,
Love hither makes his best retreat.
The gods, that mortal beauty chase,
Still in a tree did end their race.
Apollo hunted Daphne so,
Only that she might laurel grow.
And Pan did after Syrinx speed,
Not as a nymph, but for a reed.

5

What wondrous life in this I lead!
Ripe apples drop about my head;
The luscious clusters of the vine
Upon my mouth do crush their wine;
The nectarine, and curious peach,
Into my hands themselves do reach;
Stumbling on melons, as I pass,
Ensnared with flowers, I fall on grass.

6

Meanwhile the mind, from pleasures less,
Withdraws into its happiness:
The mind, that ocean where each kind
Does straight its own resemblance find;
Yet it creates, transcending these,
Far other worlds, and other seas;
Annihilating all that's made
To a green thought in a green shade.

7

Here at the fountain's sliding foot,
Or at some fruit-tree's mossy root,
Casting the body's vest aside,
My soul into the boughs does glide:
There like a bird it sits, and sings,
Then whets, and combs its silver wings;

And, till prepared for longer flight,
Waves in its plumes the various light.

8

Such was that happy garden-state,
While man there walked without a mate:
After a place so pure, and sweet,
What other help could yet be meet!
But 'twas beyond a mortal's share
To wander solitary there:
Two paradises 'twere in one
To live in paradise alone.

9

How well the skilful gardener drew
Of flowers and herbs this dial new;
Where from above the milder sun
Does through a fragrant zodiac run;
And, as it works, th' industrious bee
Computes its time as well as we.
How could such sweet and wholesome hours
Be reckoned but with herbs and flowers!

BERMUDAS

Where the remote Bermudas ride
In th' ocean's bosom unespied,
From a small boat, that rowed along,
The list'ning winds received this song.
'What should we do but sing his praise
That led us through the wat'ry maze,
Unto an isle so long unknown,
And yet far kinder than our own!
Where he the huge sea-monsters wracks,
That lift the deep upon their backs,
He lands us on a grassy stage;
Safe from the storms, and prelate's rage.

He gave us this eternal spring,
Which here enamels everything;
And sends the fowl to us in care,
On daily visits through the air.
He hangs in shades the orange bright,
Like golden lamps in a green night;
And does in the pom'granates close
Jewels more rich than Ormus shows.
He makes the figs our mouths to meet;
And throws the melons at our feet:
But apples plants of such a price,
No tree could ever bear them twice.
With cedars, chosen by his hand,
From Lebanon, he stores the land;
And makes the hollow seas, that roar,
Proclaim the ambergris on shore.
He cast (of which we rather boast)
The gospel's pearl upon our coast.
And in these rocks for us did frame
A temple, where to sound his name.
Oh let our voice his praise exalt,
Till it arrive at heaven's vault:
Which thence (perhaps) rebounding, may
Echo beyond the Mexique Bay.'
  Thus sung they, in the English boat,
An holy and a cheerful note,
And all the way, to guide their chime,
With falling oars they kept the time.

FLECKNOE, AN ENGLISH PRIEST AT ROME

Obliged by frequent visits of this man,
Whom as priest, poet, and musician,
I for some branch of Melchizadek took
(Though he derives himself from my Lord Brooke);
I sought his lodging, which is at the sign

Of the Sad Pelican; subject divine
For poetry. There, three staircases high,
Which signifies his triple property,
I found at last a chamber, as 'twas said,
But seemed a coffin set on the stairs' head,
Not higher than seven, nor larger than three feet;
Only there was nor ceiling, nor a sheet,
Save that th' ingenious door did as you come
Turn in, and show to wainscot half the room.
Yet of his state no man could have complained;
There being no bed where he entertained:
And though within one cell so narrow pent,
He'd *stanzas* for a whole *appartament*.
  Straight, without further information,
In hideous verse, he, in a dismal tone,
Begins to exorcise, as if I were
Possessed; and sure the Devil brought me there.
But I, who now imagined myself brought
To my last trial, in a serious thought
Calmed the disorders of my youthful breast,
And to my martyrdom prepared rest.
Only this frail ambition did remain,
The last distemper of the sober brain,
That there had been some present to assure
The future ages how I did endure:
And how I, silent, turned my burning ear
Towards the verse; and when that could not hear,
Held him the other; and unchanged yet,
Asked still for more, and prayed him to repeat:
Till the tyrant, weary to persecute,
Left off, and tried t' allure me with his lute.
  Now as two instruments, to the same key
Being tuned by art, if the one touched be
The other opposite as soon replies,
Moved by the air and hidden sympathies;
So while he with his gouty fingers crawls
Over the lute, his murmuring belly calls,

Whose hungry guts to the same straitness twined
In echo to the trembling strings repined.
  I, that perceived now what his music meant,
Asked civilly if he had eat this Lent.
He answered yes, with such and such an one;
For he has this of gen'rous, that alone
He never feeds, save only when he tries
With gristly tongue to dart the passing flies.
I asked if he eat flesh. And he, that was
So hungry that though ready to say Mass
Would break his fast before, said he was sick,
And th' Ordinance was only politic.
Nor was I longer to invite him scant,
Happy at once to make him Protestant,
And silent. Nothing now our dinner stayed
But till he had himself a body made
(I mean till he were dressed): for else so thin
He stands, as if he only fed had been
With consecrated wafers: and the Host
Hath sure more flesh and blood than he can boast.
This *basso relievo* of a man,
Who as a camel tall, yet eas'ly can
The needle's eye thread without any stitch,
(His only impossible is to be rich),
Lest his too subtle body, growing rare,
Should leave his soul to wander in the air,
He therefore circumscribes himself in rhymes;
And swaddled in 's own papers seven times,
Wears a close jacket of poetic buff,
With which he doth his third dimension stuff.
Thus armed underneath, he over all
Does make a primitive *sottana* fall;
And above that yet casts an antique cloak,
Torn at the first Council of Antioch;
Which by the Jews long hid, and disesteemed,
He heard of by tradition, and redeemed.
But were he not in this black habit decked,

This half-transparent man would soon reflect
Each colour that he passed by; and be seen
As the chameleon, yellow, blue, or green.
He dressed, and ready to disfurnish now
His chamber, whose compactness did allow
No empty place for complimenting doubt,
But who came last is forced first to go out;
I meet one on the stairs who made me stand,
Stopping the passage, and did him demand.
I answered, 'He is here, Sir; but you see
You cannot pass to him but thorough me.'
He thought himself affronted, and replied,
'I whom the palace never has denied
Will make the way here.' I said, 'Sir, you'll do
Me a great favour, for I seek to go.'
He gath'ring fury still made sign to draw;
But himself there closed in a scabbard saw
As narrow as his sword's; and I, that was
Delightful, said, 'There can no body pass
Except by penetration hither, where
Two make a crowd; nor can three persons here
Consist but in one substance.' Then, to fit
Our peace, the priest said I too had some wit:
To prove 't, I said, 'The place doth us invite
By its own narrowness, Sir, to unite.'
He asked me pardon; and to make me way
Went down, as I him followed to obey.
But the propitiatory priest had straight
Obliged us, when below, to celebrate
Together our atonement: so increased
Betwixt us two the dinner to a feast.
Let it suffice that we could eat in peace;
And that both poems did and quarrels cease
During the table; though my new-made friend
Did, as he threatened, ere 'twere long intend
To be both witty and valiant: I, loath,
Said 'twas too late, he was already both.

But now, Alas, my first tormentor came,
Who satisfied with eating, but not tame,
Turns to recite; though judges most severe
After th' assize's dinner mild appear,
And on full stomach do condemn but few:
Yet he more strict my sentence doth renew,
And draws out of the black box of his breast
Ten quire of paper in which he was dressed.
Yet that which was a greater cruelty
Than Nero's poem, he calls charity:
And so the pelican at his door hung
Picks out the tender bosom to its young.
Of all his poems there he stands ungirt
Save only two foul copies for his shirt:
Yet these he promises as soon as clean.
But how I loathed to see my neighbour glean
Those papers, which he peeled from within
Like white flakes rising from a leper's skin!
More odious than those rags which the French youth
At ordinaries after dinner show'th,
When they compare their *chancres* and *poulains*.
Yet he first kissed them, and after takes pains
To read; and then, because he understood
Not one word, thought and swore that they were good.
But all his praises could not now appease
The provoked author, whom it did displease
To hear his verses, by so just a curse,
That were ill made, condemned to be read worse:
And how (impossible) he made yet more
Absurdities in them than were before.
For he his untuned voice did fall or raise
As a deaf man upon a viol plays,
Making the half points and the periods run
Confus'der than the atoms in the sun.
Thereat the poet swelled with anger full,
And roared out, like Perillus in 's own bull:
'Sir, you read false.' 'That, any one but you

Should know the contrary.' Whereat, I, now
Made mediator, in my room, said, 'Why?
To say that you read false, Sir, is no lie.'
Thereat the waxen youth relented straight;
But saw with sad despair that 'twas too late.
For the disdainful poet was retired
Home, his most furious satire to have fired
Against the rebel; who, at this struck dead,
Wept bitterly as disinherited.
Who should commend his mistress now? Or who
Praise him? both difficult indeed to do
With truth. I counselled him to go in time,
Ere the fierce poet's anger turned to rhyme.
He hasted; and I, finding myself free,
As one 'scaped strangely from captivity,
Have made the chance be painted; and go now
To hang it in Saint Peter's for a vow.

TO HIS NOBLE FRIEND MR RICHARD LOVELACE, UPON HIS POEMS

Sir,
Our times are much degenerate from those
Which your sweet muse, which your fair fortune chose,
And as complexions alter with the climes,
Our wits have drawn th' infection of our times.
That candid age no other way could tell
To be ingenious, but by speaking well.
Who best could praise, had then the greatest praise,
'Twas more esteemed to give than wear the bays:
Modest ambition studied only then
To honour not herself, but worthy men.
These virtues now are banished out of town,
Our Civil Wars have lost the civic crown.
He highest builds, who with most art destroys,
And against others' fame his own employs.
I see the envious caterpillar sit

On the fair blossom of each growing wit.
The air's already tainted with the swarms
Of insects which against you rise in arms.
Word-peckers, paper-rats, book-scorpions,
Of wit corrupted, the unfashioned sons.
The barbed censurers begin to look
Like the grim consistory on thy book;
And on each line cast a reforming eye,
Severer than the young Presbytery.
Till when in vain they have thee all perused,
You shall for being faultless be accused.
Some reading your *Lucasta*, will allege
You wronged in her the House's privilege.
Some that you under sequestration are,
Because you writ when going to the war;
And one the book prohibits, because Kent
Their first petition by the author sent.
But when the beauteous ladies came to know
That their dear Lovelace was endangered so –
Lovelace that thawed the most congealed breast,
He who loved best and them defended best;
Whose hand so rudely grasps the steely brand,
Whose hand so gently melts the lady's hand –
They all in mutiny though yet undressed
Sallied, and would in his defence contest.
And one, the loveliest that was yet e'er seen,
Thinking that I too of the rout had been,
Mine eyes invaded with a female spite,
(She knew what pain 'twould be to lose that sight).
'O no, mistake not,' I replied, 'for I
In your defence, or in his cause would die.
But he, secure of glory and of time,
Above their envy, or mine aid doth climb.
Him, valiant'st men, and fairest nymphs approve;
His book in them finds judgement, with you love.'

AN HORATIAN ODE UPON CROMWELL'S RETURN FROM IRELAND

The forward youth that would appear
Must now forsake his Muses dear,
   Nor in the shadows sing
   His numbers languishing.
'Tis time to leave the books in dust,
And oil th' unused armour's rust:
   Removing from the wall
   The corslet of the hall.
So restless Cromwell could not cease
In the inglorious arts of peace,
   But through advent'rous war
   Urged his active star.
And, like the three-forked lightning, first
Breaking the clouds where it was nursed,
   Did thorough his own side
   His fiery way divide.
For 'tis all one to courage high
The emulous or enemy;
   And with such to inclose
   Is more than to oppose.
Then burning through the air he went,
And palaces and temples rent:
   And Caesar's head at last
   Did through his laurels blast.
'Tis madness to resist or blame
The force of angry heaven's flame:
   And, if we would speak true,
   Much to the man is due,
Who, from his private gardens, where
He lived reserved and austere,
   As if his highest plot
   To plant the bergamot,
Could by industrious valour climb
To ruin the great work of time,

And cast the kingdoms old
Into another mould.
Though Justice against Fate complain,
And plead the ancient rights in vain:
But those do hold or break
As men are strong or weak.
Nature, that hateth emptiness,
Allows of penetration less:
And therefore must make room
Where greater spirits come.
What field of all the Civil Wars,
Where his were not the deepest scars?
And Hampton shows what part
He had of wiser art;
Where, twining subtle fears with hope,
He wove a net of such a scope,
That Charles himself might chase
To Carisbrooke's narrow case:
That thence the royal actor borne
The tragic scaffold might adorn:
While round the armed bands
Did clap their bloody hands.
He nothing common did or mean
Upon that memorable scene:
But with his keener eye
The axe's edge did try:
Nor called the gods with vulgar spite
To vindicate his helpless right,
But bowed his comely head
Down as upon a bed.
This was that memorable hour
Which first assured the forced power.
So when they did design
The Capitol's first line,
A bleeding head where they begun,
Did fright the architects to run;
And yet in that the state

Foresaw its happy fate.
And now the Irish are ashamed
To see themselves in one year tamed:
So much one man can do,
That does both act and know.
They can affirm his praises best,
And have, though overcome, confessed
How good he is, how just,
And fit for highest trust:
Nor yet grown stiffer with command,
But still in the Republic's hand:
How fit he is to sway
That can so well obey.
He to the Commons' feet presents
A kingdom, for his first year's rents:
And, what he may, forbears
His fame to make it theirs:
And has his sword and spoils ungirt,
To lay them at the public's skirt.
So when the falcon high
Falls heavy from the sky,
She, having killed, no more does search,
But on the next green bough to perch;
Where, when he first does lure,
The falc'ner has her sure.
What may not then our isle presume
While Victory his crest does plume!
What may not others fear
If thus he crowns each year!
A Caesar he ere long to Gaul,
To Italy an Hannibal,
And to all states not free
Shall climacteric be.
The Pict no shelter now shall find
Within his parti-coloured mind;
But from this valour sad
Shrink underneath the plaid:

Happy if in the tufted brake
The English hunter him mistake;
  Nor lay his hounds in near
  The Caledonian deer.
But thou, the Wars' and Fortune's son,
March indefatigably on;
  And for the last effect
  Still keep thy sword erect:
Besides the force it has to fright
The spirits of the shady night,
  The same arts that did *gain*
  A power must it *maintain*.

TOM MAY'S DEATH

As one put drunk into the packet-boat,
Tom May was hurried hence and did not know't.
But was amazed on the Elysian side,
And with an eye uncertain, gazing wide,
Could not determine in what place he was,
(For whence in Stephen's Alley trees or grass?)
Nor where the Pope's Head, nor the Mitre lay,
Signs by which still he found and lost his way.
At last while doubtfully he all compares,
He saw near hand, as he imagined, Ares.
Such did he seem for corpulence and port,
But 'twas a man much of another sort;
'Twas Ben that in the dusky laurel shade
Amongst the chorus of old poets laid,
Sounding of ancient heroes, such as were
The subject's safety, and the rebel's fear;
But how a double-headed vulture eats
Brutus and Cassius the people's cheats.
But seeing May, he varied straight his song,
Gently to signify that he was wrong.
'Cups more than civil of Emathian wine,
I sing,' said he, 'and the Pharsalian sign,

Where the historian of the commonwealth
In his own bowels sheathed the conquering health.'
By this, May to himself and them was come,
He found he was translated, and by whom.
Yet then with foot as stumbling as his tongue
Pressed for his place among the learned throng.
But Ben, who knew not neither foe nor friend,
Sworn enemy to all that do pretend,
Rose, more than ever he was seen severe,
Shook his gray locks, and his own bays did tear
At this intrusion. Then with laurel wand –
The awful sign of his supreme command,
At whose dread whisk Virgil himself does quake,
And Horace patiently its stroke does take –
As he crowds in, he whipped him o'er the pate
Like Pembroke at the masque, and then did rate:
'Far from these blessed shades tread back again
Most servile wit, and mercenary pen;
Polydore, Lucan, Alan, Vandal, Goth,
Malignant poet and historian both.
Go seek the novice statesmen, and obtrude
On them some Roman cast similitude;
Tell them of liberty, the stories fine,
Until you all grow consuls in your wine.
Or thou, Dictator of the glass, bestow
On him the Cato, this the Cicero;
Transferring old Rome hither in your talk,
As Bethlem's house did to Loreto walk.
Foul architect that hadst not eye to see
How ill the measures of these states agree;
And who by Rome's example England lay,
Those but to Lucan do continue May.
But thee nor ignorance nor seeming good
Misled, but malice fixed and understood.
Because some one than thee more worthy wears
The sacred laurel, hence are all these tears?
Must therefore all the world be set on flame,

Because a gazette writer missed his aim?
And for a tankard-bearing muse must we
As for the basket, Guelphs and Ghib'llines be?
When the sword glitters o'er the judge's head,
And fear has coward churchmen silenced,
Then is the poet's time, 'tis then he draws,
And single fights forsaken virtue's cause.
He, when the wheel of empire whirleth back,
And though the world's disjointed axle crack,
Sings still of ancient rights and better times,
Seeks wretched good, arraigns successful crimes.
But thou, base man, first prostituted hast
Our spotless knowledge and the studies chaste,
Apostatizing from our arts and us,
To turn the chronicler to Spartacus.
Yet wast thou taken hence with equal fate,
Before thou couldst great Charles his death relate.
But what will deeper wound thy little mind,
Hast left surviving Davenant still behind,
Who laughs to see in this thy death renewed,
Right Roman poverty and gratitude.
Poor poet thou, and grateful senate they,
Who thy last reck'ning did so largely pay;
And with the public gravity would come,
When thou hadst drunk thy last to lead thee home –
If that can be thy home where Spenser lies,
And reverend Chaucer – but their dust does rise
Against thee, and expels thee from their side,
As th' eagle's plumes from other birds divide.
Nor here thy shade must dwell. Return, return,
Where sulphury Phlegethon does ever burn.
Thee Cerberus with all his jaws shall gnash,
Megaera thee with all her serpents lash.
Thou riveted unto Ixion's wheel
Shalt break, and the perpetual vulture feel.
'Tis just, what torments poets ere did feign,
Thou first historically shouldst sustain.'

Thus by irrevocable sentence cast,
May only Master of these Revels passed.
And straight he vanished in a cloud of pitch,
Such as unto the Sabbath bears the witch.

UPON THE HILL AND GROVE AT BILBROUGH: TO THE LORD FAIRFAX

1

See how the arched earth does here
Rise in a perfect hemisphere!
The stiffest compass could not strike
A line more circular and like;
Nor softest pencil draw a brow
So equal as this Hill does bow.
It seems as for a model laid,
And that the world by it was made.

2

Here learn, ye mountains more unjust,
Which to abrupter greatness thrust,
That do with your hook-shouldered height
The earth deform and heaven fright,
For whose excrescence ill-designed,
Nature must a new centre find,
Learn here those humble steps to tread,
Which to securer glory lead.

3

See what a soft access and wide
Lies open to its grassy side;
Nor with the rugged path deters
The feet of breathless travellers.
See then how courteous it ascends,
And all the way it rises bends;

Nor for itself the height does gain,
But only strives to raise the plain.

4

Yet thus it all the field commands,
And in unenvied greatness stands,
Discerning further than the cliff
Of heaven-daring Tenerife.
How glad the weary seamen haste
When they salute it from the mast!
By night the Northern Star their way
Directs, and this no less by day.

5

Upon its crest this mountain grave
A plume of aged trees does wave.
No hostile hand durst ere invade
With impious steel the sacred shade.
For something always did appear
Of the great Master's terror there:
And men could hear his armour still
Rattling through all the grove and hill.

6

Fear of the Master, and respect
Of the great Nymph did it protect;
Vera the Nymph that him inspired,
To whom he often here retired,
And on these oaks engraved her name;
Such wounds alone these woods became:
But ere he well the barks could part
'Twas writ already in their heart.

7

For they ('tis credible) have sense,
As we, of love and reverence,

And underneath the courser rind
The genius of the house do bind.
Hence they successes seem to know,
And in their Lord's advancement grow;
But in no memory were seen,
As under this, so straight and green.

8

Yet now no further strive to shoot,
Contented if they fix their root.
Nor to the wind's uncertain gust,
Their prudent heads too far intrust.
Only sometimes a flutt'ring breeze
Discourses with the breathing trees;
Which in their modest whispers name
Those acts that swelled the cheek of fame.

9

'Much other groves', say they, 'than these
And other hills him once did please.
Through groves of pikes he thundered then,
And mountains raised of dying men.
For all the civic garlands due
To him, our branches are but few.
Nor are our trunks enough to bear
The trophies of one fertile year.'

10

'Tis true, ye trees, nor ever spoke
More certain oracles in oak.
But peace (if you his favour prize):
That courage its own praises flies.
Therefore to your obscurer seats
From his own brightness he retreats:
Nor he the hills without the groves,
Nor height but with retirement loves.

UPON APPLETON HOUSE: TO MY LORD FAIRFAX

1

Within this sober frame expect
Work of no foreign architect,
That unto caves the quarries drew,
And forests did to pastures hew;
Who of his great design in pain
Did for a model vault his brain,
Whose columns should so high be raised
To arch the brows that on them gazed.

2

Why should of all things man unruled
Such unproportioned dwellings build?
The beasts are by their dens expressed:
And birds contrive an equal nest;
The low-roofed tortoises do dwell
In cases fit of tortoise-shell:
No creature loves an empty space;
Their bodies measure out their place.

3

But he, superfluously spread,
Demands more room alive than dead.
And in his hollow palace goes
Where winds (as he) themselves may lose.
What need of all this marble crust
T' impark the wanton mote of dust,
That thinks by breadth the world t' unite
Though the first builders failed in height?

4

But all things are composed here
Like Nature, orderly and near:
In which we the dimensions find
Of that more sober age and mind,
When larger-sized men did stoop

To enter at a narrow loop;
As practising, in doors so strait,
To strain themselves through heaven's gate.

5

And surely when the after age
Shall hither come in pilgrimage,
These sacred places to adore,
By Vere and Fairfax trod before,
Men will dispute how their extent
Within such dwarfish confines went:
And some will smile at this, as well
As Romulus his bee-like cell.

6

Humility alone designs
Those short but admirable lines,
By which, ungirt and unconstrained,
Things greater are in less contained.
Let others vainly strive t' immure
The circle in the quadrature!
These holy mathematics can
In every figure equal man.

7

Yet thus the laden house does sweat,
And scarce endures the Master great:
But where he comes the swelling hall
Stirs, and the square grows spherical;
More by his magnitude distressed,
Than he is by its straitness pressed:
And too officiously it slights
That in itself which him delights.

8

So honour better lowness bears,
Than that unwonted greatness wears;

Height with a certain grace does bend,
But low things clownishly ascend.
And yet what needs there here excuse,
Where everything does answer use?
Where neatness nothing can condemn,
Nor pride invent what to contemn?

9

A stately frontispiece of poor
Adorns without the open door:
Nor less the rooms within commends
Daily new furniture of friends.
The house was built upon the place
Only as for a mark of grace;
And for an inn to entertain
Its Lord a while, but not remain.

10

Him Bishop's Hill, or Denton may,
Or Bilbrough, better hold than they:
But Nature here hath been so free
As if she said, 'Leave this to me.'
Art would more neatly have defaced
What she had laid so sweetly waste;
In fragrant gardens, shady woods,
Deep meadows, and transparent floods.

11

While with slow eyes we these survey,
And on each pleasant footstep stay,
We opportunely may relate
The progress of this house's fate.
A nunnery first gave it birth
(For virgin buildings oft brought forth);
And all that neighbour-ruin shows
The quarries whence this dwelling rose.

12

Near to this gloomy cloister's gates
There dwelt the blooming virgin Thwaites;
Fair beyond measure, and an heir
Which might deformity make fair.
And oft she spent the summer suns
Discoursing with the subtle nuns.
Whence in these words one to her weaved,
(As 'twere by chance) thoughts long conceived.

13

'Within this holy leisure we
Live innocently as you see.
These walls restrain the world without,
But hedge our liberty about.
These bars inclose that wider den
Of those wild creatures, called men.
The cloister outward shuts its gates,
And, from us, locks on them the grates.

14

'Here we, in shining armour white,
Like virgin Amazons do fight.
And our chaste lamps we hourly trim,
Lest the great Bridegroom find them dim.
Our orient breaths perfumed are
With incense of incessant prayer.
And holy-water of our tears
Most strangely our complexion clears.

15

'Not tears of grief; but such as those
With which calm pleasure overflows;
Or pity, when we look on you
That live without this happy vow.
How should we grieve that must be seen

Each one a spouse, and each a queen;
And can in heaven hence behold
Our brighter robes and crowns of gold?

16

'When we have prayed all our beads,
Someone the holy Legend reads;
While all the rest with needles paint
The face and graces of the saint.
But what the linen can't receive
They in their lives do interweave.
This work the saints best represents;
That serves for altar's ornaments.

17

'But much it to our work would add
If here your hand, your face we had:
By it we would Our Lady touch;
Yet thus She you resembles much.
Some of your features, as we sewed,
Through every shrine should be bestowed.
And in one beauty we would take
Enough a thousand saints to make.

18

'And (for I dare not quench the fire
That me does for your good inspire)
'Twere sacrilege a man t' admit
To holy things, for heaven fit.
I see the angels in a crown
On you the lilies showering down:
And round about you glory breaks,
That something more than human speaks.

19

'All beauty, when at such a height,
Is so already consecrate.

Fairfax I know; and long ere this
Have marked the youth, and what he is.
But can he such a rival seem
For whom you heav'n should disesteem?
Ah, no! and 'twould more honour prove
He your *devoto* were, than love.

20

'Here live beloved, and obeyed:
Each one your sister, each your maid.
And, if our rule seem strictly penned,
The rule itself to you shall bend.
Our Abbess too, now far in age,
Doth your succession near presage.
How soft the yoke on us would lie,
Might such fair hands as yours it tie!

21

'Your voice, the sweetest of the choir,
Shall draw heaven nearer, raise us higher.
And your example, if our head,
Will soon us to perfection lead.
Those virtues to us all so dear,
Will straight grow sanctity when here:
And that, once sprung, increase so fast
Till miracles it work at last.

22

'Nor is our order yet so nice,
Delight to banish as a vice.
Here pleasure piety doth meet;
One perfecting the other sweet.
So through the mortal fruit we boil
The sugar's uncorrupting oil:
And that which perished while we pull,
Is thus preserved clear and full.

23

'For such indeed are all our arts;
Still handling Nature's finest parts.
Flowers dress the altars; for the clothes,
The sea-born amber we compose;
Balms for the grieved we draw; and pastes
We mould, as baits for curious tastes.
What need is here of man? unless
These as sweet sins we should confess.

24

'Each night among us to your side
Appoint a fresh and virgin bride;
Whom if Our Lord at midnight find,
Yet neither should be left behind.
Where you may lie as chaste in bed,
As pearls together billeted;
All night embracing arm in arm,
Like crystal pure with cotton warm.

25

'But what is this to all the store
Of joys you see, and may make more!
Try but a while, if you be wise:
The trial neither costs, nor ties.'
Now, Fairfax, seek her promised faith:
Religion that dispensed hath,
Which she henceforward does begin;
The nun's smooth tongue has sucked her in.

26

Oft, though he knew it was in vain,
Yet would he valiantly complain.
'Is this that sanctity so great,
An art by which you finelier cheat?
Hypocrite witches, hence avaunt,
Who though in prison yet enchant!

Death only can such thieves make fast,
As rob though in the dungeon cast.

27

'Were there but, when this house was made,
One stone that a just hand had laid,
It must have fall'n upon her head
Who first thee from thy faith misled.
And yet, how well soever meant,
With them 'twould soon grow fraudulent:
For like themselves they alter all,
And vice infects the very wall.

28

'But sure those buildings last not long,
Founded by folly, kept by wrong.
I know what fruit their gardens yield,
When they it think by night concealed.
Fly from their vices. 'Tis thy 'state,
Not thee, that they would consecrate.
Fly from their ruin. How I fear
Though guiltless lest thou perish there.'

29

What should he do? He would respect
Religion, but not right neglect:
For first religion taught him right,
And dazzled not but cleared his sight.
Sometimes resolved his sword he draws,
But reverenceth then the laws:
For justice still that courage led;
First from a judge, then soldier bred.

30

Small honour would be in the storm.
The Court him grants the lawful form;
Which licensed either peace or force,

To hinder the unjust divorce.
Yet still the nuns his right debarred,
Standing upon their holy guard.
Ill-counselled women, do you know
Whom you resist, or what you do?

31

Is not this he whose offspring fierce
Shall fight through all the universe;
And with successive valour try
France, Poland, either Germany;
Till one, as long since prophesied,
His horse through conquered Britain ride?
Yet, against fate, his spouse they kept,
And the great race would intercept.

32

Some to the breach against their foes
Their wooden saints in vain oppose.
Another bolder stands at push
With their old holy-water brush.
While the disjointed Abbess threads
The jingling chain-shot of her beads.
But their loud'st cannon were their lungs;
And sharpest weapons were their tongues.

33

But, waving these aside like flies,
Young Fairfax through the wall does rise.
Then th' unfrequented vault appeared,
And superstitions vainly feared.
The relics false were set to view;
Only the jewels there were true –
But truly bright and holy Thwaites
That weeping at the altar waits.

34

But the glad youth away her bears,
And to the nuns bequeaths her tears:
Who guiltily their prize bemoan,
Like gypsies that a child had stol'n.
Thenceforth (as when th' enchantment ends
The castle vanishes or rends)
The wasting cloister with the rest
Was in one instant dispossessed.

35

At the demolishing, this seat
To Fairfax fell as by escheat.
And what both nuns and founders willed
'Tis likely better thus fulfilled.
For if the virgin proved not theirs,
The cloister yet remained hers.
Though many a nun there made her vow,
'Twas no *religious house* till now.

36

From that blest bed the hero came,
Whom France and Poland yet does fame:
Who, when retired here to peace,
His warlike studies could not cease;
But laid these gardens out in sport
In the just figure of a fort;
And with five bastions it did fence,
As aiming one for every sense.

37

When in the east the morning ray
Hangs out the colours of the day,
The bee through these known alleys hums,
Beating the *dian* with its drums.
Then flowers their drowsy eyelids raise,
Their silken ensigns each displays,

And dries its pan yet dank with dew,
And fills its flask with odours new.

38

These, as their Governor goes by,
In fragrant volleys they let fly;
And to salute their Governess
Again as great a charge they press:
None for the virgin Nymph; for she
Seems with the flowers a flower to be.
And think so still! though not compare
With breath so sweet, or cheek so fair.

39

Well shot ye firemen! Oh how sweet,
And round your equal fires do meet;
Whose shrill report no ear can tell,
But echoes to the eye and smell.
See how the flowers, as at parade,
Under their colours stand displayed:
Each regiment in order grows,
That of the tulip, pink, and rose.

40

But when the vigilant patrol
Of stars walks round about the pole,
Their leaves, that to the stalks are curled,
Seem to their staves the ensigns furled.
Then in some flower's beloved hut
Each bee as sentinel is shut;
And sleeps so too: but, if once stirred,
She runs you through, or asks the word.

41

Oh thou, that dear and happy isle
The garden of the world ere while,

Thou paradise of four seas,
Which heaven planted us to please,
But, to exclude the world, did guard
With wat'ry if not flaming sword;
What luckless apple did we taste,
To make us mortal, and thee waste?

42

Unhappy! shall we never more
That sweet militia restore,
When gardens only had their towers,
And all the garrisons were flowers;
When roses only arms might bear,
And men did rosy garlands wear?
Tulips, in several colours barred,
Were then the Switzers of our Guard.

43

The gard'ner had the soldier's place,
And his more gentle forts did trace.
The nursery of all things green
Was then the only magazine.
The winter quarters were the stoves,
Where he the tender plants removes.
But war all this doth overgrow:
We ordnance plant and powder sow.

44

And yet there walks one on the sod
Who, had it pleased him and God,
Might once have made our gardens spring
Fresh as his own and flourishing.
But he preferred to the Cinque Ports
These five imaginary forts:
And, in those half-dry trenches, spanned
Power which the ocean might command.

45

For he did, with his utmost skill,
Ambition weed, but conscience till –
Conscience, that heaven-nursed plant,
Which most our earthy gardens want.
A prickling leaf it bears, and such
As that which shrinks at every touch;
But flowers eternal, and divine,
That in the crowns of saints do shine.

46

The sight does from these bastions ply,
Th' invisible artillery;
And at proud Cawood Castle seems
To point the batt'ry of its beams.
As if it quarrelled in the seat
Th' ambition of its prelate great.
But o'er the meads below it plays,
Or innocently seems to graze.

47

And now to the abyss I pass
Of that unfathomable grass,
Where men like grasshoppers appear,
But grasshoppers are giants there:
They, in their squeaking laugh, contemn
Us as we walk more low than them:
And, from the precipices tall
Of the green spires, to us do call.

48

To see men through this meadow dive,
We wonder how they rise alive;
As, under water, none does know
Whether he fall through it or go.
But, as the mariners that sound,
And show upon their lead the ground,

They bring up flowers so to be seen,
And prove they've at the bottom been.

49

No scene that turns with engines strange
Does oft'ner than these meadows change.
For when the sun the grass hath vexed,
The tawny mowers enter next;
Who seem like Israelites to be,
Walking on foot through a green sea.
To them the grassy deeps divide,
And crowd a lane to either side.

50

With whistling scythe, and elbow strong,
These massacre the grass along:
While one, unknowing, carves the rail,
Whose yet unfeathered quills her fail.
The edge all bloody from its breast
He draws, and does his stroke detest;
Fearing the flesh untimely mowed
To him a fate as black forebode.

51

But bloody Thestylis, that waits
To bring the mowing camp their cates,
Greedy as kites has trussed it up,
And forthwith means on it to sup:
When on another quick she lights,
And cries, 'He called us Israelites;
But now, to make his saying true,
Rails rain for quails, for manna, dew.'

52

Unhappy birds! what does it boot
To build below the grass's root;
When lowness is unsafe as height,

And chance o'ertakes what scapeth spite?
And now your orphan parents' call
Sounds your untimely funeral.
Death-trumpets creak in such a note,
And 'tis the sourdine in their throat.

53

Or sooner hatch or higher build:
The mower now commands the field;
In whose new traverse seemeth wrought
A camp of battle newly fought:
Where, as the meads with hay, the plain
Lies quilted o'er with bodies slain:
The women that with forks it fling,
Do represent the pillaging.

54

And now the careless victors play,
Dancing the triumphs of the hay;
Where every mower's wholesome heat
Smells like an Alexander's sweat.
Their females fragrant as the mead
Which they in fairy circles tread:
When at their dance's end they kiss,
Their new-made hay not sweeter is.

55

When after this 'tis piled in cocks,
Like a calm sea it shows the rocks:
We wond'ring in the river near
How boats among them safely steer.
Or, like the desert Memphis sand,
Short pyramids of hay do stand.
And such the Roman camps do rise
In hills for soldiers' obsequies.

56

This scene again withdrawing brings
A new and empty face of things;
A levelled space, as smooth and plain
As cloths for Lely stretched to stain.
The world when first created sure
Was such a table rase and pure.
Or rather such is the *toril*
Ere the bulls enter at Madril.

57

For to this naked equal flat,
Which Levellers take pattern at,
The villagers in common chase
Their cattle, which it closer rase;
And what below the scythe increased
Is pinched yet nearer by the beast.
Such, in the painted world, appeared
Davenant with th' universal herd.

58

They seem within the polished grass
A landskip drawn in looking-glass;
And shrunk in the huge pasture show
As spots, so shaped, on faces do.
Such fleas, ere they approach the eye,
In multiplying glasses lie.
They feed so wide, so slowly move,
As constellations do above.

59

Then, to conclude these pleasant acts,
Denton sets ope its cataracts;
And makes the meadow truly be
(What it but seemed before) a sea.
For, jealous of its Lord's long stay,
It tries t' invite him thus away.

The river in itself is drowned,
And isles th' astonished cattle round.

60

Let others tell the paradox,
How eels now bellow in the ox;
How horses at their tails do kick,
Turned as they hang to leeches quick;
How boats can over bridges sail;
And fishes do the stables scale.
How salmons trespassing are found;
And pikes are taken in the pound.

61

But I, retiring from the flood,
Take sanctuary in the wood;
And, while it lasts, myself embark
In this yet green, yet growing ark;
Where the first carpenter might best
Fit timber for his keel have pressed.
And where all creatures might have shares,
Although in armies, not in pairs.

62

The double wood of ancient stocks
Linked in so thick, an union locks,
It like two pedigrees appears,
On one hand Fairfax, th' other Vere's:
Of whom though many fell in war,
Yet more to heaven shooting are:
And, as they Nature's cradle decked,
Will in green age her hearse expect.

63

When first the eye this forest sees
It seems indeed as wood not trees:

As if their neighbourhood so old
To one great trunk them all did mould.
There the huge bulk takes place, as meant
To thrust up a fifth element;
And stretches still so closely wedged
As if the night within were hedged.

64

Dark all without it knits; within
It opens passable and thin;
And in as loose an order grows,
As the Corinthian porticoes.
The arching boughs unite between
The columns of the temple green;
And underneath the winged choirs
Echo about their tuned fires.

65

The nightingale does here make choice
To sing the trials of her voice.
Low shrubs she sits in, and adorns
With music high the squatted thorns.
But highest oaks stoop down to hear,
And list'ning elders prick the ear.
The thorn, lest it should hurt her, draws
Within the skin its shrunken claws.

66

But I have for my music found
A sadder, yet more pleasing sound:
The stock-doves, whose fair necks are graced
With nuptial rings, their ensigns chaste;
Yet always, for some cause unknown,
Sad pair unto the elms they moan.
O why should such a couple mourn,
That in so equal flames do burn!

67

Then as I careless on the bed
Of gelid strawberries do tread,
And through the hazels thick espy
The hatching throstle's shining eye,
The heron from the ash's top,
The eldest of its young lets drop,
As if it stork-like did pretend
That tribute to its Lord to send.

68

But most the hewel's wonders are,
Who here has the *holtfelster's* care.
He walks still upright from the root,
Meas'ring the timber with his foot;
And all the way, to keep it clean,
Doth from the bark the woodmoths glean.
He, with his beak, examines well
Which fit to stand and which to fell.

69

The good he numbers up, and hacks;
As if he marked them with the axe.
But where he, tinkling with his beak,
Does find the hollow oak to speak,
That for his building he designs,
And through the tainted side he mines.
Who could have thought the tallest oak
Should fall by such a feeble stroke!

70

Nor would it, had the tree not fed
A traitor-worm, within it bred.
(As first our flesh corrupt within
Tempts impotent and bashful sin.)
And yet that worm triumphs not long,
But serves to feed the hewel's young.

While the oak seems to fall content,
Viewing the treason's punishment.

71

Thus I, easy philosopher,
Among the birds and trees confer:
And little now to make me wants
Or of the fowls, or of the plants.
Give me but wings as they, and I
Straight floating on the air shall fly:
Or turn me but, and you shall see
I was but an inverted tree.

72

Already I begin to call
In their most learned original:
And where I language want, my signs
The bird upon the bough divines;
And more attentive there doth sit
Than if she were with lime-twigs knit.
No leaf does tremble in the wind
Which I returning cannot find.

73

Out of these scattered Sibyl's leaves
Strange prophecies my fancy weaves:
And in one history consumes,
Like Mexique paintings, all the plumes.
What Rome, Greece, Palestine, ere said
I in this light mosaic read.
Thrice happy he who, not mistook,
Hath read in Nature's mystic book.

74

And see how chance's better wit
Could with a mask my studies hit!
The oak-leaves me embroider all,

Between which caterpillars crawl:
And ivy, with familiar trails,
Me licks, and clasps, and curls, and hales.
Under this antic cope I move
Like some great prelate of the grove.

75

Then, languishing with ease, I toss
On pallets swoll'n of velvet moss;
While the wind, cooling through the boughs,
Flatters with air my panting brows.
Thanks for my rest ye mossy banks,
And unto you cool zephyrs thanks,
Who, as my hair, my thoughts too shed,
And winnow from the chaff my head.

76

How safe, methinks, and strong, behind
These trees have I encamped my mind;
Where beauty, aiming at the heart,
Bends in some tree its useless dart;
And where the world no certain shot
Can make, or me it toucheth not.
But I on it securely play,
And gall its horsemen all the day.

77

Bind me, ye woodbines, in your twines,
Curl me about ye gadding vines,
And O so close your circles lace,
That I may never leave this place:
But, lest your fetters prove too weak,
Ere I your silken bondage break,
Do you, O brambles, chain me too,
And, courteous briars, nail me through.

78

Here in the morning tie my chain,
Where the two woods have made a lane;
While, like a guard on either side,
The trees before their Lord divide;
This, like a long and equal thread,
Betwixt two labyrinths does lead.
But, where the floods did lately drown,
There at the evening stake me down.

79

For now the waves are fall'n and dried,
And now the meadow's fresher dyed;
Whose grass, with moister colour dashed,
Seems as green silks but newly washed.
No serpent new nor crocodile
Remains behind our little Nile;
Unless itself you will mistake,
Among these meads the only snake.

80

See in what wanton harmless folds
It everywhere the meadow holds;
And its yet muddy back doth lick,
Till as a crystal mirror slick;
Where all things gaze themselves, and doubt
If they be in it or without.
And for his shade which therein shines,
Narcissus-like, the sun too pines.

81

Oh what a pleasure 'tis to hedge
My temples here with heavy sedge;
Abandoning my lazy side,
Stretched as a bank unto the tide;
Or to suspend my sliding foot

On the osier's undermined root,
And in its branches tough to hang,
While at my lines the fishes twang!

82

But now away my hooks and quills,
And angles, idle utensils.
The young Maria walks tonight:
Hide, trifling youth, thy pleasures slight.
'Twere shame that such judicious eyes
Should with such toys a man surprise;
She that already is the law
Of all her sex, her age's awe.

83

See how loose Nature, in respect
To her, itself doth recollect;
And everything so whisht and fine,
Starts forthwith to its *bonne mine*.
The sun himself, of her aware,
Seems to descend with greater care;
And lest she see him go to bed,
In blushing clouds conceals his head.

84

So when the shadows laid asleep
From underneath these banks do creep,
And on the river as it flows
With eben shuts begin to close;
The modest halcyon comes in sight,
Flying betwixt the day and night;
And such an horror calm and dumb,
Admiring Nature does benumb.

85

The viscous air, wheres'e'er she fly,
Follows and sucks her azure dye;

The jellying stream compacts below,
If it might fix her shadow so;
The stupid fishes hang, as plain
As flies in crystal overta'en;
And men the silent scene assist,
Charmed with the sapphire-winged mist.

86

Maria such, and so doth hush
The world, and through the evening rush.
No new-born comet such a train
Draws through the sky, nor star new-slain.
For straight those giddy rockets fail,
Which from the putrid earth exhale,
But by her flames, in heaven tried,
Nature is wholly vitrified.

87

'Tis she that to these gardens gave
That wondrous beauty which they have;
She straightness on the woods bestows;
To her the meadow sweetness owes;
Nothing could make the river be
So crystal-pure but only she;
She yet more pure, sweet, straight, and fair,
Than gardens, woods, meads, rivers are.

88

Therefore what first she on them spent,
They gratefully again present:
The meadow carpets where to tread;
The garden flowers to crown her head;
And for a glass the limpid brook,
Where she may all her beauties look;
But, since she would not have them seen,
The wood about her draws a screen.

89

For she, to higher beauties raised,
Disdains to be for lesser praised.
She counts her beauty to converse
In all the languages as hers;
Nor yet in those herself employs
But for the wisdom, not the noise;
Nor yet that wisdom would affect,
But as 'tis heaven's dialect.

90

Blest Nymph! that couldst so soon prevent
Those trains by youth against thee meant;
Tears (wat'ry shot that pierce the mind);
And sighs (Love's cannon charged with wind);
True praise (that breaks through all defence);
And feigned complying innocence;
But knowing where this ambush lay,
She 'scaped the safe, but roughest way.

91

This 'tis to have been from the first
In a domestic heaven nursed,
Under the discipline severe
Of Fairfax, and the starry Vere;
Where not one object can come nigh
But pure, and spotless as the eye;
And goodness doth itself entail
On females, if there want a male.

92

Go now, fond sex, that on your face
Do all your useless study place,
Nor once at vice your brows dare knit
Lest the smooth forehead wrinkled sit:
Yet your own face shall at you grin,
Thorough the black-bag of your skin;

When knowledge only could have filled
And virtue all those furrows tilled.

93

Hence she with graces more divine
Supplies beyond her sex the line;
And, like a sprig of mistletoe,
On the Fairfacian oak does grow;
Whence, for some universal good,
The priest shall cut the sacred bud;
While her glad parents most rejoice,
And make their destiny their choice.

94

Meantime, ye fields, springs, bushes, flowers,
Where yet she leads her studious hours,
(Till Fate her worthily translates,
And find a Fairfax for our Thwaites),
Employ the means you have by her,
And in your kind yourselves prefer;
That, as all virgins she precedes,
So you all woods, streams, gardens, meads.

95

For you Thessalian Tempe's seat
Shall now be scorned as obsolete;
Aranjuez, as less, disdained;
The Bel-Retiro as constrained;
But name not the Idalian grove,
For 'twas the seat of wanton love;
Much less the dead's Elysian Fields,
Yet nor to them your beauty yields.

96

'Tis not, what once it was, the world;
But a rude heap together hurled;
All negligently overthrown,

Gulfs, deserts, precipices, stone.
Your lesser world contains the same,
But in more decent order tame;
You heaven's centre, Nature's lap,
And paradise's only map.

97

But now the salmon-fishers moist
Their leathern boats begin to hoist;
And, like Antipodes in shoes,
Have shod their heads in their canoes.
How tortoise-like, but not so slow,
These rational amphibii go!
Let's in: for the dark hemisphere
Does now like one of them appear.

ON MR MILTON'S 'PARADISE LOST'

When I beheld the poet blind, yet bold,
In slender book his vast design unfold,
Messiah crowned, God's reconciled decree,
Rebelling Angels, the Forbidden Tree,
Heaven, Hell, Earth, Chaos, all; the argument
Held me a while misdoubting his intent,
That he would ruin (for I saw him strong)
The sacred truths to fable and old song,
(So Samson groped the temple's posts in spite)
The world o'erwhelming to revenge his sight.
  Yet as I read, soon growing less severe,
I liked his project, the success did fear;
Through that wide field how he his way should find
O'er which lame Faith leads Understanding blind;
Lest he perplexed the things he would explain,
And what was easy he should render vain.
  Or if a work so infinite he spanned,

Jealous I was that some less skilful hand
(Such as disquiet always what is well,
And by ill imitating would excel)
Might hence presume the whole Creation's day
To change in scenes, and show it in a play.
  Pardon me, Mighty Poet, nor despise
My causeless, yet not impious, surmise.
But I am now convinced that none will dare
Within thy labours to pretend a share.
Thou hast not missed one thought that could be fit,
And all that was improper dost omit:
So that no room is here for writers left,
But to detect their ignorance or theft.
  That majesty which through thy work doth reign
Draws the devout, deterring the profane.
And things divine thou treat'st of in such state
As them preserves, and thee, inviolate.
At once delight and horror on us seize,
Thou sing'st with so much gravity and ease;
And above human flight dost soar aloft,
With plume so strong, so equal, and so soft.
The bird named from that paradise you sing
So never flags, but always keeps on wing.
  Where couldst thou words of such a compass find?
Whence furnish such a vast expense of mind?
Just heaven thee, like Tiresias, to requite,
Rewards with prophecy thy loss of sight.
  Well mightst thou scorn thy readers to allure
With tinkling rhyme, of thine own sense secure;
While the *Town-Bays* writes all the while and spells,
And like a pack-horse tires without his bells.
Their fancies like our bushy points appear,
The poets tag them; we for fashion wear.
I too transported by the mode offend,
And while I meant to *praise* thee, must *commend*.
Thy verse created like thy theme sublime,
In number, weight, and measure, needs not rhyme.

THE FIRST ANNIVERSARY OF THE GOVERNMENT UNDER HIS HIGHNESS THE LORD PROTECTOR

Like the vain curlings of the wat'ry maze,
Which in smooth streams a sinking weight does raise;
So man, declining always, disappears
In the weak circles of increasing years;
And his short tumults of themselves compose,
While flowing Time above his head does close.
  Cromwell alone with greater vigour runs,
(Sun-like) the stages of succeeding suns:
And still the day which he doth next restore,
Is the just wonder of the day before.
Cromwell alone doth with new lustre spring,
And shines the jewel of the yearly ring.
  'Tis he the force of scattered time contracts,
And in one year the work of ages acts:
While heavy monarchs make a wide return,
Longer, and more malignant than Saturn:
And though they all Platonic years should reign,
In the same posture would be found again.
Their earthy projects under ground they lay,
More slow and brittle than the China clay:
Well may they strive to leave them to their son,
For one thing never was by one king done.
Yet some more active for a frontier town
Took in by proxy, begs a false renown;
Another triumphs at the public cost,
And will have won, if he no more have lost;
They fight by others, but in person wrong,
And only are against their subjects strong;
Their other wars seem but a feigned contest,
This common enemy is still oppressed;
If conquerors, on them they turn their might;
If conquered, on them they wreak their spite:
They neither build the temple in their days,

Nor matter for succeeding founders raise;
Nor sacred prophecies consult within,
Much less themselves to perfect them begin;
No other care they bear of things above,
But with astrologers divine, and Jove,
To know how long their planet yet reprieves
From the deserved fate their guilty lives:
Thus (image-like) an useless time they tell,
And with vain sceptre, strike the hourly bell;
Nor more contribute to the state of things,
Than wooden heads unto the viol's strings.
  While indefatigable Cromwell hies,
And cuts his way still nearer to the skies,
Learning a music in the region clear,
To tune this lower to that higher sphere.
  So when Amphion did the lute command,
Which the god gave him, with his gentle hand,
The rougher stones, unto his measures hewed,
Danced up in order from the quarries rude;
This took a lower, that an higher place,
As he the treble altered, or the bass:
No note he struck, but a new storey laid,
And the great work ascended while he played.
  The list'ning structures he with wonder eyed,
And still new stops to various time applied:
Now through the strings a martial rage he throws,
And joining straight the Theban tower arose;
Then as he strokes them with a touch more sweet,
The flocking marbles in a palace meet;
But, for he most the graver notes did try,
Therefore the temples reared their columns high:
Thus, ere he ceased, his sacred lute creates
Th' harmonious city of the seven gates.
  Such was that wondrous order and consent,
When Cromwell tuned the ruling Instrument;
While tedious statesmen many years did hack,
Framing a liberty that still went back;

Whose num'rous gorge could swallow in an hour
That island, which the sea cannot devour:
Then our Amphion issues out and sings,
And once he struck, and twice, the powerful strings.
 The Commonwealth then first together came,
And each one entered in the willing frame;
All other matter yields, and may be ruled;
But who the minds of stubborn men can build?
No quarry bears a stone so hardly wrought,
Nor with such labour from its centre brought;
None to be sunk in the foundation bends,
Each in the house the highest place contends,
And each the hand that lays him will direct,
And some fall back upon the architect;
Yet all composed by his attractive song,
Into the animated city throng.
 The Commonwealth does through their centres all
Draw the circumf'rence of the public wall;
The crossest spirits here do take their part,
Fast'ning the contignation which they thwart;
And they, whose nature leads them to divide,
Uphold, this one, and that the other side;
But the most equal still sustain the height,
And they as pillars keep the work upright;
While the resistance of opposed minds,
The fabric as with arches stronger binds,
Which on the basis of a senate free,
Knit by the roof's protecting weight agree.
 When for his foot he thus a place had found,
He hurls e'er since the world about him round;
And in his sev'ral aspects, like a star,
Here shines in peace, and thither shoots a war.
While by his beams observing princes steer,
And wisely court the influence they fear;
O would they rather by his pattern won
Kiss the approaching, nor yet angry Son;
And in their numbered footsteps humbly tread

The path where holy oracles do lead;
How might they under such a captain raise
The great designs kept for the latter days!
But mad with reason, so miscalled, of state
They know them not, and what they know not, hate.
Hence still they sing Hosanna to the Whore,
And her whom they should massacre adore:
But Indians, whom they should convert, subdue;
Not teach, but traffic with, or burn the Jew.
  Unhappy princes, ignorantly bred,
By malice some, by error more misled;
If gracious heaven to my life give length,
Leisure to time, and to my weakness strength,
Then shall I once with graver accents shake
Your regal sloth, and your long slumbers wake:
Like the shrill huntsman that prevents the east,
Winding his horn to kings that chase the beast.
  Till then my muse shall hollo far behind
Angelic Cromwell who outwings the wind;
And in dark nights, and in cold days alone
Pursues the Monster thorough every throne:
Which shrinking to her Roman den impure,
Gnashes her gory teeth; nor there secure.
  Hence oft I think, if in some happy hour
High grace should meet in one with highest power,
And then a seasonable people still
Should bend to his, as he to heaven's will,
What might we hope, what wonderful effect
From such a wished conjuncture might reflect.
Sure, the mysterious work, where none withstand,
Would forthwith finish under such a hand:
Foreshortened time its useless course would stay,
And soon precipitate the latest day.
But a thick cloud about that morning lies,
And intercepts the beams of mortal eyes,
That 'tis the most which we determine can,
If these the times, then this must be the man.

And well he therefore does, and well has guessed,
Who in his age has always forward pressed:
And knowing not where heaven's choice may light,
Girds yet his sword, and ready stands to fight;
But men, alas, as if they nothing cared,
Look on, all unconcerned, or unprepared;
And stars still fall, and still the Dragon's tail
Swinges the volumes of its horrid flail.
For the great justice that did first suspend
The world by sin, does by the same extend.
Hence that blest day still counterpoised wastes,
The ill delaying what th' elected hastes;
Hence landing nature to new seas is tossed,
And good designs still with their authors lost.
  And thou, great Cromwell, for whose happy birth
A mould was chosen out of better earth;
Whose saint-like mother we did lately see
Live out an age, long as a pedigree;
That she might seem, could we the Fall dispute,
T' have smelled the blossom, and not eat the fruit;
Though none does of more lasting parents grow,
But never any did them honour so;
Though thou thine heart from evil still unstained,
And always hast thy tongue from fraud refrained;
Thou, who so oft through storms of thund'ring lead
Hast borne securely thine undaunted head,
Thy breast through poniarding conspiracies,
Drawn from the sheath of lying prophecies;
Thee proof beyond all other force or skill,
Our sins endanger, and shall one day kill.
  How near they failed, and in thy sudden fall
At once assayed to overturn us all.
Our brutish fury struggling to be free,
Hurried thy horses while they hurried thee.
When thou hadst almost quit thy mortal cares,
And soiled in dust thy crown of silver hairs.
  Let this one sorrow interweave among

The other glories of our yearly song.
Like skilful looms, which through the costly thread
Of purling ore, a shining wave do shed:
So shall the tears we on past grief employ,
Still as they trickle, glitter in our joy.
So with more modesty we may be true,
And speak as of the dead the praises due:
While impious men deceived with pleasure short,
On their own hopes shall find the fall retort.
But the poor beasts wanting their noble guide,
(What could they more?) shrunk guiltily aside.
First winged fear transports them far away,
And leaden sorrow then their flight did stay.
See how they each his tow'ring crest abate,
And the green grass, and their known mangers hate,
Nor through wide nostrils snuff the wanton air,
Nor their round hooves, or curled manes compare;
With wand'ring eyes, and restless ears they stood,
And with shrill neighings asked him of the wood.
  Thou Cromwell falling, not a stupid tree,
Or rock so savage, but it mourned for thee:
And all about was heard a panic groan,
As if that Nature's self were overthrown.
It seemed the earth did from the centre tear;
It seemed the sun was fall'n out of the sphere:
Justice obstructed lay, and reason fooled;
Courage disheartened, and religion cooled.
A dismal silence through the palace went,
And then loud shrieks the vaulted marbles rent.
Such as the dying chorus sings by turns,
And to deaf seas, and ruthless tempests mourns,
When now they sink, and now the plundering streams
Break up each deck, and rip the oaken seams.
  But thee triumphant hence the fiery car,
And fiery steeds had borne out of the war,
From the low world, and thankless men above,
Unto the kingdom blest of peace and love:

We only mourned ourselves, in thine ascent,
Whom thou hadst left beneath with mantle rent.
  For all delight of life thou then didst lose,
When to command, thou didst thyself depose;
Resigning up thy privacy so dear,
To turn the headstrong people's charioteer;
For to be Cromwell was a greater thing,
Than ought below, or yet above a king:
Therefore thou rather didst thyself depress,
Yielding to rule, because it made thee less.
  For, neither didst thou from the first apply
Thy sober spirit unto things too high,
But in thine own fields exercised'st long,
An healthful mind within a body strong;
Till at the seventh time thou in the skies,
As a small cloud, like a man's hand didst rise;
Then did thick mists and winds the air deform,
And down at last thou poured'st the fertile storm;
Which to the thirsty land did plenty bring,
But though forewarned, o'ertook and wet the King.
  What since he did, an higher force him pushed
Still from behind, and it before him rushed,
Though undiscerned among the tumult blind,
Who think those high decrees by man designed.
'Twas heaven would not that his power should cease,
But walk still middle betwixt war and peace;
Choosing each stone, and poising every weight,
Trying the measures of the breadth and height;
Here pulling down, and there erecting new,
Founding a firm state by proportions true.
  When Gideon so did from the war retreat,
Yet by the conquest of two kings grown great,
He on the peace extends a warlike power,
And Israel silent saw him raze the tower;
And how he Succoth's elders durst suppress,
With thorns and briars of the wilderness.
No king might ever such a force have done;

Yet would not he be Lord, nor yet his son.
  Thou with the same strength, and an heart as plain,
Didst (like thine olive) still refuse to reign;
Though why should others all thy labour spoil,
And brambles be anointed with thine oil,
Whose climbing flame, without a timely stop,
Had quickly levelled every cedar's top?
Therefore first growing to thyself a law,
Th' ambitious shrubs thou in just time didst awe.
  So have I seen at sea, when whirling winds
Hurry the bark, but more the seamen's minds,
Who with mistaken course salute the sand,
And threat'ning rocks misapprehend for land;
While baleful Tritons to the shipwreck guide,
And corposants along the tacklings slide,
The passengers all wearied out before,
Giddy, and wishing for the fatal shore;
Some lusty mate, who with more careful eye
Counted the hours, and every star did spy,
The helm does from the artless steersman strain,
And doubles back unto the safer main.
What though a while they grumble discontent,
Saving himself, he does their loss prevent.
  'Tis not a freedom, that where all command;
Nor tyranny, where one does them withstand:
But who of both the bounders knows to lay
Him as their father must the state obey.
  Thou, and thine house, like Noah's eight, did rest,
Left by the war's flood on the mountain's crest:
And the large vale lay subject to thy will,
Which thou but as an husbandman wouldst till:
And only didst for others plant the vine
Of liberty, not drunken with its wine.
  That sober liberty which men may have,
That they enjoy, but more they vainly crave:
And such as to their parent's tents do press,
May show their own, not see his nakedness.

Yet such a Chammish issue still does rage,
The shame and plague both of the land and age,
Who watched thy halting, and thy fall deride,
Rejoicing when thy foot had slipped aside;
That their new king might the fifth sceptre shake,
And make the world, by his example, quake:
Whose frantic army should they want for men
Might muster heresies, so one were ten.
What thy misfortune, they the spirit call,
And their religion only is to fall.
O Mahomet! now couldst thou rise again,
Thy falling-sickness should have made thee reign,
While Feake and Simpson would in many a tome
Have writ the comments of thy sacred foam:
For soon thou mightst have passed among their rant
Were't but for thine unmoved tulipant;
As thou must needs have owned them of thy band
For prophecies fit to be *Alcoraned*.
Accursed locusts, whom your king does spit
Out of the centre of th' unbottomed pit;
Wanderers, adult'rers, liars, Munser's rest,
Sorcerers, atheists, Jesuits, possessed;
You who the scriptures and the laws deface
With the same liberty as points and lace;
Oh race most hypocritically strict!
Bent to reduce us to the ancient Pict;
Well may you act the Adam and the Eve;
Ay, and the serpent too that did deceive.
But the great captain, now the danger's o'er,
Makes you for his sake tremble one fit more;
And, to your spite, returning yet alive,
Does with himself all that is good revive.
So when first man did through the morning new
See the bright sun his shining race pursue,
All day he followed with unwearied sight,
Pleased with that other world of moving light;
But thought him when he missed his setting beams,

Sunk in the hills, or plunged below the streams.
While dismal blacks hung round the universe,
And stars (like tapers) burned upon his hearse:
And owls and ravens with their screeching noise
Did make the funerals sadder by their joys.
His weeping eyes the doleful vigils keep
Not knowing yet the night was made for sleep:
Still to the west, where he him lost, he turned,
And with such accents, as despairing, mourned:
'Why did mine eyes once see so bright a ray;
Or why day last no longer than a day?'
When straight the sun behind him he descried,
Smiling serenely from the further side.
  So while our star that gives us light and heat,
Seemed now a long and gloomy night to threat,
Up from the other world his flame he darts,
And princes, shining through their windows, starts;
Who their suspected counsellors refuse,
And credulous ambassadors accuse.
  'Is this,' saith one, 'the nation that we read
Spent with both wars, under a captain dead?
Yet rig a navy while we dress us late;
And ere we dine, raze and rebuild their state.
What oaken forests, and what golden mines!
What mints of men, what union of designs!
(Unless their ships do, as their fowl, proceed
Of shedding leaves, that with their ocean breed.)
Theirs are not ships, but rather arks of war,
And beaked promontories sailed from far;
Of floating islands a new hatched nest;
A fleet of worlds, of other worlds in quest;
An hideous shoal of wood-leviathans,
Armed with three tier of brazen hurricanes;
That through the centre shoot their thund'ring side
And sink the earth that does at anchor ride.
What refuge to escape them can be found,
Whose wat'ry leaguers all the world surround?

Needs must we all their tributaries be,
Whose navies hold the sluices of the sea.
The ocean is the fountain of command,
But that once took, we captives are on land.
And those that have the waters for their share,
Can quickly leave us neither earth nor air.
Yet if through these our fears could find a pass;
Through double oak, and lined with treble brass;
That one man still, although but named, alarms
More than all men, all navies, and all arms.
Him, all the day, him, in late nights I dread,
And still his sword seems hanging o'er my head.
The nation had been ours, but his one soul
Moves the great bulk, and animates the whole.
He secrecy with number hath enchased,
Courage with age, maturity with haste:
The valiant's terror, riddle of the wise;
And still his falchion all our knots unties.
Where did he learn those arts that cost us dear?
Where below earth, or where above the sphere?
He seems a king by long succession born,
And yet the same to be a king does scorn.
Abroad a king he seems, and something more,
At home a subject on the equal floor.
O could I once him with our title see,
So should I hope yet he might die as we.
But let them write his praise that love him best,
It grieves me sore to have thus much confessed.'
  Pardon, great Prince, if thus their fear or spite
More than our love or duty do thee right.
I yield, nor further will the prize contend;
So that we both alike may miss our end:
While thou thy venerable head dost raise
As far above their malice as my praise.
And as the Angel of our Commonweal,
Troubling the waters, yearly mak'st them heal.

A POEM UPON THE DEATH OF HIS LATE HIGHNESS THE LORD PROTECTOR

That Providence which had so long the care
Of Cromwell's head, and numbered every hair,
Now in itself (the glass where all appears)
Had seen the period of his golden years:
And thenceforth only did attend to trace
What death might least so fair a life deface.
The people, which what most they fear esteem,
Death when more horrid, so more noble deem;
And blame the last act, like spectators vain,
Unless the prince whom they applaud be slain;
Nor Fate indeed can well refuse that right
To those that lived in war, to die in fight.
But long his valour none had left that could
Endanger him, or clemency that would:
And he whom Nature all for peace had made,
But angry Heaven unto war had swayed,
And so less useful where he most desired,
For what he least affected was admired,
Deserved yet an end whose every part
Should speak the wondrous softness of his heart.
To Love and Grief the fatal writ was signed
(Those nobler weaknesses of human kind,
From which those powers that issued the decree,
Although immortal, found they were not free),
That they, to whom his breast still open lies,
In gentle passions should his death disguise:
And leave succeeding ages cause to mourn,
As long as Grief shall weep, or Love shall burn.
Straight does a slow and languishing disease
Eliza, Nature's and his darling, seize:
Her when an infant, taken with her charms,
He oft would flourish in his mighty arms;
And, lest their force the tender burden wrong,
Slacken the vigour of his muscles strong;

Then to the mother's breast her softly move,
Which, while she drained of milk, she filled with love.
But as with riper years her virtue grew,
And every minute adds a lustre new;
When with meridian height her beauty shined,
And thorough that sparkled her fairer mind;
When she with smiles serene in words discreet
His hidden soul at every turn could meet;
Then might y' ha' daily his affection spied,
Doubling that knot which destiny had tied;
While they by sense, not knowing, comprehend
How on each other both their fates depend.
With her each day the pleasing hours he shares,
And at her aspect calms his growing cares;
Or with a grandsire's joy her children sees
Hanging about her neck or at his knees.
Hold fast, dear infants, hold them both or none!
This will not stay when once the other's gone.
  A silent fire now wastes those limbs of wax,
And him within his tortured image racks.
So the flower with'ring which the garden crowned,
The sad root pines in secret under ground.
Each groan he doubled and each sigh he sighed,
Repeated over to the restless night.
No trembling string composed to numbers new,
Answers the touch in notes more sad, more true.
She, lest he grieve, hides what she can her pains,
And he to lessen hers his sorrow feigns:
Yet both perceived, yet both concealed their skills,
And so diminishing increased their ills:
That whether by each other's grief they fell,
Or on their own redoubled, none can tell.
  And now Eliza's purple locks were shorn,
Where she so long her father's fate had worn:
And frequent lightning to her soul that flies,
Divides the air and opens all the skies:
And now his life, suspended by her breath,

Ran out impetuously to hasting death.
Like polished mirrors, so his steely breast
Had every figure of her woes expressed;
And with the damp of her last gasps obscured,
Had drawn such stains as were not to be cured.
Fate could not either reach with single stroke,
But, the dear image fled, the mirror broke.
  Who now shall tell us more of mournful swans,
Of halcyons kind, or bleeding pelicans?
No downy breast did ere so gently beat,
Or fan with airy plumes so soft an heat.
For he no duty by his height excused,
Nor, though a *prince*, to be a *man* refused:
But rather than in his Eliza's pain
Not love, not grieve, would neither live nor reign:
And in himself so oft immortal tried,
Yet in compassion of another died.
  So have I seen a vine, whose lasting age
Of many a winter hath survived the rage;
Under whose shady tent men every year
At its rich blood's expense their sorrows cheer,
If some dear branch where it extends its life
Chance to be pruned by an untimely knife,
The parent tree unto the grief succeeds,
And through the wound its vital humour bleeds;
Trickling in wat'ry drops, whose flowing shape
Weeps that it falls ere fixed into a grape.
So the dry stock, no more that spreading vine,
Frustrates the autumn and the hopes of wine.
  A secret cause does sure those signs ordain
Foreboding princes' falls, and seldom vain:
Whether some kinder powers, that wish us well,
What they above cannot prevent, foretell;
Or the great world do by consent presage,
As hollow seas with future tempests rage:
Or rather Heaven, which us so long foresees,
Their funerals celebrates while it decrees.

But never yet was any human fate
By Nature solemnized with so much state.
He unconcerned the dreadful passage crossed;
But oh what pangs that death did Nature cost!
  First the great thunder was shot off, and sent
The signal from the starry battlement:
The winds receive it, and its force outdo,
As practising how they could thunder too:
Out of the binder's hand the sheaves they tore,
And thrashed the harvest in the airy floor;
Or of huge trees, whose growth with his did rise,
The deep foundations opened to the skies.
Then heavy showers the winged tempests lead,
And pour the deluge o'er the chaos' head.
The race of warlike horses at his tomb
Offer themselves in many a hecatomb;
With pensive head towards the ground they fall,
And helpless languish at the tainted stall.
Numbers of men decrease with pains unknown,
And hasten, not to see his death, their own.
Such tortures all the elements unfixed,
Troubled to part where so exactly mixed:
And as through air his wasting spirits flowed,
The universe laboured beneath their load.
  Nature it seemed with him would Nature vie;
He with Eliza, it with him would die.
  He without noise still travelled to his end,
As silent suns to meet the night descend.
The stars that for him fought had only power
Left to determine now his fatal hour;
Which, since they might not hinder, yet they cast
To choose it worthy of his glories past.
  No part of time but bare his mark away
Of honour; all the year was Cromwell's day:
But this, of all the most auspicious found,
Twice had in open field him victor crowned:
When up the armed mountains of Dunbar

He marched, and through deep Severn ending war.
What day should him eternize but the same
That had before immortalized his name?
That so who ere would at his death have joyed,
In their own griefs might find themselves employed;
But those that sadly his departure grieved,
Yet joyed rememb'ring what he once achieved.
And the last minute his victorious ghost
Gave chase to Ligny on the Belgic coast.
Here ended all his mortal toils; he laid
And slept in peace under the laurel shade.
  O Cromwell, Heaven's Favourite! To none
Have such high honours from above been shown:
For whom the elements we mourners see,
And Heaven itself would the great herald be;
Which with more care set forth his obsequies
Than those of Moses hid from human eyes:
As jealous only here lest all be less,
That we could to his memory express.
  Then let us too our course of mourning keep:
Where Heaven leads, 'tis piety to weep.
Stand back, ye seas, and shrunk beneath the veil
Of your abyss, with covered head bewail
Your monarch: we demand not your supplies
To compass in our isle; our tears suffice;
Since him away the dismal tempest rent,
Who once more joined us to the continent;
Who planted England on the Flandric shore,
And stretched our frontier to the Indian ore;
Whose greater truths obscure the fables old,
Whether of British saints or worthies told;
And in a valour less'ning Arthur's deeds,
For holiness the Confessor exceeds.
  He first put arms into Religion's hand,
And tim'rous Conscience unto Courage manned:
The soldier taught that inward mail to wear,
And fearing God how they should nothing fear.

'Those strokes,' he said, 'will pierce through all below
Where those that strike from Heaven fetch their blow.'
Astonished armies did their flight prepare,
And cities strong were stormed by his prayer.
Of that forever Preston's field shall tell
The story, and impregnable Clonmel;
And where the sandy mountain Fenwick scaled,
The sea between, yet hence his prayer prevailed.
What man was ever so in Heaven obeyed
Since the commanded sun o'er Gibeon stayed?
In all his wars needs must he triumph, when
He conquered God still ere he fought with men.
  Hence, though in battle none so brave or fierce,
Yet him the adverse steel could never pierce:
Pity it seemed to hurt him more that felt
Each wound himself which he to others dealt;
Danger itself refusing to offend
So loose an enemy, so fast a friend.
  Friendship, that sacred virtue, long does claim
The first foundation of his house and name:
But within one its narrow limits fall;
His tenderness extended unto all:
And that deep soul through every channel flows,
Where kindly nature loves itself to lose.
More strong affections never reason served,
Yet still affected most what best deserved.
If he Eliza loved to that degree,
(Though who more worthy to be loved than she?)
If so indulgent to his own, how dear
To him the children of the Highest were?
For her he once did nature's tribute pay:
For these his life adventured every day.
And 'twould be found, could we his thoughts have cast,
Their griefs struck deepest, if Eliza's last.
  What prudence more than human did he need
To keep so dear, so diff'ring minds agreed?
The worser sort, as conscious of their ill,

Lie weak and easy to the ruler's will;
But to the good (too many or too few),
All law is useless, all reward is due.
Oh ill advised! if not for love, for shame,
Spare yet your own, if you neglect his fame;
Lest others dare to think your zeal a mask,
And you to govern only *Heaven's* task.
  Valour, religion, friendship, prudence died
At once with him, and all that's good beside;
And we, death's refuse, nature's dregs, confined
To loathsome life, alas! are left behind,
Where we (so once we used) shall now no more,
To fetch day, press about his chamber door;
From which he issued with that awful state,
It seemed Mars broke through Janus' double gate:
Yet always tempered with an air so mild,
No April suns that e'er so gently smiled;
No more shall hear that powerful language charm,
Whose force oft spared the labour of his arm;
No more shall follow where he spent the days
In war, in counsel, or in prayer, and praise;
Whose meanest acts he would himself advance,
As ungirt David to the ark did dance.
All, all is gone of ours or his delight
In horses fierce, wild deer, or armour bright.
Francisca fair can nothing now but weep,
Nor with soft notes shall sing his cares asleep.
  I saw him dead. A leaden slumber lies,
And mortal sleep, over those wakeful eyes:
Those gentle rays under the lids were fled,
Which through his looks that piercing sweetness shed;
That port which so majestic was and strong,
Loose and deprived of vigour, stretched along:
All withered, all discoloured, pale and wan,
How much another thing, no more that man?
Oh human glory vain, Oh death, Oh wings,
Oh worthless world, Oh transitory things!

Yet dwelt that greatness in his shape decayed,
That still, though dead, greater than death he laid;
And in his altered face you something feign
That threatens death he yet will live again.
Not much unlike the sacred oak which shoots
To heaven its branches and through earth its roots,
Whose spacious boughs are hung with trophies round,
And honoured wreaths have oft the victor crowned.
When angry Jove darts lightning through the air
At mortals' sins, nor his own plant will spare;
(It groans, and bruises all below, that stood
So many years the shelter of the wood.)
The tree erewhile foreshortened to our view,
When fall'n shows taller yet than as it grew.
So shall his praise to after times increase,
When truth shall be allowed, and faction cease,
And his own shadows with him fall. The eye
Detracts from objects than itself more high:
But when death takes them from that envied seat,
Seeing how little, we confess how great.
Thee, many ages hence in martial verse
Shall th' English soldier, ere he charge, rehearse:
Singing of thee, inflame themselves to fight,
And with the name of Cromwell armies fright.
As long as rivers to the seas shall run,
As long as Cynthia shall relieve the sun,
While stags shall fly unto the forests thick,
While sheep delight the grassy downs to pick,
As long as future time succeeds the past,
Always thy honour, praise, and name shall last.
Thou in a pitch how far beyond the sphere
Of human glory tower'st, and, reigning there,
Despoiled of mortal robes, in seas of bliss
Plunging dost bathe, and tread the bright abyss:
There thy great soul at once a world does see
Spacious enough and pure enough for thee.
How soon thou Moses hast, and Joshua found,

And David for the sword and harp renowned!
How straight canst to each happy mansion go!
(Far better known above than here below)
And in those joys dost spend the endless day,
Which in expressing we ourselves betray.
  For we, since thou art gone, with heavy doom
Wander like ghosts about thy loved tomb;
And lost in tears have neither sight nor mind
To guide us upward through this region blind.
Since thou art gone, who best that way could'st teach,
Only our sighs, perhaps, may thither reach.
  And Richard yet, where his great parent led,
Beats on the rugged track: he virtue dead
Revives, and by his milder beams assures;
And yet how much of them his grief obscures!
  He, as his father, long was kept from sight,
In private to be viewed by better light;
But opened once, what splendour does he throw?
A Cromwell in an hour a prince will grow!
How he becomes that seat, how strongly strains,
How gently winds at once the ruling reins!
Heaven to this choice prepared a diadem,
Richer than any eastern silk or gem:
A pearly rainbow, where the sun enchased
His brows, like an imperial jewel graced.
  We find already what those omens mean,
Earth ne'er more glad, nor heaven more serene:
Cease now our griefs, calm peace succeeds a war;
Rainbows to storms, Richard to Oliver.
Tempt not his clemency to try his power,
He threats no deluge, yet foretells a shower.

THE LAST INSTRUCTIONS TO A PAINTER

After two sittings, now our Lady State,
To end her picture, does the third time wait.
But ere thou fall'st to work, first, Painter, see
It ben't too slight grown or too hard for thee.
Canst thou paint without colours? Then 'tis right:
For so we too without a fleet can fight.
Or canst thou daub a sign-post, and that ill?
'Twill suit our great debauch and little skill.
Or hast thou marked how antique masters limn
The alley-roof with snuff of candle dim,
Sketching in shady smoke prodigious tools?
'Twill serve this race of drunkards, pimps, and fools.
But if to match our crimes thy skill presumes,
As th' Indians, draw our luxury in plumes.
Or if to score out our compendious fame,
With Hooke, then, through the microscope take aim,
Where, like the new Comptroller, all men laugh
To see a tall louse brandish the white staff.
Else shalt thou oft thy guiltless pencil curse,
Stamp on thy palette, nor perhaps the worse.
The painter so, long having vexed his cloth,
Of his hound's mouth to feign the raging froth,
His desp'rate pencil at the work did dart:
His anger reached that rage which passed his art;
Chance finished that which art could but begin,
And he sat smiling how his dog did grin.
So mayst thou perfect by a lucky blow
What all thy softest touches cannot do.
  Paint then St Albans, full of soup and gold,
The new Court's pattern, stallion of the old.
Him neither wit nor courage did exalt,
But Fortune chose him for her pleasure salt.
Paint him with drayman's shoulders, butcher's mien,
Membered like mules, with elephantine chine.
Well he the title of St Albans bore,

For Bacon never studied Nature more.
But age, allaying now that youthful heat,
Fits him in France to play at cards and treat.
Draw no commission lest the Court should lie,
That disavowing treaty, asks supply.
He needs no seal but to St James's lease,
Whose breeches wear the Instrument of Peace;
Who, if the French dispute his power, from thence
Can straight produce them a plenipotence.
Nor fears he the *Most Christian* should trepan
Two saints at once, St Germain, St Alban,
But thought the Golden Age was now restored,
When men and women took each other's word.
  Paint then again Her Highness to the life,
Philosopher beyond Newcastle's wife.
She, nak'd, can Archimedes' self put down,
For an experiment upon the crown.
She perfected that engine, oft assayed,
How after childbirth to renew a maid,
And found how royal heirs might be matured
In fewer months than mothers once endured.
Hence Crowther made the rare inventress free
Of's Highness's Royal Society:
Happiest of women, if she were but able
To make her glassen Dukes once malleable!
Paint her with oyster lip and breath of fame,
Wide mouth that 'sparagus may well proclaim;
With Chancellor's belly and so large a rump,
There, not behind the coach, her pages jump.
Express her studying now if China clay
Can, without breaking, venomed juice convey,
Or how a mortal poison she may draw
Out of the cordial meal of the cacao.
Witness, ye stars of night, and thou the pale
Moon, that o'ercome with the sick steam didst fail;
Ye neighb'ring elms, that your green leaves did shed,
And fawns, that from the womb abortive fled!

Not unprovoked, she tries forbidden arts,
But in her soft breast love's hid cancer smarts,
While she revolves at once Sidney's disgrace
And her self scorned for emulous Denham's face;
And nightly hears the hated guards away
Galloping with the Duke to other prey.
  Paint Castlemaine in colours that will hold
(Her, not her picture, for she now grows old).
She through her lackey's drawers, as he ran,
Discerned love's cause, and a new flame began.
Her wonted joys thenceforth and Court she shuns,
And still within her mind the footman runs:
His brazen calves, his brawny thighs (the face
She slights), his feet shaped for a smoother race.
Poring within her glass she readjusts
Her looks, and oft-tried beauty now distrusts;
Fears lest he scorn a woman once assayed,
And now first wished she e'er had been a maid.
Great Love, how dost thou triumph and how reign,
That to a groom couldst humble her disdain!
Stripped to her skin, see how she stooping stands,
Nor scorns to rub him down with those fair hands,
And washing (lest the scent her crime disclose)
His sweaty hooves, tickles him 'twixt the toes.
But envious Fame, too soon, began to note
More gold in's fob, more lace upon his coat;
And he, unwary, and of tongue too fleet,
No longer could conceal his fortune sweet.
Justly the rogue was whipped in Porter's Den,
And Jermyn straight has leave to come again.
Ah, Painter, now could Alexander live,
And this Campaspe thee, Apelles, give!
  Draw next a pair of tables opening, then
The House of Commons clatt'ring like the men.
Describe the Court and Country, both set right
On opposite points, the black against the white.
Those having lost the nation at tric-trac,

These now advent'ring how to win it back.
The dice betwixt them must the fate divide
(As chance doth still in multitudes decide).
But here the Court does its advantage know,
For the cheat Turner for them both must throw.
As some from boxes, he so from the Chair
Can strike the die and still with them goes share.
  Here, Painter, rest a little, and survey
With what small arts the public game they play.
For so too Rubens, with affairs of state
His labouring pencil oft would recreate.
  The close Cabal marked how the navy eats
And thought all lost that goes not to the cheats;
So therefore secretly for peace decrees,
Yet as for war the Parliament would squeeze,
And fix to the revenue such a sum
Should Goodrick silence, and strike Paston dumb,
Should pay land armies, should dissolve the vain
Commons, and ever such a Court maintain;
Hyde's avarice, Bennet's luxury should suffice,
And what can these defray but the Excise?
Excise, a monster worse than e'er before
Frighted the midwife and the mother tore.
A thousand hands she has, and thousand eyes,
Breaks into shops and into cellars pries,
With hundred rows of teeth the shark exceeds,
And on all trade like cassowar she feeds:
Chops off the piece wheres'e'er she close the jaw,
Else swallows all down her indented maw.
She stalks all day in streets concealed from sight
And flies like bats with leathern wings by night.
She wastes the country and on cities preys:
Her, of a female harpy, in dog-days,
Black Birch, of all the earth-born race most hot
And most rapacious, like himself begot.
And, of his brat enamoured, as't increased,
Buggered in incest with the mongrel beast.

Say, Muse, for nothing can escape thy sight
(And, Painter, wanting other, draw this fight),
Who, in an English senate, fierce debate
Could raise so long for this new whore of State.
Of early wittols first the troop marched in,
For diligence renowned and discipline:
In loyal haste they left young wives in bed,
And Denham these by one consent did head.
Of the old courtiers next a squadron came,
That sold their master, led by Ashburnham.
To them succeeds a despicable rout,
But know the word and well could face about;
Expectants pale, with hopes of spoil allured,
Though yet but pioneers, and led by Stew'rd.
Then damning cowards ranged the vocal plain,
Wood these commands, Knight of the Horn and Cane.
Still his hook-shoulder seems the blow to dread,
And under's armpit he defends his head.
The posture strange men laughed at of his poll,
Hid with his elbow like the spice he stole.
Headless St Denys so his head does bear,
And both of them alike French martyrs were.
Court officers, as used, the next place took,
And followed Fox, but with disdainful look.
His birth, his youth, his brokage all dispraise,
In vain, for always he commands that pays.
Then the procurers under Progers filed,
Gentlest of men, and his lieutenant mild,
Brouncker, Love's squire; through all the field arrayed,
No troop was better clad nor so well paid.
Then marched the troop of Clarendon, all full,
Haters of fowl, to teal preferring bull:
Gross bodies, grosser minds, and grossest cheats,
And bloated Wren conducts them to their seats.
Charlton advances next, whose coif does awe
The Mitre troop, and with his looks gives law.
He marched with beaver cocked of bishop's brim,

And hid much fraud under an aspect grim.
Next th' lawyers' mercenary band appear:
Finch in the front, and Thurland in the rear.
The troop of privilege, a rabble bare
Of debtors deep, fell to Trelawny's care.
Their fortune's error they supplied in rage,
Nor any further would than these engage.
Then marched the troop, whose valiant acts before
(Their public acts) obliged them still to more.
For chimney's sake they all Sir Pool obeyed,
Or in his absence him that first it laid.
Then comes the thrifty troop of privateers,
Whose horses each with other interferes:
Before them Higgons rides with brow compact,
Mourning his Countess, anxious for his Act.
Sir Frederick and Sir Solomon draw lots
For the command of politics or sots;
Thence fell to words, but, quarrel to adjourn,
Their friends agreed they should command by turn.
Carteret the rich did the accountants guide,
And in ill English all the world defied.
The Papists – but of these the House had none,
Else Talbot offered to have led them on.
Bold Duncombe next, of the projectors chief,
And old Fitz-harding of the Eaters Beef.
Late and disordered out the drinkers drew;
Scarce them their leaders, they their leaders knew.
Before them entered, equal in command,
Apsley and Brod'rick, marching hand in hand.
Last then but one, Powell, that could not ride,
Led the French standard, welt'ring in his stride.
He to excuse his slowness, truth confessed
That 'twas so long before he could be dressed.
The Lords' sons, last, all these did reinforce:
Cornb'ry before them managed hobby-horse.
  Never, before nor since, an host so steeled
Trooped on to muster in the Tothill Field.

Not the first cock-horse that with cork were shod
To rescue Albemarle from the sea-cod,
Nor the late feather-men, whom Tomkins fierce
Shall with one breath, like thistledown disperse.
All the two Coventrys their generals chose,
For one had much, the other nought to lose;
Nor better choice all accidents could hit,
While *Hector Harry* steers by *Will the Wit*.
They both accept the charge with merry glee,
To fight a battle from all gunshot free.
  Pleased with their numbers, yet in valour wise,
They feign a parley, better to surprise;
They, that ere long shall the rude Dutch upbraid,
Who in a time of treaty durst invade.
  Thick was the morning, and the House was thin,
The Speaker early, when they all fell in.
Propitious heavens, had not you them crossed,
Excise had got the day, and all been lost!
For th' other side all in loose quarters lay,
Without intelligence, command, or pay:
A scattered body, which the foe ne'er tried,
But oft'ner did among themselves divide.
And some ran o'er each night while others sleep,
And undescried returned ere morning peep.
But Strangeways, that all night still walked the round
(For vigilance and courage both renowned)
First spied the enemy and gave th' alarm:
Fighting it single till the rest might arm.
Such Roman Cocles strid before the foe,
The falling bridge behind, the stream below.
  Each ran, as chance him guides, to sev'ral post,
And all to pattern his example boast.
Their former trophies they recall to mind,
And to new edge their angry courage grind.
First entered forward Temple, conqueror
Of Irish cattle and Solicitor;
Then daring Seymour, that with spear and shield

Had stretched the monster Patent on the field;
Keen Whorwood next, in aid of damsel frail,
That pierced the giant Mordaunt through his mail;
And surly Williams, the accountants' bane,
And Lovelace young, of chimney-men the cane.
Old Waller, trumpet-gen'ral, swore he'd write
This combat truer than the naval fight.
How'rd on's birth, wit, strength, courage much presumes,
And in his breast wears many Montezumes.
These and some more with single valour stay
The adverse troops, and hold them all at bay.
Each thinks his person represents the whole,
And with that thought does multiply his soul,
Believes himself an army, theirs one man,
As eas'ly conquered, and, believing, can;
With heart of bees so full, and head of mites,
That each, though duelling, a battle fights.
Such once Orlando, famous in romance,
Broached whole brigades like larks upon his lance.
  But strength at last still under number bows,
And the faint sweat trickled down Temple's brows.
E'en iron Strangeways, chafing, yet gave back,
Spent with fatigue, to breathe a while toback.
When, marching in, a seas'nable recruit
Of citizens and merchants held dispute;
And, charging all their pikes, a sullen band
Of Presbyterian Switzers made a stand.
  Nor could all these the field have long maintained
But for th' unknown reserve that still remained:
A gross of English gentry, nobly born,
Of clear estates, and to no faction sworn;
Dear lovers of their king, and death to meet
For country's cause, that glorious think and sweet;
To speak not forward, but in action brave,
In giving gen'rous, but in counsel grave;
Candidly credulous for once, nay twice,
But sure the Devil cannot cheat them thrice.

The van and battle, though retiring, falls
Without disorder in their intervals:
Then, closing all in equal front, fall on,
Led by great Garway and great Littleton.
Lee, ready to obey or to command,
Adjutant-general, was still at hand.
The martial standard, Sandys displaying, shows
St Dunstan in it, tweaking Satan's nose.
See sudden chance of war! To paint or write
Is longer work and harder than to fight.
At the first charge the enemy give out,
And the Excise receives a total rout.
  Broken in courage, yet the men the same,
Resolve henceforth upon their other game:
Where force had failed, with stratagem to play,
And what haste lost, recover by delay.
St Albans straight is sent to, to forbear,
Lest the sure peace, forsooth, too soon appear.
The seamen's clamour to three ends they use:
To cheat their pay, feign want, the House accuse.
Each day they bring the tale, and that too true,
How strong the Dutch their equipage renew.
Meantime through all the yards their orders run
To lay the ships up, cease the keels begun.
The timber rots, and useless axe doth rust,
Th' unpractised saw lies buried in its dust;
The busy hammer sleeps, the ropes untwine;
The stores and wages all are thine and mine.
Along the coast and harbours they take care
That money lack, nor forts be in repair.
Long thus they could against the House conspire,
Load them with envy, and with sitting tire:
And the loved king, and never yet denied,
Is brought to beg in public and to chide.
But when this failed, and months enow were spent,
They with the first day's proffer seem content:
And to Land-tax from the Excise turn round,

Bought off with eighteen-hundred-thousand pound.
Thus, like fair thieves, the Commons' purse they share,
But all the Members' lives, consulting, spare.
  Blither than hare that hath escaped the hounds,
The House prorogued, the Chancellor rebounds.
Not so decrepit Aeson, hashed and stewed
With bitter herbs, rose from the pot renewed,
And with fresh age felt his glad limbs unite;
His gout (yet still he cursed) had left him quite.
What frosts to fruit, what ars'nic to the rat,
What to fair Denham, mortal chocolate,
What an account to Carteret, that, and more,
A Parliament is to the Chancellor.
So the sad tree shrinks from the morning's eye,
But blooms all night and shoots its branches high.
So, at the sun's recess, again returns
The comet dread, and earth and heaven burns.
  Now Mordaunt may, within his castle tower,
Imprison parents, and the child deflower.
The Irish herd is now let loose, and comes
By millions over, not by hecatombs;
And now, now the Canary Patent may
Be broached again for the great holiday.
  See how he reigns in his new palace culminant,
And sits in state divine like Jove the fulminant!
First Buckingham, that durst to him rebel,
Blasted with lightning, struck with thunder, fell.
Next the twelve Commons are condemned to groan,
And roll in vain at Sisyphus's stone.
But still he cared, while in revenge he braved,
That peace secured, and money might be saved:
Gain and revenge, revenge and gain are sweet:
United most, else when by turns they meet.
France had St Albans promised (so they sing),
St Albans promised him, and he the King.
The Count forthwith is ordered all to close,
To play for Flanders, and the stake to lose.

While, chained together, two ambassadors
Like slaves shall beg for peace at Holland's doors.
This done, among his Cyclops he retires,
To forge new thunder and inspect their fires.
The Court, as once of war, now fond of peace,
All to new sports their wanton fears release.
From Greenwich (where intelligence they hold)
Comes news of pastime martial and old:
A punishment invented first to awe
Masculine wives, transgressing Nature's law,
Where, when the brawny female disobeys,
And beats the husband till for peace he prays,
No concerned jury for him damage finds,
Nor partial justice her behaviour binds;
But the just street does the next house invade,
Mounting the neighbour couple on lean jade;
The distaff knocks, the grains from kettle fly,
And boys and girls in troops run hooting by.
Prudent antiquity, that knew by shame,
Better than law, domestic crimes to tame,
And taught youth by spectacle innocent!
So thou and I, dear Painter, represent
In quick effigy, others' faults, and feign
By making them ridic'lous, to restrain.
With homely sight, they chose thus to relax
The joys of state, for the new Peace and Tax.
So Holland with us had the mast'ry tried,
And our next neighbours, France and Flanders, ride.
But a fresh news the great designment nips,
Of, at the Isle of Candy, Dutch and ships!
Bab May and Arlington did wisely scoff,
And thought all safe, if they were so far off.
Modern geographers, 'twas there, they thought,
Where Venice twenty years the Turk had fought;
While the first year our navy is but shown,
The next divided, and the third we've none.
They, by the name, mistook it for that isle

Where Pilgrim Palmer travelled in exile,
With the bull's horn to measure his own head,
And on Pasiphae's tomb to drop a bead.
But Morice learn'd demonstrates, by the post,
This Isle of Candy was on Essex coast.
  Fresh messengers still the sad news assure,
More tim'rous now we are, than first secure.
False terrors our believing fears devise,
And the French army one from Calais spies.
Bennet and May and those of shorter reach
Change all for guineas, and a crown for each;
But wiser men, and well foreseen in chance,
In Holland theirs had lodged before, and France.
Whitehall's unsafe, the Court all meditates
To fly to Windsor, and mure up the gates.
Each does the other blame, and all distrust;
But Mordaunt, new obliged, would sure be just.
Not such a fatal stupefaction reigned
At London's flame, nor so the Court complained.
The Bloodworth-Chancellor gives, then does recall
Orders; amazed at last gives none at all.
  St Albans writ to that he may bewail
To Master Louis, and tell coward tale,
How yet the Hollanders do make a noise,
Threaten to beat us, and are naughty boys.
Now Dolman's disobedient, and they still
Uncivil; his unkindness would us kill.
Tell him our ships unrigged, our forts unmanned,
Our money spent; else 'twere at his command.
Summon him therefore of his word, and prove
To move him out of pity, if not love.
Pray him to make De Witt and Ruyter cease,
And whip the Dutch unless they'll hold their peace.
But Louis was of memory but dull,
And to St Albans too undutiful;
Nor word nor near relation did revere,
But asked him bluntly for his character.

The gravelled Count did with the answer faint
(His character was that which thou didst paint)
And so enforced, like enemy or spy,
Trusses his baggage and the camp does fly.
Yet Louis writes, and lest our hearts should break,
Consoles us morally out of *Seneque*.
  Two letters next unto Breda are sent,
In cipher one to Harry Excellent.
The first instructs our (verse the name abhors)
Plenipotentiary ambassadors
To prove by Scripture, treaty does imply
Cessation, as the look adultery;
And that, by law of arms, in martial strife,
Who yields his sword has title to his life.
Presbyter Holles the first point should clear;
The second Coventry the Cavalier.
But, would they not be argued back from sea,
Then to return home straight, *infecta re*.
But Harry's ordered, if they won't recall
Their fleet, to threaten, we will grant them all.
The Dutch are then in proclamation shent
For sin against th' eleventh commandment.
Hyde's flippant style there pleasantly curvets;
Still his sharp wit on states and princes whets
(So Spain could not escape his laughter's spleen:
None but himself must choose the King a Queen);
But when he came the odious clause to pen
That summons up the Parliament again,
His writing-master many a time he banned,
And wished himself the gout to seize his hand.
Never old lecher more repugnance felt,
Consenting, for his rupture, to be gelt;
But still in hope he solaced, ere they come,
To work the peace and so to send them home,
Or in their hasty call to find a flaw,
Their acts to vitiate, and them overawe;
But most relied upon this Dutch pretence,

To raise a two-edged army for's defence.
   First then he marched our whole militia's force
(As if indeed we ships or Dutch had horse);
Then from the usual commonplace, he blames
These, and in standing army's praise declaims.
And the wise Court, that always loved it dear,
Now thinks all but too little for their fear.
Hyde stamps, and straight upon the ground the swarms
Of current Myrmidons appear in arms,
And for their pay he writes, as from the King,
With that cursed quill plucked from a vulture's wing,
Of the whole nation now to ask a loan.
(The eighteen-hundred-thousand pound was gone.)
   This done, he pens a proclamation stout,
In rescue of the *banquiers banquerouts*:
His minion imps that, in his secret part,
Lie nuzzling at the sacramental wart,
Horse-leeches circling at the haem'rrhoid vein:
He sucks the King, they him, he them again.
The kingdom's farm he lets to them bid least:
Greater the bribe, and that's at interest.
Here men, induced by safety, gain, and ease,
Their money lodge; confiscate when he please.
These can at need, at instant, with a scrip
(This liked him best) his cash beyond sea whip.
When Dutch invade, when Parliament prepare,
How can he engines so convenient spare?
Let no man touch them or demand his own,
Pain of displeasure of great Clarendon.
   The state affairs thus marshalled, for the rest
Monck in his shirt against the Dutch is pressed.
Often, dear Painter, have I sat and mused
Why he should still be 'n all adventures used:
If they for nothing ill, like ashen wood,
Or think him, like Herb John, for nothing good.
Whether his valour they so much admire,
Or that for cowardice they all retire,

As heaven in storms, they call, in gusts of state,
On Monck and Parliament, yet both do hate.
All causes sure concur, but most they think
Under Herculean labours he may sink.
Soon then the independent troops would close,
And Hyde's last project would his place dispose.
  Ruyter the while, that had our ocean curbed,
Sailed now among our rivers undisturbed:
Surveyed their crystal streams and banks so green,
And beauties ere this never naked seen.
Through the vain sedge, the bashful nymphs he eyed:
Bosoms and all which from themselves they hide.
The sun much brighter, and the skies more clear,
He finds the air and all things sweeter here.
The sudden change, and such a tempting sight,
Swells his old veins with fresh blood, fresh delight.
Like am'rous victors he begins to shave,
And his new face looks in the English wave.
His sporting navy all about him swim,
And witness their complacence in their trim:
Their streaming silks play through the weather fair,
And with inveigling colours court the air,
While the red flags breathe on their topmasts high
Terror and war, but want an enemy.
Among the shrouds the seamen sit and sing,
And wanton boys on every rope do cling.
Old Neptune springs the tides and water lent
(The gods themselves do help the provident),
And, where the deep keel on the shallow cleaves,
With trident's lever and great shoulder heaves.
Aeolus their sails inspires with eastern wind,
Puffs them along, and breathes upon them kind.
With pearly shell the Tritons all the while
Sound the sea-march, and guide to Sheppey Isle.
  So have I seen, in April's bud, arise
A fleet of clouds, sailing along the skies:
The liquid region with their squadrons filled,

Their airy sterns the sun behind does gild;
And gentle gales them steer, and heaven drives,
When, all on sudden, their calm bosom rives
With thunder and lightning from each armed cloud;
Shepherds themselves in vain in bushes shroud.
Such up the stream the Belgic navy glides,
And at Sheerness unloads its stormy sides.
  Spragge there, though practised in the sea-command,
With panting heart lay like a fish on land,
And quickly judged the fort was not tenable,
Which, if a house, yet were not tenantable.
No man can sit there safe: the cannon pours
Thorough the walls untight and bullet showers,
The neighbourhood ill, and an unwholesome seat,
So at the first salute resolves retreat,
And swore that he would never more dwell there
Until the city put it in repair.
So he in front, his garrison in rear,
March straight to Chatham to increase the fear.
  There our sick ships unrigged in summer lay,
Like moulting fowl, a weak and easy prey;
For whose strong bulk earth scarce could timber find,
The ocean water, or the heavens wind;
Those oaken giants of the ancient race,
That ruled all seas and did our Channel grace.
The conscious stag so, once the forest's dread,
Flies to the wood and hides his armless head.
Ruyter forthwith a squadron does untack;
They sail securely through the river's track.
An English pilot too (O shame, O sin!)
Cheated of pay, was he that showed them in.
Our wretched ships within their fate attend,
And all our hopes now on frail chain depend:
Engine so slight to guard us from the sea,
It fitter seemed to captivate a flea.
A skipper rude shocks it without respect,
Filling his sails, more force to recollect.

Th' English from shore the iron deaf invoke
For its last aid: 'Hold chain, or we are broke!'
But with her sailing weight the Holland keel,
Snapping the brittle links, does thorough reel,
And to the rest the opened passage show.
Monck from the bank the dismal sight does view.
Our feathered gallants, which came down that day
To be spectators safe of the new play,
Leave him alone when first they hear the gun
(Cornb'ry the fleetest) and to London run.
Our seamen, whom no danger's shape could fright,
Unpaid, refuse to mount our ships for spite,
Or to their fellows swim on board the Dutch,
Which show the tempting metal in their clutch.
Oft had he sent of Duncombe and of Legge
Cannon and powder, but in vain, to beg:
And Upnor Castle's ill-deserted wall,
Now needful, does for ammunition call.
He finds, wheres'e'er he succour might expect,
Confusion, folly, treach'ry, fear, neglect.
But when the *Royal Charles* (what rage, what grief!)
He saw seized, and could give her no relief –
That sacred keel which had, as he, restored
His exiled sovereign on its happy board,
And thence the British Admiral became,
Crowned, for that merit, with their master's name;
That pleasure-boat of war, in whose dear side
Secure so oft he had his foe defied:
Now a cheap spoil and the mean victor's slave,
Taught the Dutch colours from its top to wave –
Of former glories the reproachful thought,
With present shame compared, his mind distraught.
Such, from Euphrates bank, a tigress fell
After the robber for her whelps doth yell;
But sees enraged the river flow between;
Frustrate revenge and love, by loss more keen,
At her own breast her useless claws does arm:

She tears herself since him she cannot harm.
  The guards, placed for the chain's and fleet's defence,
Long since were fled on many a feigned pretence.
Daniel had there adventured, man of might;
Sweet Painter, draw his picture while I write.
Paint him of person tall, and big of bone,
Large limbs, like ox not to be killed but shown.
Scarce can burnt iv'ry feign an hair so black,
Or face so red, thine ochre and thy lac.
Mix a vain terror in his martial look,
And all those lines by which men are mistook;
But when, by shame constrained to go on board,
He heard how the wild cannon nearer roared,
And saw himself confined like sheep in pen,
Daniel then thought he was in lion's den;
And when the frightful fire-ships he saw,
Pregnant with sulphur, to him nearer draw,
Captain, lieutenant, ensign, all make haste
Ere in the fiery furnace they be cast:
Three children tall, unsinged, away they row,
Like Shadrack, Meschak, and Abednego.
  Not so brave Douglas, on whose lovely chin
The early down but newly did begin,
And modest beauty yet his sex did veil,
While envious virgins hope he is a male.
His yellow locks curl back themselves to seek,
Nor other courtship knew but to his cheek.
Oft as he in chill Esk or Seine by night
Hardened and cooled his limbs, so soft, so white,
Among the reeds, to be espied by him,
The nymphs would rustle; he would forward swim.
They sighed and said, 'Fond boy, why so untame,
That fliest love's fires, reserved for other flame?'
Fixed on his ship, he faced that horrid day,
And wondered much at those that run away;
Nor other fear himself could comprehend
Than lest heaven fall ere thither he ascend,

But entertains the while his time too short
With birding at the Dutch, as if in sport,
Or waves his sword, and could he them conjure
Within its circle, knows himself secure.
The fatal bark him boards with grappling fire,
And safely through its port the Dutch retire:
That precious life he yet disdains to save,
Or with known art to try the gentle wave.
Much him the honours of his ancient race
Inspire, nor would he his own deeds deface,
And secret joy in his calm soul does rise
That Monck looks on to see how Douglas dies.
Like a glad lover, the fierce flames he meets,
And tries his first embraces in their sheets.
His shape exact, which the bright flames enfold,
Like the sun's statue stands of burnished gold.
Round the transparent fire about him glows,
As the clear amber on the bee does close;
And, as on angels' heads their glories shine,
His burning locks adorn his face divine.
But when in his immortal mind he felt
His alt'ring form and soldered limbs to melt,
Down on the deck he laid himself and died,
With his dear sword reposing by his side;
And on the flaming plank, so rests his head
As one that's warmed himself and gone to bed.
His ship burns down and with his relics sinks,
And the sad stream beneath his ashes drinks.
Fortunate boy! If either pencil's fame,
Or if my verse can propagate thy name,
When Oeta and Alcides are forgot,
Our English youth shall sing the valiant Scot.
  Each doleful day still with fresh loss returns:
The *Loyal London* now a third time burns,
And the true *Royal Oak* and *Royal James*,
Allied in fate, increase with theirs her flames.
Of all our navy none should now survive,

But that the ships themselves were taught to dive,
And the kind river in its creek them hides,
Fraughting their piercèd keels with oozy tides.
  Up to the Bridge contagious terror struck:
The Tower itself with the near danger shook,
And were not Ruyter's maw with ravage cloyed,
E'en London's ashes had been then destroyed.
Officious fear, however, to prevent
Our loss does so much more our loss augment:
The Dutch had robbed those jewels of the crown;
Our merchant-men, lest they be burned, we drown.
So when the Fire did not enough devour,
The houses were demolished near the Tower.
Those ships that yearly from their teeming howl
Unloaded here the birth of either Pole –
Furs from the north, and silver from the west,
Wines from the south, and spices from the east,
From Gambo gold, and from the Ganges gems –
Take a short voyage underneath the Thames,
Once a deep river, now with timber floored,
And shrunk, lest navigable, to a ford.
  Now (nothing more at Chatham left to burn)
The Holland squadron leisurely return,
And, spite of Ruperts and of Albemarles,
To Ruyter's triumph lead the captive *Charles*.
The pleasing sight he often does prolong:
Her masts erect, tough cordage, timbers strong,
Her moving shapes, all these he does survey,
And all admires, but most his easy prey.
The seamen search her all within, without:
Viewing her strength, they yet their conquest doubt.
Then with rude shouts, secure, the air they vex,
With gamesome joy insulting on her decks.
Such the feared Hebrew, captive, blinded, shorn,
Was led about in sport, the public scorn.
  Black day accursed! On thee let no man hale
Out of the port, or dare to hoist a sail,

Nor row a boat in thy unlucky hour.
Thee, the year's monster, let thy dam devour:
And constant time, to keep his course yet right,
Fill up thy space with a redoubled night.
When aged Thames was bound with fetters base,
And Medway chaste ravished before his face,
And their dear offspring murdered in their sight,
Thou and thy fellows held'st the odious light.
Sad change since first that happy pair was wed,
When all the rivers graced their nuptial bed,
And Father Neptune promised to resign
His empire, old, to their immortal line!
Now with vain grief their vainer hopes they rue,
Themselves dishonoured, and the gods untrue,
And to each other, helpless couple, moan,
As the sad tortoise for the sea does groan.
But most they for their darling *Charles* complain,
And were it burnt, yet less would be their pain.
To see that fatal pledge of sea-command
Now in the ravisher De Ruyter's hand,
The Thames roared, swooning Medway turned her tide,
And, were they mortal, both for grief had died.
  The Court in farthing yet itself does please,
And female Stuart there rules the four seas,
But Fate does still accumulate our woes,
And Richmond her commands, as Ruyter those.
  After this loss, to relish discontent,
Someone must be accused by punishment.
All our miscarriages on Pett must fall:
His name alone seems fit to answer all.
Whose counsel first did this mad war beget?
Who all commands sold through the navy? *Pett.*
Who would not follow when the Dutch were beat?
Who treated out the time at Bergen? *Pett.*
Who the Dutch fleet with storms disabled met?
And, rifling prizes, them neglected? *Pett.*
Who with false news prevented the Gazette?

The fleet divided, writ for Rupert? *Pett*.
Who all our seamen cheated of their debt?
And all our prizes who did swallow? *Pett*.
Who did advise no navy out to set?
And who the forts left unrepaired? *Pett*.
Who to supply with powder did forget
Languard, Sheerness, Gravesend and Upnor? *Pett*.
Who all our ships exposed in Chatham's net?
Who should it be but the *Fanatic Pett*?
Pett, the sea-architect, in making ships,
Was the first cause of all these naval slips:
Had he not built, none of these faults had been;
If no Creation, there had been no Sin.
But, his great crime, one boat away he sent:
That lost our fleet and did our flight prevent.
Then (that reward might in its turn take place,
And march with punishment in equal pace),
Southampton dead, much of the Treasure's care
And place in council fell to Duncombe's share.
All men admired he to that pitch could fly:
Powder ne'er blew man up so soon so high;
But sure his late good husbandry in petre
Showed him to manage the Exchequer meeter;
And who the forts would not vouchsafe a corn,
To lavish the King's money more would scorn.
Who hath no chimneys, to give all is best,
And ablest speaker, who of law has least;
Who less estate, for Treasurer most fit,
And for a couns'llor, he that has least wit.
But the true cause was that, in's brother May,
The Exchequer might the Privy Purse obey.
But now draws near the Parliament's return:
Hyde and the Court again begin to mourn.
Frequent in council, earnest in debate,
All arts they try how to prolong its date.
Grave Primate Sheldon (much in preaching there)
Blames the last Session and this more does fear:

With Boynton or with Middleton 'twere sweet,
But with a Parliament abhors to meet,
And thinks 'twill ne'er be well within this nation
Till it be governed by a Convocation.
But in the Thames's mouth still Ruyter laid;
The peace not sure, new army must be paid.
Hyde saith he hourly waits for a dispatch;
Harry came post just as he showed his watch,
All to agree the articles were clear,
The Holland fleet and Parliament so near;
Yet Harry must job back and all mature,
Binding, ere th' Houses meet, the treaty sure.
And 'twixt necessity and spite, till then,
Let them come up so to go down again.
  Up ambles country justice on his pad,
And vest bespeaks to be more seemly clad.
Plain gentlemen in stage-coach are o'erthrown,
And deputy-lieutenants in their own.
The portly burgess, through the weather hot,
Does for his corporation sweat and trot;
And all with sun and choler come adust
And threaten Hyde to raise a greater dust.
But, fresh as from the Mint, the courtiers fine
Salute them, smiling at their vain design,
And Turner gay up to his perch does march
With face new bleached, smoothened and stiff with starch;
Tells them he at Whitehall had took a turn,
And for three days thence moves them to adjourn.
'Not so!' quoth Tomkins, and straight drew his tongue,
Trusty as steel, that always ready hung;
And so, proceeding in his motion warm,
Th' army soon raised, he doth as soon disarm.
True Trojan! while this town can girls afford,
And long as cider lasts in Hereford;
The girls shall always kiss thee, though grown old,
And in eternal healths thy name be trolled.
  Meanwhile the certain news of peace arrives

At Court, and so reprieves their guilty lives.
Hyde orders Turner that he should come late,
Lest some new Tomkins spring a fresh debate.
The King, that day raised early from his rest,
Expects, as at a play, till Turner's dressed.
At last, together Ayton come and he:
No dial more could with the sun agree.
The Speaker, summoned, to the Lords repairs,
Nor gave the Commons leave to say their prayers,
But like his prisoners to the bar them led,
Where mute they stand to hear their sentence read:
Trembling with joy and fear, Hyde them prorogues,
And had almost mistook and called them rogues.
  Dear Painter, draw this Speaker to the foot:
Where pencil cannot, there my pen shall do't;
That may his body, this his mind explain.
Paint him in golden gown, with mace's brain,
Bright hair, fair face, obscure and dull of head,
Like knife with iv'ry haft and edge of lead.
At prayers, his eyes turn up the pious white,
But all the while his private bill's in sight.
In chair, he smoking sits like master-cook,
And a poll bill does like his apron look.
Well was he skilled to season any question,
And made a sauce fit for Whitehall's digestion:
Whence every day, the palate more to tickle,
Court-mushrumps ready are, sent in in pickle.
When grievance urged, he swells like squatted toad,
Frisks like a frog, to croak a tax's load;
His patient piss he could hold longer than
An urinal, and sit like any hen;
At table jolly as a country host
And soaks his sack with Norfolk, like a toast;
At night, than Chanticleer more brisk and hot,
And Sergeant's wife serves him for Pertelotte.
  Paint last the King, and a dead shade of night
Only dispersed by a weak taper's light,

And those bright gleams that dart along and glare
From his clear eyes (yet these too dark with care).
There, as in the calm horror all alone
He wakes, and muses of th' uneasy throne,
Raise up a sudden shape with virgin's face
(Though ill agree her posture, hour, or place),
Naked as born, and her round arms behind
With her own tresses interwove and twined;
Her mouth locked up, a blind before her eyes;
Yet from beneath the veil her blushes rise,
And silent tears her secret anguish speak;
Her heart throbs and with very shame would break.
The object strange in him no terror moved:
He wondered first, then pitied, then he loved,
And with kind hand does the coy vision press
(Whose beauty greater seemed by her distress),
But soon shrunk back, chilled with her touch so cold,
And th' airy picture vanished from his hold.
In his deep thoughts the wonder did increase,
And he divined 'twas England or the Peace.
  Express him startling next with list'ning ear,
As one that some unusual noise does hear:
With cannon, trumpets, drums, his door surround,
But let some other painter draw the sound.
Thrice did he rise, thrice the vain tumult fled,
But again thunders when he lies in bed.
His mind secure does the known stroke repeat
And finds the drums Louis's march did beat.
  Shake then the room and all his curtains tear,
And with blue streaks infect the taper clear,
While the pale ghosts his eye does fixed admire
Of grandsire Harry and of Charles his sire.
Harry sits down, and in his open side
The grisly wound reveals of which he died;
And ghastly Charles, turning his collar low,
The purple thread about his neck does show:
Then whisp'ring to his son in words unheard,

Through the locked door both of them disappeared.
The wondrous night the pensive King revolves,
And rising straight on Hyde's disgrace resolves.
  At his first step, he Castlemaine does find,
Bennet and Coventry, as 't were designed;
And they, not knowing, the same thing propose
Which his hid mind did in its depth enclose.
Through their feigned speech their secret hearts he knew:
To her own husband, Castlemaine untrue;
False to his master Bristol, Arlington;
And Coventry, falser than anyone,
Who to the brother, brother would betray;
Nor therefore trusts himself to such as they.
His father's ghost, too, whispered him one note,
That who does cut his purse will cut his throat;
But in wise anger he their crimes forbears,
As thieves reprieved for executioners;
While Hyde, provoked, his foaming tusk does whet,
To prove them traitors and himself the *Pett*.
  Painter, adieu, how well our arts agree!
Poetic picture, painted poetry!
But this great work is for our Monarch fit,
And henceforth Charles only to Charles shall sit.
His master-hand the ancients shall outdo,
Himself the painter and the poet too.

To the King

So his bold tube, man to the sun applied
And spots unknown to the bright star descried:
Showed they obscure him, while too near they please,
And seem his courtiers, are but his disease.
Through optic trunk the planet seemed to hear,
And hurls them off, e'er since, in his career.
  And you, Great Sir, that with him empire share,
Sun of our world, as he the Charles is there:
Blame not the Muse that brought those spots to sight,
Which, in your splendour hid, corrode your light.

(Kings in the country oft have gone astray,
Nor of a peasant scorned to learn the way.)
Would she the unattended throne reduce,
Banishing love, trust, ornament, and use,
Better it were to live in cloister's lock,
Or in fair fields to rule the easy flock.
She blames them only who the Court restrain,
And, where all England serves, themselves would reign.
Bold and accursed are they that all this while
Have strove to isle our Monarch from his isle,
And to improve themselves, on false pretence,
About the Common-Prince have raised a fence;
The kingdom from the crown distinct would see
And peel the bark to burn at last the tree.
(But Ceres corn, and Flora is the spring,
Bacchus is wine, the Country is the King.)
Not so does rust insinuating wear,
Nor powder so the vaulted bastion tear,
Nor earthquake so an hollow isle o'erwhelm,
As scratching courtiers undermine a realm
And through the palace's foundations bore,
Burr'wing themselves to hoard their guilty store.
The smallest vermin make the greatest waste,
And a poor warren once a city razed.
But they whom, born to virtue and to wealth,
Nor guilt to flatt'ry binds, nor want to stealth;
Whose gen'rous conscience and whose courage high
Does with clear counsels their large souls supply;
That serve the King with their estates and care,
And, as in love, on Parliaments can stare,
(Where few the number, choice is there less hard):
Give us this Court, and rule without a Guard.

UPON SIR ROBERT VINER'S SETTING UP THE KING'S STATUE IN WOOL-CHURCH MARKET

1

As cities that to the fierce conqueror yield
Do at their own charges their citadels build,
So Sir Robert advanced the King's statue, in token
Of banker defeated, and Lombard Street broken.

2

Some thought it a knightly and generous deed,
Obliging the city with a king and a steed,
When with honour he might from his word ha' gone back:
He that vows for a calm is absolved by a wrack.

3

But now it appears from the first to the last
To be all a revenge and malice forecast,
Upon the King's birthday to set up a thing
That shows him a monster more like than a king.

4

When each one that passes finds fault with the horse,
Yet all do affirm the King is much worse;
And some by the likeness Sir Robert suspect,
That he did for the King's his own statue erect.

5

To see him so disfigured the herb-women chide,
Who upon their panniers more decently ride;
And so loose is his seat, that all men agree:
Even Sir William Peak sits much firmer than he.

6

But a market, they say, does suit the King well,
Who the Parliament buys and revenue does sell;
And others, to make the similitude hold,
Say his Majesty himself is bought too and sold.

7

This statue is surely more scandalous far
Than all the Dutch pictures that caused the War,
And what the Exchequer for that took on trust
May be henceforth confiscate for reason more just.

8

But Sir Robert, to take the scandal away,
Does the fault upon the artificer lay;
And alleges the workmanship was not his own,
For he counterfeits only in gold, not in stone.

9

But, Sir Knight of the Vine, how came 't in your thought
That when to the scaffold your liege you had brought,
With canvas and deal you e'er since do him cloud,
As if you it meant for his coffin and shroud?

10

Has Blood him away, as his crown once, conveyed,
Or is he to Clayton's gone in masquerade;
Or is he in cabal in this Cabinet set?
Or have you to the Counter removed him for debt?

11

Methinks by the equipage of this vile scene,
That to change him into a jackpudding you mean;
Or else thus expose him to popular flouts,
As if we'd as good have a king made of clouts.

12

Or do you his beams out of modesty veil
With three shattered planks and the rag of a sail,
To express how his navy was tattered and torn,
The day that he was both restored and born?

13

Sure the King will ne'er think of repaying his bankers,
Whose loyalty all expires with his spankers,
Now the Indies or Smirna do not him enrich,
They'll scarcely afford a rag to his breech.

14

But Sir Robert affirms that we do him much wrong,
For the 'graver's at work to reform him thus long;
But, alas! he will never arrive at his end,
For 'tis such a king as no chisel can mend.

15

But with all his faults, pray restore us our king,
As ever you hope in December for spring;
For though the whole world cannot show such another,
Yet we'd better by far have him than his brother.

THE REHEARSAL TRANSPROS'D: THE FIRST PART (EXTRACTS)

But before I commit myself to the dangerous depths of his discourse, which I am now upon the brink of, I would with his leave make a motion: that, instead of Author, I may henceforth indifferently call him *Mr Bayes* as oft as I shall see occasion. And that, first, because he hath no name or at least will not own it, though he himself writes under the greatest security, and gives us the first letters of other men's names before he be asked them. Secondly, because he is I perceive a lover of elegancy of style, and can endure no man's tautologies but his own, and therefore I would not distaste him with too frequent repetition of one word. But chiefly, because Mr Bayes and he do very much symbolize: in their understandings, in their expressions, in their humour, in their contempt and quarrelling of all others, though of their own profession; because our divine, the Author, manages his contest with the same prudence and civility, which the players and poets have practised of late in their several divisions; and, lastly, because both their talents do peculiarly lie in exposing and personating the Nonconformists. I would therefore give our Author a name, the memory of which may perpetually excite him to the exercise and highest improvement of that virtue. For our Cicero doth not yet equal our Roscius, and one turn of Lacy's face hath more Ecclesiastical Policy in it than all the books of our Author put together. Besides, to say 'Mr Bayes' is more civil than to say 'Villain' and 'Caitiff', though these indeed are more *tuant*. And, to conclude: the irrefragable Doctor of School Divinity, page 460 of his *Defence*, determining concerning symbolical ceremonies, hath warranted me that not only Governors, but anything else, may have power to appropriate new names to things, without having absolute authority over the things themselves. And therefore, henceforward, seeing I am on such sure ground, *Author*, or *Mr Bayes*, whether I please. Now, having had our dance, let us advance to our more serious counsels. [. . .]

And so, thinking himself now ripe and qualified for the greatest undertakings and highest fortune, he therefore exchanged the narrowness of the University for the Town. But coming out of the confinement of the square-cap and the quadrangle into the open air, the world began to turn round with him, which he imagined, though it were his own giddiness, to be nothing less than the *quadrature* of the *circle*. This accident concurring so happily to increase the good opinion which he naturally had of himself, he thenceforward applied to gain a like reputation with others. He followed the town life, haunted the best companies; and, to polish himself from any pedantic roughness, he read and saw the plays, with much care and more proficiency than most of the auditory. But all this while he forgot not the main chance, but hearing of a vacancy with a nobleman, he clapped in and easily obtained to be his chaplain. From that day, you may take the date of his preferments and his ruin. For having soon wrought himself dexterously into his patron's favour, by short graces and sermons, and a mimical way of drolling upon the Puritans, which he knew would take both at chapel and table, he gained a great authority likewise among all the domestics. They all listened to him as an oracle; and they allowed him by common consent to have not only all the Divinity, but more wit too than all the rest of the family put together. This thing alone elevated him exceedingly in his own conceit, and raised his hypochondria into the region of the brain: that his head swelled like any bladder with wind and vapour. But after he was stretched to such an height in his own fancy, that he could not look down from top to toe but his eyes dazzled at the precipice of his stature, there fell out, or in, another natural chance which pushed him headlong. For being of an amorous complexion, and finding himself (as I told you) the Cock-Divine and the Cock Wit of the family, he took the privilege to walk among the hens; and thought it was not impolitic to establish his new-acquired reputation upon the gentlewomen's side. And they that perceived he was a rising man, and of pleasant conversation, dividing his day among them into Canonical hours, of reading now the Common-prayer and now the Romances, were very much taken with him. The sympathy of silk began to stir and attract the tippet to the petticoat and the petticoat toward the tippet. The innocent ladies found a strange unquietness in their minds, and could not distinguish whether it were love or devotion. Neither was he wanting on his part to carry on the work; but shifted himself every day with a clean surplice, and, as oft as he had occasion to bow, he directed his reverence towards the gentlewomen's pew. Till, having before had enough of the libertine, and undertaken his calling only for preferment, he was transported now with the sanctity of his office, even to ecstasy; and like the bishop over Magdalen College altar, or like Maudlin de la Croix, he was seen in his prayers to be lifted up sometimes in the air, and once particularly so high that he cracked his skull against the chapel ceiling. I do not hear for all this that he had ever practised upon the honour of the ladies, but that he preserved always the civility of a Platonic knight errant. For all this courtship had no other operation than to make him still more in love with himself; and if he frequented their company, it was only to speculate his own baby in their eyes. But being thus without competitor or rival, the darling of both sexes in the family and his own minion, he grew beyond all measure elated, and that crack of his skull, as in broken looking-glasses, multiplied him in self-conceit and imagination. [. . .]

And now, though I intend not to be longer than the nature of *Animadversions* requires (this also being but collateral to my work of examining the Preface, and having been so abundantly performed already), yet neither can I proceed well without some preface. For, as I am obliged to ask pardon if I speak of serious things ridiculously, so I must now beg excuse if I should hap to discourse of ridiculous things seriously. But I shall, so far as possible, observe decorum, and, whatever I talk of, not commit such an absurdity as to be grave with a buffoon. But the principal cause of my apology is, because I see I am drawn in to mention kings and princes, and even our own; whom, as I think of with all duty and reverence, so I avoid speaking of either in jest or earnest, lest by reason of my private condition and breeding, I should, though most unwillingly, trip in a word, or fail in the mannerliness of an expression. But Mr Bayes, because princes sometimes hear men of his quality play their part, or preach a sermon, grows so insolent that he thinks himself fit to be their governor. So dangerous it is to let such creatures be too familiar. They know not their distance, and like the ass in the fable, because they see the spaniel play with their master's legs, they think themselves privileged to paw and ramp upon his shoulders. Yet though I must follow his track now I am in, I hope I shall not write after his copy. [. . .]

I should not have been so large in these particulars, had they been only single and volatile sermons, but because this was then the doctrine of those persons that pretended to be the Church of England. The whole choir sung that tune, and instead of the Common Law of England and the Statutes of Parliament, that part of the clergy had invented these Ecclesiastical Laws, which according to their predominancy, were sure to be put in execution. So that between their own revenue, which must be held *Jure Divino*, as everything else that belonged to them, and the Prince's that was *Jure Regio*, they had not left an inch of propriety for the subject. It seemed that they had granted themselves Letters of Reprisal against the laity, for the losses of the Church under Henry the Eighth, and that they would make a greater havoc upon their temporalities in retaliation. And indeed, having many times since pondered with my greatest and earnest impartiality, what could be the true reason of the spleen that they manifested in those days, on the one hand against the Puritans, and on the other against the gentry (for it was come, they tell me, to *Jack Gentleman*), I could not devise any cause, but that the Puritans had ever since the Reformation obstructed that laziness and splendour which they enjoyed under the Pope's supremacy, and the gentry had (sacrilegiously) divided the abbey lands and other fat morsels of the Church at the Dissolution, and now was the time to be revenged on them.

While therefore the kingdom was turned into a prison, upon occasion of this ecclesiastical loan, and many of the eminentest of the gentry of England were under restraint, they thought it seasonable to recover once again their ancient glory and to magnificate the Church with triumphal pomp and ceremony. The three ceremonies that have the countenance of law would not suffice, but they were all upon new inventions, and happy was he that was endued with that capacity, for he was sure before all others to be preferred. There was a second service, the table set altar-wise, and to be called the altar; candles, crucifixes, paintings, images, copes, bowing to the east, bowing to the altar, and so many several cringes and genuflexions that a man unpractised stood in need to entertain both a dancing-master and a remembrancer. And though these things were very uncouth to English Protestants, who naturally affect a plainness of fashion, especially in sacred things; yet, if those gentlemen could have contented themselves with their own formality, the innovation had been more excusable. But many of these additions, and to be sure, all that had any colour of law, were so imposed and pressed upon others, that a great part of the nation was e'en put as it were to fine and ransom upon this account. What censures, what excommunications, what deprivations, what imprisonments? I cannot represent the misery and desolation, as it hath been represented to me. But wearied out at home, many thousands of his Majesty's subjects, to his and the nation's great loss, thought themselves constrained to seek another habitation, and every country, even though it were among savages and cannibals, appeared more hospitable to them than their own.

And, although I have been told by those that have seen both, that our Church did even then exceed the Romish in ceremonies and decorations; and indeed, several of our Church did thereby frequently mistake their way, and from a Popish kind of worship, fell into the Roman religion; yet I cannot upon my best judgement believe, that that party had generally a design to alter the religion so far, but rather to set up a new kind of papacy of their own, here in England. And it seemed they had, to that purpose, provided themselves of a new religion in Holland. It was Arminianism, which though it were the Republican opinion there, and so odious to King James that it helped on the death of Barneveldt, yet now they undertook to accommodate it to Monarchy and Episcopacy. And the choice seemed not imprudent. For on the one hand, it was removed at so moderate a distance from Popery that they should not disoblige the Papists more than formerly, neither yet could the Puritans with justice reproach these men, as Romish Catholics; and yet, on the other hand, they knew it was so contrary to the ancient reformed doctrine of the Church of England, that the Puritans would never embrace it, and so they should gain this pretence further to keep up that convenient and necessary quarrel against Nonconformity. And accordingly it happened, so that here again was a new shibboleth. And the Calvinists were all studiously discountenanced, and none but an Arminian was judged capable and qualified for employment in the Church. And though the King did declare, as I have before mentioned, that Montague's Arminian book had been the occasion of the schisms in the Church; yet care was immediately taken, by those of the same robe and party, that he should be the more rewarded and advanced. As also it was in Manwaring's case, who, though by censure in Parliament made incapable of any ecclesiastical preferment, was straight made Rector of Stamford Rivers in Essex, with a dispensation to hold too his living in St Giles's. And all dexterity was practised to propagate the same opinions and to suppress all writings or discourses to the contrary.

So that those who were of understanding in those days tell me, that a man would wonder to have heard their kind of preachings. How instead of the practical doctrine which tends to the reforming of men's lives and manners, all their sermons were a very mash of Arminian subtleties, of ceremonies, and decency, and of Manwaring and Sibthorpianism brewed together. Besides that in their conversation they thought fit to take some more licence the better to dis-Ghibelline themselves from the Puritans. And though there needed nothing more to make them unacceptable to the sober part of the nation, yet moreover they were so exceedingly pragmatical, so intolerably ambitious, and so desperately proud, that scarce any gentleman might come near the tail of their mules. And many things I perceive of that nature do even yet stick upon the stomachs of the Old Gentlemen of those times. For the English have been always very tender of their religion, their liberty, their propriety, and (I was going to say) no less of their reputation. Neither yet do I speak of these things with passion, considering at more distance how natural it is for men to desire to be in office, and no less natural to grow proud and intractable in office; and the less a clergyman is so, the more he deserves to be commended. But these things before mentioned grew yet higher after that Bishop Laud was once not only exalted to the See of Canterbury, but to be chief minister. Happy had it been for the King, happy for the nation, and happy for himself, had he never climbed that pinnacle. For whether it be or no that the clergy are not so well fitted by education as others for political affairs, I know not; though I should rather think they have advantage above others, and even if they would but keep to their Bibles, might make the best Ministers of State in the world; yet it is generally observed that things miscarry under their government. If there be any counsel more precipitate, more violent, more rigorous, more extreme than other, that is theirs. Truly I think the reason that God does not bless them in affairs of state is, because he never intended them for that employment. Or if government and the preaching of the Gospel may well concur in the same person, God therefore frustrates him, because though knowing better, he seeks and manages his greatness by the lesser and meaner maxims. I am confident the Bishop studied to do both God and His Majesty good service, but alas how utterly was he mistaken. Though so learned, so pious, so wise a man, he seemed to know nothing beyond ceremonies, Arminianism, and Manwaring. With that he began, and with that ended, and thereby deformed the whole reign of the best prince that ever wielded the English sceptre.

For his late Majesty, being a prince truly pious and religious, was thereby the more inclined to esteem and favour the clergy. And thence, though himself of a most exquisite understanding, yet thought he could not trust it better than in their keeping. Whereas every man is best in his own post, and so the preacher in the pulpit. But he that will do the clergy's drudgery, must look for his reward in another world. For they having gained this ascendant upon him, resolved whatever became on't to make their best of him; and having made the whole business of State their Arminian jangles and the persecution for ceremonies, did for recompense assign him that imaginary absolute government, upon which rock we all ruined.

For now was come the last part of the Archbishop's indiscretion; who having strained those strings so high here, and all at the same time, which no wise man ever did, he moreover had a mind to try the same dangerous experiment in Scotland, and sent thither the book of the English liturgy, to be imposed upon them. What followed thereupon is yet within the compass of most men's memory. And how the war broke out, and then to be sure Hell's broke loose. Whether it were a war of religion, or of liberty, is not worth the labour to enquire. Whichsoever was at the top, the other was at the bottom; but upon considering all, I think the Cause was too good to have been fought for. Men ought to have trusted God; they ought and might have trusted the King with that whole matter. The *arms of the church are prayers and tears*, the arms of the subjects are patience and petitions. The King himself being of so accurate and piercing a judgement, would soon have felt where it stuck. For men may spare their pains where Nature is at work, and the world will not go the faster for our driving. Even as his present Majesty's happy Restoration did itself, so all things else happen in their best and proper time, without any need of our officiousness.

But after all the fatal consequences of that rebellion, which can only serve as sea-marks unto wise princes to avoid the causes, shall this sort of men still vindicate themselves as the most zealous assertors of the rights of princes? They are but at the best well-meaning zealots. Shall, to decline so pernicious counsels and to provide better for the quiet of government, be traduced as the Author does here, under these odious terms of *forsaking the Church, and delivering up the Church*? Shall these men always presume to usurp to themselves that venerable style of the Church of England? God forbid. The Independents at that rate would not have so many distinct congregations as they. There would be Sibthorpe's Church, and Manwaring's Church, and Montague's Church, and a whole bead-roll more, whom for decency's sake I abstain from naming. And every man that could invent a new opinion, or a new ceremony, or a new tax, should be a new Church of England.

Neither, as far as I can discern, have this sort of the clergy since his Majesty's return, given him better encouragement to steer by their compass. I am told that preparatory to that, they had frequent meetings in the City, I know not whether in Grub Street, with the Divines of the other party, and that there in their Feasts of Love, they promised to forget all former offences, to lay by all animosities, that there should be a new Heaven, and a new earth, all meekness, charity, and condescension. His Majesty I am sure sent over his gracious Declaration of liberty to tender consciences, and upon his coming over, seconded it with his Commission under the broad seal, for a conference betwixt the two parties to prepare things for an accommodation, that he might confirm it by his royal authority. Hereupon what do they? Notwithstanding this happy conjuncture of his Majesty's Restoration, which had put all men into so good a humour that upon a little moderation and temper of things, the Nonconformists could not have stuck out; some of these men so contrived it, that there should not be the least abatement to bring them off with conscience and (which insinuates into all men) some little reputation. But to the contrary: several unnecessary additions were made, only because they knew they would be more ingrateful and stigmatical to the Nonconformists. I remember one in the Litany, where to *False Doctrine and Heresy*, they added *Schism*, though it were to spoil the music and cadence of the period; but these things were the best. To show that they were men like others, even cunning men, revengeful men, they drilled things on till they might procure a law, wherein besides all the Conformity that had been of former times enacted, there might be some new conditions imposed on those that should have or hold any Church-livings, such as they assured themselves, that rather than swallow, the Nonconformists would disgorge all their benefices. And accordingly it succeeded; several thousands of those ministers being upon one memorable day outed of their subsistence. His Majesty in the meantime, although they had thus far prevailed to frustrate his royal intentions, had reinstated the Church in all its former revenues, dignities, and advantages, so far from the Author's mischievous aspersion of ever thinking of converting them to his own use, that he restored them free from what was due to him by law upon their first admission. So careful was he, *because all government must owe its quiet and continuance to the Church's patronage*, to pay them even what they ought. But I have observed that if a man be in the Church's debt once, 'tis very hard to get an acquittance. And these men never think they have their full rights, unless they reign. What would they have had more? They rolled on a flood of wealth, and yet in matter of a lease would make no difference betwixt a Nonconformist and one of their own fellow-sufferers, who had ventured his life and spent his estate for the King's service. They were restored to Parliament, and to take their places with the King and the Nobility. They had a new liturgy to their own heart's desire; and to cumulate all this happiness, they had this new law against the Fanatics. All they had that could be devised in the world to make a clergyman good natured.

Nevertheless, after all their former sufferings and after all these new enjoyments and acquisitions, they have proceeded still in the same track. The matter of ceremonies, to be sure, hath not only exercised their ancient rigour and severity, but hath been a main ingredient of their public discourses, of their sermons, of their writings. [. . .]

And now I have done. And I shall think myself largely recompensed for this trouble, if anyone that hath been formerly of another mind, shall learn by this example, that it is not impossible to be merry and angry as long time as I have been writing, without profaning and violating those things which are and ought to be most sacred.

FINIS

THE REHEARSAL TRANSPROS'D: THE SECOND PART (EXTRACTS)

Those that take upon themselves to be writers are moved to it either by ambition or charity, imagining that they shall do therein something to make themselves famous, or that they can communicate something that may be delightful and profitable to mankind. But therefore it is either way an envious and dangerous employment. For, how well soever it be intended, the world will have some pretence to suspect, that the author hath both too good a conceit of his own sufficiency, and that by undertaking to teach them, he implicitly accuses their ignorance. So that not to write at all is much the safer course of life.

But if a man's fate or genius prompt him otherwise, 'tis necessary that he be copious in matter, solid in reason, methodical in the order of his work; and that the subject be well chosen, the season well fixed, and, to be short, that his whole production be matured to see the light by a just course of time and judicious deliberation. Otherwise, though with some of these conditions he may perhaps attain commendation, yet without them all he cannot deserve pardon. For indeed whosoever he be that comes in print whereas he might have sat at home in quiet, does either make a treat, or send a challenge to all readers; in which cases, the first, it concerns him to have no scarcity of provisions, and in the other to be completely armed. For if anything be amiss on either part, men are subject to scorn the weakness of the attack or laugh at the meanness of the entertainment. In conclusion, the Author of the *Ecclesiastical Polity* hath in his own particular very fully stated and comprehended this whole matter. For he saith here in his Preface to the Reader, that *if his Book have any effect* (I suppose he means any good effect) *he hath a double reward* (that is, both the public and his private satisfaction); *but if it have none* (that is impossible) *that then he hath his own reward* (that is sure to be accounted none of the wisest); and indeed this reward too is double; for if he fails of his design, he saith *he must confess that he has lost both his labour and his understanding*. This is the common condition to which every man that will write a book must be content with patience to submit.

But, among all the differences of writing, he that does publish an invective, does it at his utmost peril, and 'tis but just that it should be so. For a man's credit is of so natural and high concernment to him, that the preserving of it better was perhaps none of the least inducements at first to enter into the bonds of society and civil government; as that government too must at one time or other be dissolved where men's reputation cannot be under security. 'Tis dearer than life itself, and (to use a thought something perhaps too delicate, yet not altogether unreasonable) if beside the laws of murder men have thought fit, out of respect to human nature, that whatsoever else moves to the death of man should be forfeit to pious uses, why should there not as well be deodands for reputation? And this I intend not only of those who publish ignominious falsehoods, to whom no quarter ought to be granted, but even of such partly who by a truth too officious shall procure any man's infamy. For 'tis better that evil men should be left in an undisturbed possession of their repute, how unjustly soever they may have acquired it, than that the exchange and credit of mankind should be universally shaken, wherein the best too will suffer and be involved. It is one thing to do that which is justifiable, but another that which is commendable, and I suppose every prudent writer aims at both. But how can the author of an invective, though never so truly founded, expect approbation (unless from such as love to see mischief at other men's expense) who, in a world all furnished with subjects of praise, instruction and learned inquiry, shall studiously choose and set himself apart to comment upon the blemishes and imperfections of some particular person? Such men do seldom miss too of their own reward: for whereas those that treat of innocent and benign argument are represented by the Muses, they that make it their business to set out others ill-favouredly do pass for satyrs, and themselves are sure to be personated with prick-ears, wrinkled horns, and cloven feet.

Yet if for once to write in that style may be lawful, discreet or necessary, to do it a second time is liable to greater censure. Not so much because the aftermath seldom or never equals the first herbage (a caution not unfit, however, for all authors), as that by-standers will begin then to suspect that what they looked on first as an accident with some divertisement does rather proceed from a natural malignity of temper. For few readers are so ill natured but that they are quickly tired with personal and passionate discourses; and when the contest comes to be continued and repeated, if they interest themselves at all, they usually incline and think that the justice lies on the weaker side. But whether the last appeal of writers lie to the readers or to a man's own ultimate recollection, this invective way cannot be truly satisfactory either to themselves or others. For it is a predatory course of life, and indeed but a privateering upon reputation, wherein all that stock of credit, which an honest man perhaps hath all his age been toiling for, is in an hour or two's reading plundered from him by a free-booter. So that whatsoever be the success, he that chances in these contests to be superior, can at best (for that too is disputable) be accounted of the two the less unfortunate. And certainly (as it was usual of old for any man who had but casually acted in an unlucky rencounter), he that hath had his pen once in the reputation of another, ought to withdraw, and disappear for some time, till he has undergone and passed through all the ceremonies of expiation.

But if the credit of all men whatsoever be, and ought to be so well guarded both by Nature, law, and discretion, the clergy certainly of all others ought to be kept and preserved sacred in their reputation. For they being men of the same spirit with others, and no less subject to human passions, but confined within the regularity of their function, it is indeed unmanly, whatsoever scuffle others may make among themselves, to vilify or treat them with those affronts which nothing but the respect of decency or conscience could hinder them from resenting as well as others. But (which is more considerable) whoever too shall fix upon them an ill report, does thereby frustrate the very effect of their ministry in proportion. For though Baptism is not to be vacated by the contrary intention of him that officiates, yet few men will or can be persuaded by his doctrine, whose practice they conceive to be opposite. A conversation differing from doctrine is spiritual nonsense: neither will men believe by the ear, when their eye informs them otherwise. If an artificer indeed make his work fit for men's wearing, 'tis sufficient; or if he that sells have good of the kind, men inquire no further. No man's shoe wrings him the more because of the heterodoxy or the tippling of his shoe-maker; and a billet burns as well though bought of whatsoever wood-monger. But the clergy being men dedicate by their vocation to teach what is truth, what falsehood, to deter men from vice, and lead them unto all virtue: 'tis expected from them, and with good reason, that they should define their opinion by their manners. And therefore men ought to be chary of aspersing them on either account, but even reflect upon their failings with some reverence. A clergyman ought to have treble damages both for his tithes and his credit; and it were to be wished that with the same ease that their maintenance comes in from the fruits of men's labour, they had too no less proportion out of the yearly increase of every man's reputation. The rest would thrive the better for it. Their virtues are to be celebrated with all encouragement; and, if their vices be not notoriously palpable, let the eye as it defends its organ, so conceal the object by connivance.

And yet nevertheless, and all that has been said before being granted, it may so chance that to write, and that satirically, and that a second time and a third; and this too even against a clergyman, may be not only excusable but necessary. That I may spare a tedious recapitulation, I shall prove all the rest upon the strongest instance, that is in the case of a clergyman. For it is not impossible that a man by evil arts may have crept into the Church, through the belfry or at the windows. 'Tis not improbable that having so got in he should foul the pulpit and afterwards the press with opinions destructive to human society and the Christian religion. That he should illustrate so corrupt doctrines with as ill a conversation, and adorn the lasciviousness of his life with an equal petulancy of style and language. In such a concurrence of misdemeanours what is to be done? Why certainly, how pernicious soever this must be in the example and consequence, yet, before any private man undertake to obviate it, he ought to expect the judgement of the diocesan and the method of the ecclesiastical discipline. There was in the ancient times of Christianity a wholesome usage, but now obsolete, which went very far in preventing all these occasions. For whosoever was to receive ordination, his name was first published to the congregation in the same way as the banns of those that enter into matrimony; and if any could object a sufficient cause against him that was proposed, he was not to be admitted to the ministry. He that would be a preacher was to be first himself commented upon by the people, and in the style of those ages was said *praedicari*. But since that circumspection has been devolved into the single oversight of the later bishops, it cannot be otherwise, but some one or other may sometimes escape into the Church, who were much fitter to be shut out of doors. Yet then if our great pastors should but exercise the wisdom of common shepherds, by parting with one to stop the infection of the whole flock, when his rottenness grew notorious; or if our clergy would but use the instinct of other creatures, and chase the blown deer out of their herd; such mischiefs might quickly be remedied. But on the contrary, it happens not seldom that this necessary duty (which is so great a part of true *ecclesiastical polity*) is not only neglected, but that persons so dangerous are rather encouraged by their superiors, and he that, upon their omission, shall but single out one of them, yet shall be exposed to the general out-cry of the Faculty, and be pursued with bell, book, and candle, as a declared and public enemy of the clergy. Whereas they ought to consider that by this way of proceeding, they themselves do render that universal which was but individual, and affix a personal crime upon their whole order, and, for want of separating from one obnoxious, do contribute to the causes of separation, justifying so far that schism which they condemn. In this case, and supposing such a failure of justice in those whose province it is to prevent or punish, I ask again what is to be done? Why certainly the next thing had been to admonish him in particular as a friend does his friend, or one Christian another. But he that hath once printed an ill book has thereby condensed his words on purpose lest they should be carried away by the wind; he has diffused his poison so publicly in design that it might be beyond his own recollection; and put himself deliberately past the reach of any private admonition. In this case it is that I think a clergyman is laid open to the pen of anyone that knows how to manage it; and that every person who has either wit, learning or sobriety is licensed, if debauched to curb him, if erroneous to catechize him, and if foul-mouthed and biting to muzzle him. For they do but abuse themselves who shall any longer consider or reverence such an one as a clergyman, who as oft as he undresses degrades himself and would never have come into the Church but to take sanctuary. Rather, wheresoever men shall find the footing of so wanton a satyr out of his own bounds, the neighbourhood ought, notwithstanding all his pretended capering divinity, to hunt him through the woods with hounds and horn home to his harbour. [. . .]

You do three times at least in your *Reproof*, and in your *Transproser Rehears'd* well nigh half the book through, run upon an author J.M. which does not a little offend me. For why should any other man's reputation suffer in a contest betwixt you and me? But it is because you resolved to suspect that he had an hand in my former book, wherein, whether you deceive yourself or no, you deceive others extremely. For by chance I had not seen him of two years before; but after I undertook writing, I did more carefully avoid either visiting or sending to him, lest I should any way involve him in my consequences. And you might have understood, or I am sure your friend the author of the *Common Places* could have told you (he too had a slash at J.M. upon my account), that had he took you in hand, you would have had cause to repent the occasion, and not escaped so easily as you did under my *Transprosal*. But I take it moreover very ill that you should have so mean an opinion of me, as not to think me competent to write such a simple book as that without any assistance. It is a sign (however you upbraid me often as your old acquaintance) that you did not know me well, and that we had not much conversation together. But because in your 125 *p.* you are so particular *you know a friend of ours*, &c., intending that J.M. and his answer to *Salmasius*, I think it here seasonable to acquit my promise to you in giving the reader a short trouble concerning my first acquaintance with you. J.M. was, and is, a man of great learning and sharpness of wit as any man. It was his misfortune, living in a tumultuous time, to be tossed on the wrong side, and he writ *flagrante bello* certain dangerous treatises. His books of *Divorce* I know not whether you may have use of; but those upon which you take him at advantage were of no other nature than that which I mentioned to you, writ by your own father, only with this difference, that your father's, which I have by me, was written with the same design, but with much less wit or judgement, for which there was no remedy: unless you will supply his judgement with his High Court of Justice. At His Majesty's happy return, J.M. did partake, even as you yourself did for all your huffing, of his regal clemency and has ever since expiated himself in a retired silence. It was after that, I well remember it, that being one day at his house, I there first met you and accidentally. Since that I have been scarce four or five times in your company, but, whether it were my foresight or my good fortune, I never contracted any friendship or confidence with you. But then it was, when you, as I told you, wandered up and down Moorfields astrologizing upon the duration of His Majesty's government, that you frequented J.M. incessantly and haunted his house day by day. What discourses you there used he is too generous to remember. But he never having in the least provoked you, for you to insult thus over his old age, to traduce him by your *Scaramuccios*, and in your own person, as a school-master, who was born and hath lived much more ingenuously and liberally than yourself; to have done all this, and lay at last my simple book to his charge, without ever taking care to inform yourself better, which you had so easy opportunity to do; nay, when you yourself too have said, to my knowledge, that you saw no such great matter in it but that I might be the author. It is inhumanely and inhospitably done, and will I hope be a warning to all others as it is to me, to avoid (I will not say such a Judas) but a man that creeps into all companies, to jeer, trepan, and betray them.

HIS MAJESTY'S MOST GRACIOUS SPEECH TO BOTH HOUSES OF PARLIAMENT

My Lords and Gentlemen,

I told you, at our last meeting, the winter was the fittest time for business, and truly I thought so, till my Lord Treasurer assured me the spring was the best season for salads and subsidies. I hope therefore that April will not prove so unnatural a month as not to afford some kind showers on my parched Exchequer, which gapes for want of them. Some of you, perhaps, will think it dangerous to make me too rich; but I do not fear it, for I promise you faithfully, whatever you give me I will always want. And although in other things my word may be thought a slender authority, yet in that, you may rely on me, I will never break it.

My Lords and Gentlemen,

I can bear my straits with patience, but my Lord Treasurer does protest to me, that the Revenue, as it now stands, will not serve him and me too. One of us must pinch for it, if you do not help me. I must speak freely to you, I am under bad circumstances, for besides my harlots in service, my reformado concubines lie heavy upon me. I have a passable good estate, I confess, but, God's-fish, I have a great charge upon 't. Here's my Lord Treasurer can tell, that all the money designed for next summer's Guards must, of necessity, be applied to the next year's cradles and swaddling-clothes. What shall we do for ships, then? I hint this only to you, it being your business, not mine. I know, by experience, I can live without ships. I lived ten years abroad without, and never had my health better in my life; but how you will be without, I leave to yourselves to judge, and therefore hint this only by the by: I do not insist upon it. There's another thing I must press more earnestly, and that is this: it seems a good part of my revenue will expire in two or three years, except you will be pleased to continue it. I have to say for 't, Pray, why did you give me so much as you have done, unless you resolve to give on as fast as I call for it? The nation hates you already for giving so much, and I'll hate you too, if you do not give me more. So that if you stick not to me, you must not have a friend in England. On the other hand, if you will give me the revenue I desire, I shall be able to do those things for your religion and liberty that I have had long in my thoughts, but cannot effect them without a little more money to carry me through. Therefore look to 't, and take notice that if you do not make me rich enough to undo you, it shall lie at your doors. For my part, I wash my hands on 't. But that I may gain your good opinion, the best way is to acquaint you what I have done to deserve it, out of my royal care for your religion and your property. For the first, my proclamation is a true picture of my mind. He that cannot, as in glass, see my zeal for the Church of England, does not deserve any farther satisfaction, for I declare him wilful, abominable, and not good. Some may, perhaps, be startled, and cry, 'How comes this sudden change?' To which I answer, I am a changeling, and that's sufficient, I think. But to convince men farther that I mean what I say, there are these arguments.

First, I tell you so, and you know I never break my word.

Secondly, my Lord Treasurer says so, and he never told a lie in his life.

Thirdly, my Lord Lauderdale will undertake it for me; and I should be loath, by any act of mine, he should forfeit the credit he has with you.

If you desire more instances of my zeal, I have them for you. For example, I have converted my natural sons from Popery; and I may say, without vanity, it was my own work, so much the more peculiarly mine than the begetting them. 'Twould do one's heart good to hear how prettily George can read already in the Psalter. They are all fine children, God bless 'em, and so like me in their understandings! But, as I was saying, I have, to please you, given a pension to your favourite, my Lord Lauderdale; not so much that I thought he wanted it, as that you would take it kindly. I have made Carwel Duchess of Portsmouth, and married her sister to the Earl of Pembroke. I have, at my brother's request, sent my Lord Inchiquin into Barbary, to settle the Protestant religion among the Moors, and an English interest at Tangier. I have made Crewe Bishop of Durham, and, at the first word of my Lady Portsmouth, Prideaux Bishop of Chichester. I know not, for my part, what factious men would have; but this I am sure of, my predecessors never did anything like this to gain the good will of their subjects. So much for your religion, and now for your property. My behaviour to the bankers is a public instance; and the proceedings between Mrs Hyde and Mrs Sutton, for private ones, are such convincing evidences that it will be needless to say any more to 't.

I must now acquaint you that by my Lord Treasurer's advice I have made a considerable retrenchment upon my expenses in candles and charcoal, and do not intend to stop there, but will, with your help, look into the late embezzlements of my drippingpans and kitchenstuffs; of which, by the way, upon my conscience, neither my Lord Treasurer nor my Lord Lauderdale are guilty. I tell you my opinion; but if you should find them dabbling in that business, I tell you plainly, I leave 'em to you. For I would have the world to know, I am not a man to be cheated.

My Lords and Gentlemen,

I desire you to believe me as you have found me; and I do solemnly promise you that whatsoever you give me shall be specially managed with the same conduct, trust, sincerity, and prudence that I have ever practised since my happy Restoration.

MR SMIRKE; OR, THE DIVINE IN MODE (EXTRACT)

It hath been the good nature (and politicians will have it the wisdom) of most governors to entertain the people with public recreations; and therefore to encourage such as could best contribute to their divertisement. And hence doubtless it is, that our ecclesiastical governors also (who as they yield to none for prudence, so in good humour they exceed all others), have not disdained of late years to afford the laity no inconsiderable pastime. Yea, so great hath been their condescension that, rather than fail, they have carried on the merriment by men of their own Faculty, who might otherwise, by the gravity of their calling, have claimed an exemption from such offices. They have ordained, from time to time, several of the most ingenious and pregnant of their clergy to supply the press continually with new books of ridiculous and facetious argument. Wherein divers of them have succeeded even to admiration; insomuch that by the reading thereof, the ancient sobriety and seriousness of the English nation hath been in some good measure discussed and worn out of fashion. Yet, though the clergy have hereby manifested that nothing comes amiss to them, and particularly that when they give their minds to it, no sort of men are more proper or capable to make sport for spectators; it hath so happened by the rewards and promotions bestowed upon those who have laboured in this province, that many others in hopes of the like preferment, although otherwise by their parts, their complexion and education unfitted for this jocular divinity, have in order to it, wholly neglected the more weighty cares of their function. And from hence it proceeds, that to the no small scandal and disreputation of our Church, a great *arcanum* of their state hath been discovered and divulged: that, albeit wit be not inconsistent and incompatible with a clergyman, yet neither is it inseparable from them. So that it is of concernment to my lords the bishops henceforward to repress those of 'em who have no wit from writing, and to take care that even those that have, do husband it better, as not knowing to what exigency they may be reduced: but however that they the bishops be not too forward in licensing and prefixing their venerable names to such pamphlets. For admitting (though I am not too positive in it) that our episcopacy is of apostolical right, yet we do not find that among all those gifts then given to men, that which we call wit is enumerated; nor yet among those qualifications requisite to a bishop. And therefore should they, out of complacency for an author, or delight in the argument, or facility of their judgements, approve of a dull book, their own understandings will be answerable, and irreverent people, that cannot distinguish, will be ready to think that such of them differ from men of wit, not only in degree, but in order. For all are not of my mind, who could never see anyone elevated to that dignity, but I presently conceived a greater opinion of his wit than ever I had formerly. But some do not stick to affirm that even they, the bishops, come by theirs not by inspiration, not by teaching, but even as the poor laity do sometimes light upon it, by a good mother; which has occasioned the homely Scotch proverb that 'an ounce of mother-wit is worth a pound of clergy.' And as they come by it as do other men, so they possess it on the same condition: that they cannot transmit it by breathing, touching, or any natural *effluvium*, to other persons; not so much as to their most domestic chaplain, or to the closest residentiary. That the King himself, who is no less the spring of that than he is the fountain of honour, yet has never used the dubbing or creating of wits as a flower of his prerogative; much less can the ecclesiastical power confer it with the same ease as they do the holy orders. That whatsoever they can do of that kind is at uttermost to empower men by their authority and commission, no otherwise than in the licensing of midwives or physicians. But that as to their collating of any internal talent or ability, they could never pretend to it; their grants and their prohibitions are alike invalid, and they can neither capacitate one man to be witty, nor hinder another from being so, further than as the press is at their devotion. Which if it be the case, they cannot be too circumspect in their management, and should be very exquisite (seeing this way of writing is found so necessary) in making choice of fit instruments. The Church's credit is more interested in an ecclesiastical droll than in a lay chancellor. It is no small trust that is reposed in him to whom the bishop shall commit *omne et omnimodum suum ingenium, tam temporale quam spirituale*: and however it goes with excommunication, they should take good heed to what manner of person they delegate the keys of laughter. It is not every man that is qualified to sustain the dignity of the Church's jester; and should they take as exact a scrutiny of them as of the Nonconformists through their dioceses, the number would appear inconsiderable upon this Easter Visitation. Before men be admitted to so important an employment, it were fit they underwent a severe examination; and that it might appear, first, whether they have any sense; for without that how can any man pretend (and yet they do) to be ingenious? Then, whether they have any modesty; for without that they can only be scurrilous and impudent. Next, whether any truth; for true jests are those that do the greatest execution. And lastly, it were not amiss that they gave some account too of their Christianity; for the world has always hitherto been so uncivil as to expect something of that from the clergy, in the design and style even of their lightest and most uncanonical writings. And though I am no rigid imposer of a discipline of mine own devising, yet had anything of this nature entered into the minds of other men, it is not impossible that a late pamphlet, published by Authority and proclaimed by the Gazette, *Animadversions upon a late pamphlet, entitled, The Naked Truth; or, The True State of the Primitive Church*, might have been spared.

That book so called, *The Naked Truth*, is a treatise that, were it not for this its opposer, needs no commendation; being writ with that evidence and demonstration of Spirit, that all sober men cannot but give their assent and consent to it, unasked. It is a book of that kind, that no Christian scarce can peruse it without wishing himself had been the author, and almost imagining that he is so; the conceptions therein being of so eternal an idea, that every man finds it to be but the copy of an original in his own mind, and though he never read it till now, wonders it could be so long before he remembered it. Neither, although there be a time whenas they say all truths are not to be spoken, could there ever have come forth anything more seasonable; when the sickly nation had been so long indisposed and knew not the remedy, but (having taken so many things that rather did it harm than good) only longed for some moderation, and as soon as it had tasted this, seemed to itself sensibly to recover; when their representatives in Parliament had been of late so frequent in consultations of this nature, and they, the physicians of the nation, were ready to have received any wholesome advice for the cure of our malady. It appears moreover plainly that the Author is judicious, learned, conscientious, a sincere Protestant, and a true son, if not a father, of the Church of England. For the rest, the book cannot be free from the imperfections incident to all human endeavours, but those so small, and guarded everywhere with so much modesty, that it seems there was none left for the Animadverter, who might otherwise have blushed to reproach him. But some there were that thought Holy Church was concerned in it, and that no true-born son of our mother of England but ought to have it in detestation. Not only the churches but the coffee-houses rung against it. They itinerated like excise-spies from one house to another, and some of the morning and evening chaplains burnt their lips with perpetual discoursing it out of reputation, and loading the Author, whoever he were, with all contempt, malice and obloquy. Nor could this suffice them, but a lasting pillar of infamy must be erected to eternize his crime and his punishment. There must be an answer to him, in print, and that not according to the ordinary rules of civility, or in the sober way of arguing controversy, but with the utmost extremity of jeer, disdain, and indignation; and happy the man whose lot it should be to be deputed to that performance. It was Shrove Tuesday with them, and, not having yet forgot their boys-play, they had set up this cock, and would have been content some of them to have ventured their coffee-farthings, yea their Easter-pence by advance, to have a fling at him. But there was this close youth who treads always upon the heels of Ecclesiastical Preferment, but hath come nearer the heels of the Naked Truth than were for his service, that rather by favour than any tolerable sufficiency carried away this employment, as he hath done many others from them. So that being the man pitched upon, he took up an unfortunate resolution that he would be witty: unfortunate, I say, and no less criminal; for I dare aver that never any person was more manifestly guilty of the sin against nature. But however to write a book of that virulence, and at such a season, was very improper; even in the holy time of Lent, when, whether upon the sacred account, it behoved him rather to have subjugated and mortified the swelling of his passions; or whether upon the political reason, he might well have forborn his young wit, as but newly pigged or calved, in order to the growth of the yearly summer provisions. Yet to work he fell, not omitting first to sum himself up in the whole wardrobe of his function; as well because his wit consisting wholly in his dress, he would (and 'twas his concernment to) have it all about him: as to the end that being huffed up in all his ecclesiastical fluster, he might appear more formidable, and in the pride of his heart and habit out-boniface an Humble Moderator. So that there was more to do in equipping of Mr Smirke than there is about Dorimant, and the Divine in Mode might have vied with Sir Fopling Flutter. The vestry and the tiring-room were both exhausted, and 'tis hard to say whether there went more attendants toward the composing of himself, or of his pamphlet. Being thus dressed up, at last forth he comes in print. No poet either the first or the third day could be more concerned; and his little party, like men hired for the purpose, had posted themselves at every corner to feign a more numerous applause; but clapped out of time, and disturbed the whole company.

AN ACCOUNT OF THE GROWTH OF POPERY, AND ARBITRARY GOVERNMENT IN ENGLAND (EXTRACTS)

There has now for divers years a design been carried on to change the lawful government of England into an absolute tyranny, and to convert the established Protestant religion into downright Popery: than both which, nothing can be more destructive or contrary to the interest and happiness, to the constitution and being of the King and kingdom.

For if first we consider the State, the kings of England rule not upon the same terms with those of our neighbour nations, who, having by force or by address usurped that due share which their people had in the government, are now for some ages in possession of an arbitrary power (which yet no prescription can make legal) and exercise it over their persons and estates in a most tyrannical manner. But here the subjects retain their proportion in the legislature; the very meanest commoner of England is represented in Parliament, and is a party to those laws by which the prince is sworn to govern himself and his people. No money is to be levied but by the common consent. No man is for life, limb, goods, or liberty at the sovereign's discretion: but we have the same right (modestly understood) in our propriety that the prince hath in his regality; and in all cases where the King is concerned, we have our just remedy as against any private person of the neighbourhood, in the Courts of Westminster Hall or in the High Court of Parliament. His very prerogative is no more than what the law has determined. His Broad Seal, which is the legitimate stamp of his pleasure, yet is no longer current, than upon the trial it is found to be legal. He cannot commit any person by his particular warrant. He cannot himself be witness in any cause: the balance of public justice being so delicate, that not the hand only but even the breath of the prince would turn the scale. Nothing is left to the King's will, but all is subjected to his authority: by which means it follows that he can do no wrong, nor can he receive wrong; and a King of England keeping to these measures may without arrogance be said to remain the only intelligent ruler over a rational people. In recompense therefore and acknowledgement of so good a government under his influence, his person is most sacred and inviolable; and whatsoever excesses are committed against so high a trust, nothing of them is imputed to him, as being free from the necessity or temptation; but his ministers only are accountable for all, and must answer it at their perils. He hath a vast revenue constantly arising from the hearth of the householder, the sweat of the labourer, the rent of the farmer, the industry of the merchant, and consequently out of the estate of the gentleman: a large competence to defray the ordinary expense of the Crown and maintain its lustre. And if any extraordinary occasion happen, or be but with any probable decency pretended, the whole land at whatsoever season of the year does yield him a plentiful harvest. So forward are his people's affections to give, even to superfluity, that a foreigner (or Englishman that hath been long abroad) would think they could neither will nor choose, but that the asking of a supply were a mere formality, it is so readily granted. He is the fountain of all honours, and has moreover the distribution of so many profitable offices of the Household, of the Revenue, of State, of Law, of Religion, of the Navy (and, since his present Majesty's time, of the Army) that it seems as if the nation could scarce furnish honest men enough to supply all those employments. So that the Kings of England are in nothing inferior to other princes, save in being more abridged from injuring their own subjects; but have as large a field as any of external felicity, wherein to exercise their own virtue, and so reward and encourage it in others. In short, there is nothing that comes nearer in government to the Divine Perfection, than where the monarch, as with us, enjoys a capacity of doing all the good imaginable to mankind, under a disability to all that is evil.

And as we are thus happy in the constitution of our State, so are we yet more blessed in that of our Church; being free from that Romish yoke, which so great a part of Christendom do yet draw and labour under. That Popery is such a thing as cannot, but for want of a word to express it, be called a religion; nor is it to be mentioned with that civility which is otherwise decent to be used in speaking of the differences of human opinion about Divine matters. [. . .]

So that in conclusion, there is no Englishman that hath a soul, a body, or an estate to save, that loves either God, his King, or his Country, but is by all those tenures bound, to the best of his power and knowledge, to maintain the established Protestant religion.

And yet, all this notwithstanding, there are those men among us, who have undertaken, and do make it their business, under so legal and perfect a government, to introduce a French slavery, and instead of so pure a religion, to establish the Roman idolatry: both and either of which are crimes of the highest nature. For, as to matter of government, if to murder the King be, as certainly it is, a fact so horrid, how much more heinous is it to assassinate the kingdom? And as none will deny that to alter our monarchy into a commonwealth were treason, so by the same fundamental rule, the crime is no less to make that monarchy absolute.

What is thus true in regard of the State holds as well in reference to our religion. Former Parliaments have made it treason in whosoever shall attempt to seduce anyone, the meanest of the King's subjects, to the Church of Rome; and this Parliament hath, to all penalties by the common or statute law, added incapacity for any man who shall presume to say that the King is a Papist or an introducer of Popery. But what lawless and incapable miscreants then, what wicked traitors are those wretched men, who endeavour to pervert our whole Church and to bring that about in effect, which even to mention is penal, at one Italian stroke attempting to subvert the government and religion, to kill the body and damn the soul of our nation?

Yet were these men honest old Cavaliers that had suffered in his late Majesty's service, it were allowable in them, as oft as their wounds broke out at Spring or Fall, to think of a more arbitrary government, as a sovereign balsam for their aches, or to imagine that no weapon-salve but of the moss that grows on an enemy's skull could cure them. Should they mistake this Long Parliament also for rebels, and that, although all circumstances be altered, there were still the same necessity to fight it all over again in pure loyalty, yet their age and the times they have lived in might excuse them. But those worthy gentlemen are too generous, too good Christians and subjects, too affectionate to the good English government to be capable of such an impression; whereas these conspirators are such as have not one drop of Cavalier blood, or no bowels at least of a Cavalier in them, but have starved them to revel and surfeit upon their calamities, making their persons, and the very cause, by pretending to it themselves, almost ridiculous.

Or were these conspirators on the other side but avowed Papists, they were the more honest, the less dangerous, and the religion were answerable for the errors they might commit in order to promote it. [. . .] But these persons, that have since taken the work in hand, are such as lie under no temptation of religion: secure men, that are above either honour or consciences, but obliged by all the most sacred ties of malice and ambition to advance the ruin of the King and Kingdom, and qualified much better than others, under the name of good Protestants, to effect it. [. . .]

And now, should I enter into a particular retail of all former and latter transactions relating to this affair, there would be sufficient for a just volume of history. But my intention is only to write a naked narrative of some the most considerable passages in the meeting of Parliament the 15th of February 1677: such as have come to my notice, which may serve for matter to some stronger pen, and to such as have more leisure and further opportunity to discover and communicate to the public. This in the meantime will, by the progress made in so few weeks, demonstrate at what rate these men drive over the necks of King and people, of religion and government; and how near they are in all human probability to arrive triumphant at the end of their journey. Yet, that I may not be too abrupt, and leave the reader wholly destitute of a thread to guide himself by through so intriguing a labyrinth, I shall summarily, as short as so copious and redundant a matter will admit, deduce the order of affairs both at home and abroad, as it led into this Session. [. . .]

It is now come to the fourth act, and the next scene that opens may be Rome or Paris, yet men sit by, like idle spectators, and still give money towards their own tragedy. It is true, that by His Majesty and the Church's care, under God's special providence, the conspiracy hath received frequent disappointments. But it is here as in gaming, where, though the cheat may lose for a while to the skill or good fortune of a fairer player, and sometimes on purpose to draw him in deeper, yet the false dice must at the long run carry it, unless discovered, and when it comes once to a great stake, will infallibly sweep the table.

If the relator had extended all these articles in their particular instances, with several other heads, which out of respect he forbore to enumerate, it is evident there was matter sufficient to have further accused his subjects. And nevertheless, he foresees that he shall on both hands be blamed for pursuing this method. Some on the one side will expect that the very persons should have been named; whereas he only gives evidence to the fact, and leaves the malefactors to those who have the power of inquiry. It was his design indeed to give information, but not to turn informer. That these to whom he hath only a public enmity, no private animosity, might have the privilege of statesmen, to repent at the last hour and by one signal action to expiate all their former misdemeanours. But if anyone delight in the chase, he is an ill woodman that knows not the size of the beast by the proportion of his excrement.

On the other hand, some will represent this discourse (as they do all books that tend to detect their conspiracy) against His Majesty and the kingdom, as if it too were written against the government. For now of late, as soon as any man is gotten into public employment by ill acts, and by worse continues it, he, if it please the fates, is thenceforward the government, and by being criminal pretends to be sacred. These are, themselves, the men who are the living libels against the government, and who (whereas the law discharges the prince upon his ministers) do, if in danger of being questioned, plead or rather impeach his authority in their own justification. Yea, so impudent is their ingratitude, that as they entitle him to their crimes, so they arrogate to themselves his virtues, challenging whatsoever is well done, and is the pure emanation of his royal goodness, to have proceeded from their influence; objecting thereby His Majesty, if it were possible, to the hatred, and interposing as far as in them lies, betwixt the love of his people. For being conscious to themselves how inconsiderable they would be under any good government, but for their notorious wickedness, they have no other way of subsisting but by nourishing suspicions betwixt a most loyal people and most gracious sovereign. But this book, though of an extraordinary nature, as the case required, and however it may be calumniated by interested persons, was written with no other intent than of mere fidelity and service to His Majesty, and God forbid that it should have any other effect than that *the mouth of all iniquity and of flatterers may be stopped*, and that His Majesty, having discerned the disease, may with his healing touch apply the remedy. For so far is the relator himself from any sinister surmise of His Majesty, or from suggesting it to others, that he acknowledges, if it were fit for Caesar's wife to be free, much more is Caesar himself from all crime and suspicion. Let us therefore conclude with our own common devotions, *From all privy conspiracy, &c. Good Lord deliver us.*

FINIS

FOR HIS EXCELLENCY, THE LORD GENERAL CROMWELL

May it please your Excellency,

It might perhaps seem fit for me to seek out words to give your Excellency thanks for myself. But indeed the only civility which it is proper for me to practise with so eminent a person is to obey you, and to perform honestly the work that you have set me about. Therefore I shall use the time that your Lordship is pleased to allow me for writing, only to that purpose for which you have given me it: that is, to render you some account of Mr Dutton. I have taken care to examine him several times in the presence of Mr Oxenbridge, as those who weigh and tell over money before some witness ere they take charge of it. For I thought that there might possibly be some lightness in the coin, or error in the telling, which hereafter I should be bound to make good. Therefore Mr Oxenbridge is the best to make your Excellency an impartial relation thereof. I shall only say that I shall strive according to my best understanding (that is according to those rules your Lordship hath given me) to increase whatsoever talent he may have already. Truly he is of a gentle and waxen disposition; and, God be praised, I cannot say that he hath brought with him any evil impression, and I shall hope to set nothing upon his spirit but what may be of a good sculpture. He hath in him two things which make youth most easy to be managed, modesty which is the bridle to vice, and emulation which is the spur to virtue. And the care which your Excellency is pleased to take of him is no small encouragement and shall be so represented to him. But above all I shall labour to make him sensible of his duty to God. For then we begin to serve faithfully, when we consider that he is our Master. And in this both he and I owe infinitely to your Lordship, for having placed us in so godly a family as that of Mr Oxenbridge, whose doctrine and example are like a book and a map, not only instructing the ear but demonstrating to the eye which way we ought to travel. And Mrs Oxenbridge hath a great tenderness over him also in all other things. She has looked so well to him that he hath already much mended his complexion. And now she is busy in ordering his chamber, that he may delight to be in it as often as his studies require. For the rest, most of this time hitherto hath been spent in acquainting ourselves with him; and truly he is very cheerful and I hope thinks us to be good company. I shall upon occasion henceforward inform your Excellency of any particularities in our little affairs. For so I esteem it to be my duty. I have no more at present but to give thanks to God for your Lordship, and to beg grace of him, that I may approve myself

Your Excellency's most humble and faithful Servant

Andrew Marvell.

Windsor July 28 1653.

Mr Dutton presents his most humble service to your Excellency.

TO WILLIAM POPPLE

Dearest Will,

I wrote to you two letters, and paid for them from the Post-house here at Westminster; to which I have had no answer. Perhaps they miscarried. I sent you an answer to the only letter I received from Bordeaux, and having put it into Mr Nelthorpe's hand, I doubt not but it came to yours. To proceed. The same day my letter bore date there was an extraordinary thing done. The King, about ten o'clock, took boat, with Lauderdale only, and two ordinary attendants, and rowed awhile as towards the Bridge, but soon turned back to the Parliament Stairs, and so went up into the House of Lords, and took his seat. Almost all of them were amazed, but all seemed so; and the Duke of York especially was very much surprised. Being sat, he told them it was a privilege he claimed from his ancestors to be present at their deliberations. That, therefore, they should not, for his coming, interrupt their debates, but proceed, and be covered. They did so. It is true that this has been done long ago, but it is now so old, that it is new, and so disused that at any other, but so bewitched a time, as this, it would have been looked on as an high usurpation, and breach of privilege. He indeed sat still, for the most part, and interposed very little; sometimes a word or two. But the most discerning opinion was, that he did herein as he rowed, for having had his face first to the Conventicle Bill, he turned short to the Lord Ross's. So that, indeed, it is credible, the King, in prospect of diminishing the Duke of York's influence in the Lords' House, in this or any future matter, resolved, and wisely enough at present, to weigh up and lighten the Duke's efficacy, by coming himself in person. After three or four days' continuance, the Lords were very well used to the King's presence, and sent the Lord Steward and Lord Chamberlain to him, when they might wait, as an House on him, to render their humble thanks for the honour he did them. The hour was appointed them, and they thanked him, and he took it well. So this matter, of such importance on all great occasions, seems riveted to them, and us, for the future, and to all posterity. Now the Lord Ross's Bill came in order to another debate, and the King present. Nevertheless, the debate lasted an entire day; and it passed by very few voices. The King has ever since continued his session among them, and says it is better than going to a play. In this Session the Lords sent down to us a Proviso for the King, that would have restored him to all civil or ecclesiastical prerogatives which his ancestors had enjoyed at any time since the Conquest. There was never so compendious a piece of absolute universal tyranny. But the Commons made them ashamed of it, and retrenched it. The Parliament was never so embarrassed, beyond recovery. We are all venal cowards, except some few. What plots of state will go on this Interval I know not. There is a new set of Justices of Peace framing through the whole kingdom. The governing Cabal, since Ross's business, are Buckingham, Lauderdale, Ashley, Orrery, and Trevor. Not but the other Cabal too have seemingly sometimes their turn. Madame, our king's sister, during the King of France's progress in Flanders, is to come as far as Canterbury. There will doubtless be family counsels then. Some talk of a French queen to be then invented for our king. Some talk of a sister of Denmark; others of a good virtuous Protestant here at home. The King disavows it; yet he has said in public, he knew not why a woman might not be divorced for barrenness, as a man for impotence. The Lord Barclay went on Monday last for Ireland, the King to Newmarket. God keep, and increase you, in all things.

Yours, &c.

April 14 1670

TO MAYOR HOARE

Gentlemen, my very worthy friends,

The Parliament having assembled this day I must not neglect to give you account of what hath passed. His Majesty having called the Commons before him in the Lords' House told them the occasion of this session was that he might know what further he could do towards the securing of their religion and property and to establish a durable correspondence betwixt him and his people. He took notice that there were some pernicious persons who did endeavour the contrary, but testified his great satisfaction in this Parliament the most of which had in their own persons or were descended of those who had signalized themselves in his service. That for his part he should always maintain the religion and the Church of England as now established and be all his life constant in that profession. That the navy did stand in need of repairing and increasing, that something might be done in it this summer for otherwise a whole year would be lost. And that he intended, a long session not being now seasonable, to meet the Parliament again in winter. The Keeper spoke very largely to the same purpose but no account was given of that to the Commons by their Speaker. And I must desire you not by this summary relation I give you of His Majesty's speech to conceive of it accordingly. For by reason of the shortness of my memory and conception I do it much wrong both as to the matter and the expression. When printed I will send it you. The Commons in sense of so acceptable a speech after some hours' time for the wording of their thankfulness, voted That the humble thanks of this House be returned to His Majesty for the gracious promises and assurances expressed in his speech of maintaining religion and property as established by law and for calling the Parliament at this time for the said purpose. The Lords I hear also voted general thanks to His Majesty. This is what this day hath produced and I hope all the rest of this session may prove proportionable. If you have any particular commands for me I shall be very glad to obey you, being Gentlemen &c., Your most affectionate friend and humble servant

Andrew Marvell

Westminster April 13 1675

TO WILLIAM POPPLE

Dear Will,

I have time to tell you thus much of public matters. The patience of the Scots, under their oppressions, is not to be paralleled in any history. They still continue their extraordinary and numerous, but peaceable, field conventicles. One Mr Welsh is their archminister, and the last letter I saw tells, people were going forty miles to hear him. There came out, about Christmas last, here a large book concerning *The Growth of Popery and Arbitrary Government*. There have been great rewards offered in private, and considerable in the Gazette, to any who could inform of the author or printer, but not yet discovered. Three or four printed books since have described, as near as it was proper to go, the man being a Member of Parliament, Mr Marvell to have been the author; but if he had, surely he should not have escaped being questioned in Parliament, or some other place. My good wishes attend you.

Yours, etc.

June 10 1678

Critical commentary

CRITICAL POSITIONS

The poems and prose texts that make up the works of Andrew Marvell have been evaluated according to many different criteria and subjected to many different kinds of interpretation during the three hundred years since the writer's death. For a reader coming to them in the 1980s, they throw into sharp relief the contemporary debate not only about the competing claims of a number of reading strategies but also about the nature and function of the study of literature itself.

To begin with a specific example: because of its relation to a precise historical event, 'An Horatian ode upon Cromwell's return from Ireland' provided the occasion for a celebrated clash between two critical theories which were struggling for dominance in the early postwar years. Cleanth Brooks, from the formalist position of the New Critics, admitted that a reader 'may need to lean upon the historian' to a certain extent in coming to terms with such a text, but went on to insist 'that the poem has to be read as a poem – that what it "says" is a question for the critic to answer, and that no amount of historical evidence as such can finally determine what the poem says' (Brooks, 1946, pp. 134, 155). Taking up the cause of the literary biographer and historian, for whom critical attention centres upon the words that Marvell wrote 'as an Englishman of 1650',

Douglas Bush asserted in reply that 'to read the poem as poetry is also to read it as an historical document' (Bush 1952, pp. 373, 363). The assumptions which underlay Brooks's original essay were more explicitly formulated in his rejoinder to Bush:

> I am not concerned to lift Marvell out of his age into ours; I am concerned with what transcends his age. I am concerned with what is universal in the poem, and that means that I am concerned with more than seeing the 'Horatian Ode' as merely a document of its age. (Brooks, 1953, p. 133)

For the New Critic, the value of poetry as a distinct mode of discourse is to be found in those properties of language and symbol which enable it to speak across the centuries – properties which need not be part of the writer's conscious intention and which it is the function of criticism to analyse for signs of ingenuity, complexity and coherence.

Similar kinds of antagonism, or at least tension, between different critical approaches are apparent in subsequent studies. John M. Wallace declares that the enquiry into the ideological attitudes expressed in the 'Ode' 'cannot be profitably continued unless we relinquish introspection into our personal responses to the poem' in favour of a more thorough investigation into the situation created by the execution of the king in 1649 (Wallace, 1968, p. 71). Annabel Patterson enters the reservation that 'when the formidable political contexts of the [Cromwell] poems have been mastered, as they were by John Wallace, knowledge of the period and of its constitutional debates seems to overpower purely literary considerations' (Patterson, 1975, p. 251). Two more recent comments reflect developments in literary theory which transfer the focus of critical activity from the quest for the author's intended meaning or for 'what is universal in the poem' to the cultural conventions which govern the way we perceive and think about reality and to the creative role of the reader in generating meanings. Catherine Belsey cites Marvell's 'Ode' as an example of what she calls an 'interrogative text', which 'disrupts the unity of the reader' by 'discouraging identification' with an implied speaker and inviting him or her 'to produce answers to the questions it implicitly or explicitly raises'. Dismissing attempts like Wallace's to accommodate it within an internally consistent philosophy of politics, she argues that 'to smooth over the contradictions in the "Horatian Ode" by attributing to Marvell a non-contradictory ideology of Loyalism is to refuse to enter into the debates about revolution, authority and tyranny initiated in the text' (Belsey, 1980, pp. 91, 95). Robin Grove considers that the metrical form (alternating couplets of four-beat and three-beat lines) stimulates a reading experience that is at odds with any endeavour to extract a fixed set of meanings or attitudes from the words on the page: 'The voice, like the point of view, finds new possibilities opening before it with every move it makes, so that to write the verse, or to read it, you have constantly (and feelingly) to change your view. Yet still to *have* a view as well' (Grove, 1981, p. 47).

The purpose of this selective look at the controversy provoked by one of Marvell's best-known poems is not to highlight its inherently controversial qualities as a text, but to demonstrate that the practice of literary criticism in the modern world has itself become a problematic activity. Consequently, the present essay sets out to alert the new reader to some of the critical issues raised by different groups of works in the Marvell canon, rather than to offer a detailed commentary on separate items. In method, it reflects a model of literature which posits the active contribution of both writer and reader to the experience of reading a text. Without seeking to divert critical interest to the psychology or biography of the author, it is assumed that Andrew Marvell exerted a certain amount of conscious control over the choice and disposition of words, images and allusions, and therefore that the text itself can be expected to carry indications of the kind of effect it was designed to achieve. Similarly, without subscribing to those brands of contemporary theory which deny the right or power of the text to impose any constraints upon the free play of the interpretative and imaginative faculties, it is recognized that a reader will bring to the act of reading a set of preconceptions (moral, religious, political, aesthetic) derived from the age and environment in which he or she lives. An individual poem or prose work is therefore conceived as the locus of an encounter between author and reader, which contains within itself stylistic features appropriate to the nature and conditions of that encounter. The author, that is, builds into the text signals which imply the kind of reader for whom it is intended. This, in turn, involves the assumption that a responsible reading will acknowledge the historical dimension of the text and take into account the linguistic, social, political, cultural and intellectual context in which it was composed.

The selection of letters included in this volume illustrates how a written text partially prescribes the manner in which it is to be read and defines the relative stances of writer and reader. Of the four letters, written by Marvell between 1653 and 1678, one is addressed to His Excellency, the Lord General Cromwell, one to Mayor Hoare of Kingston-upon-Hull, and two to William Popple, the poet's nephew. The first, sent from the house of John Oxenbridge when Marvell had just taken up his position as tutor to William Dutton, is written from the point of view of a dependant who wishes to establish that he is conscious both of the personal obligation he is under to his employer and of his temerity in intruding upon so eminent a personage with this report on 'our little affairs'. But at the same time, the newly appointed tutor is at pains to convey the impression that he has a genuine concern for the spiritual and physical well-being of his young charge and that he is shrewd enough to know that a teacher cannot work wonders with a pupil if there should prove to be 'some lightness in the coin'. While maintaining the appropriate tone of social distance and respect, Marvell contrives to avoid servility and speaks as one man of experience to another in confiding his opinion that Dutton 'hath in him two things which make youth most easy to be managed'. The great general and politician is implicitly invited to recognize the value of a correspondent who knows his place but does not forfeit a proper sense of his own dignity and abilities.

The letter to the Mayor and Corporation of Hull is a business-like record of the latest happenings in the House by a conscientious MP who, after fifteen years representing their interests, is on easy but professional terms with those whose 'particular commands' he will be 'very glad to obey', but to whom he can unaffectedly excuse the 'shortness' of his 'memory and conception'. Only when we recall that the speech from the throne, transmitted so dispassionately in this 'summary relation', is the very one which he himself parodied with such merciless wit do we detect a possible note of irony here and there – for example, in the remark that the Commons returned a vote of 'humble thanks' to His Majesty 'in sense of so acceptable a speech after some hours' time for the wording of their thankfulness'. Did the original recipients of the letter read between the lines as we may feel compelled to do, or was the irony an entirely private joke not intended to be shared and only made available to us by an accident of history? Is the modern reader making illegitimate use of biographical inference or of knowledge extrinsic to the text in 'discovering' irony where there is no internal stylistic demand for an ironic reading?

In the letter to 'Dearest Will', dated 14 April 1670, the first three sentences sound a note of reproof tempered by a tentative explanation which may serve either to excuse the young man or to sharpen his conscience about neglecting to reply to his uncle's letters: 'Perhaps they miscarried.' The narrative of public events which follows this personal opening is spiced with the kind of commentary which is conspicuously absent from the letter to Mayor Hoare. The account of Charles II's attendance at debates in the House of Lords is coloured in advance by its introduction as 'an extraordinary thing', and Marvell goes on to charge some of the peers with complicity in this act of 'high usurpation' ('Almost all of them were amazed, but all seemed so') and to guess at the political motives behind this 'breach of privilege' by the monarch, which may have been to diminish 'the Duke of York's influence' ('indeed, it is credible') or may have been connected with his interest in the bill to allow Lord Ross to marry again after a divorce. The mood darkens as the public servant contemplates the constitutional significance of the recent turn of events and the man of conscience glances uncomfortably at his own moral implication in what is happening: 'We are all venal cowards, except some few.' His contempt for the 'governing Cabal' of statesmen and the 'other Cabal' within the royal family is bound up with his apprehensiveness about the 'plots' that may be hatched during the interval between parliamentary sessions. The private dimension which had to be suppressed or concealed behind the persona of the objective reporter in the correspondence with the aldermen of Hull is allowed into the foreground when the same individual writes to one who can be entrusted with reflections and judgements too indiscreet for a more public mode of discourse.

The final letter to William Popple furnishes an instance of irony clearly intended to be perceived by the original reader. As in the summary of the king's speech, there is nothing in the text itself to indicate an ironic undertow to the news of how the authorities had reacted to 'a large book' published 'about Christmas last' and the continuing speculation about its authorship. But because we are privileged to know, as Popple did, that the letter was written by his uncle, we can participate in the audacious humour of this straight-faced prose.

In all of these examples – the formal communication between tutor and employer, the professional report to an official body of men, the confidential disclosure of personal opinions on matters of state and the private joke at the expense of oppressive authority – the stylistic features of the text and the interpretative procedures adopted by the reader are largely determined by their status as letters. Our knowledge of when and in what context they were written and to whom they were addressed helps us to appreciate the nature of the constraints placed upon the use of language and to make significant adjustments to the way in which we interpret both the material content and the kind of persona projected in the writing. Similar adjustments are involved in reading a lyric poem, a satire or a polemical tract, with the added complication that an overtly fictional element may be much more prominent than in the linguistic construction of 'the tutor of William Dutton' or 'the MP for Hull'.

The following survey of Marvell's literary output in verse and prose is organized along broad lines according to the implied relationships among author, persona and reader and the degree of explicit engagement with the world of public affairs in which the historical Andrew Marvell lived and wrote. At one extreme are the prose pamphlets and topical satires which were designed to play an active part in influencing opinion in the political arena. At the other extreme are the pastoral, amatory and devotional lyrics spoken by mowers or nymphs and addressed to coy mistresses or the 'list'ning winds'. In between are poems to or about named individuals, which seem to fulfil a more intimate function than the exercises in satire or propaganda, but which also seem to demand an awareness of historical circumstances external to their own self-validating qualities as literary artefacts. These categories make no claim to theoretical rigour, but provide a convenient framework within which to identify the different kinds of challenge that Marvell's work offers to the modern reader.

LYRIC VOICES

Marvell's lyric poems possess characteristics which have made them particularly amenable to the 'thematic and interpretive orientation' of twentieth-century criticism which Jonathan Culler regards as the major legacy of the New Critics (Culler, 1981, p. 4). William Empson, for example, found ideal evidence for his study of how multiple meanings can be extracted from 'the same piece of language' in the pun on 'chordage' in line 44 of 'A dialogue between the Resolved Soul and Created Pleasure' and in the concentrated ambiguities of the conceit that 'all the jewels which we prize,/Melt in these pendants of the eyes' in 'Eyes and tears' (Empson, 1947, pp. 1, 105–6, 172–3), and inaugurated a long line of ingenious attempts to unpack the complex allusions and linguistic ambivalences of 'The garden' (Empson, 1935). The pursuit of meaning as the primary objective of modern literary criticism has resulted not only in an immense number of isolated raids on the secrets of individual poems, but also in more sustained campaigns, such as Ann Berthoff's demonstration that 'the major poems share the one grand theme of the soul's life in time' (Berthoff, 1970, p. 4) or Bruce King's that 'Marvell's poems on secular topics are also religious allegories' in which 'we must see the narrative as shadowing or figurative of biblical events, prophecies, or kinds of Christian experience' (King, 1977, p. 16). These approaches yield interpretations of that enigmatic poem, 'The unfortunate lover', as 'a continued metaphor by which is figured the necessary suffering of the time-bound soul' (Berthoff, 1970, p. 75), and as an allegory of the 'Incarnation, sufferings and Sacrifice' of Christ in which the Lover 'ere brought forth "cast away" in a shipwreck recalls mankind's rejection of divine love' (King, 1977, pp. 77, 80).

Others have followed the path indicated by Christopher Hill's claim 'that if we study Marvell with a knowledge of the political background of his life we can discover in the great lyrics new complexities which will increase our appreciation of those very sensitive and civilized poems' (Hill, 1968, pp. 324–5). Hill himself saw in Marvell's work evidence of profound changes in seventeenth-century England, which gave rise to 'a new type of lyric'. Having lost the 'social function' it had in the Elizabethan age, lyric poetry in the mid-century 'existed only to resolve the conflict within the poet's mind' – a conflict in Marvell 'between subjective and objective, between the idea and the reality', which attained conscious articulation in poems ostensibly about love or gardens and which may be linked '(very indirectly, of course) with the social and political problems of his time' (Hill, 1968, pp. 327–8). Like his unfortunate lover, the poet had himself been forced 'by the malignant stars' to 'live in storms and wars', and the 'iron wedges' which Fate drives between the lovers in 'A definition of love' can be seen to draw symbolic power from their association with 'one of the industries which were transforming rural Britain'. Similar connotations inhere in the 'iron gates' through which the coy mistress is urged to tear the pleasures of love, and in the iron scythe with which Damon the mower cuts down himself and the grass. Even in the pastoral fancy of 'The mower to the glow-worms', 'war and the death of kings are never very far away' (Hill, 1968, pp. 330–1, 334, 336). For Graham Parry, the solidity of Fate's iron wedges 'seems to require a more immediate reference, some glance at the iron-clad world of Civil War England, where "decrees of steel" were enforced'. 'Is there', he wonders, '(faintly suggested) some Royalist–Roundhead/Capulet–Montague situation of star-crossed lovers here to give a social basis to the abstract geometry of the poem?' Unlike those critics who bluntly enquire what 'The definition of love' is 'really about', however, Parry registers in his next sentence a recognition of the quality which has made this body of lyric poetry so inviting and so dangerous for the modern interpreter: 'Impossible to say: Marvell is a specialist in conjuring up spectral meanings in his verse' (Parry, 1985, p. 224). A lyric by Andrew Marvell does indeed have the elusive air of implying more than it is prepared to divulge, or in Bruce King's formulation, 'its explicit subject matter is not its main concern' (King, 1977,

p. 10). This is something with which the reader has to come to terms, whether by weighing the relative merits of the available interpretations and selecting the one that seems most convincing, or by revelling in the free play of the mind in generating a plurality of readings each as valid as the other, or by seeking to understand 'how it is that a work can have a variety of meanings but not just any meaning whatsoever' (Culler, 1975, p. 122).

A helpful concept to invoke at this point is that of the 'institution of literature', the complex of literary norms and conventions which operate in a given culture and within which the performances of individual writers and readers are judged to be competent or inadequate. The competent act of reading can then be seen as an interplay between a conscious effort to reconstruct the nature of a text as it was determined by the conditions prevailing at the time of its composition and the kinds of significance which can be attributed to it under the different conditions of our own time. The process of reconstruction provides a means of discriminating between possible and impossible meanings within a particular historical context. For instance, an awareness of what Alastair Fowler calls the 'linguistic horizon' within which a work was written will guard the twentieth-century reader against misconstruing the word 'needless' in line 15 of 'A dialogue between the Soul and Body' as 'unnecessary' rather than 'not subject to want', or the word 'prevent' in line 24 of 'Young love' as 'stop from happening' rather than 'act in advance of'. It will also make available a range of significance which is no longer current in such words as 'kinder' in line 8 of 'Bermudas', which could mean both 'more benign' and 'more natural' in Marvell's day, or 'impression' in line 8 of 'The unfortunate lover' which, as Empson points out, could mean 'an assault' and 'a meteor' in addition to the restricted meaning that survives in modern English (Empson, 1947, pp. 166–7).

More fruitful for investigating the source of the elusiveness of Marvell's lyric poetry is Fowler's related concept of the 'generic horizon'. On the premise that no literary text 'is intelligible without some context of familiar types', he argues that the initial task of the critic, the necessary foundation for a competent reading, is 'to construct an impression of the anterior state of literature – of the genres from which the original work took its departure' (Fowler, 1982, pp. 259–60). In this modern development of genre theory, a genre is no longer regarded as a prescriptive set of rules for writers to follow in the pursuit of excellence, or as a descriptive tool for categorizing different kinds of literary work. It is the active constituent in the reader's engagement with the text. As Culler puts it, 'The function of genre conventions is essentially to establish a contract between writer and reader so as to make certain relevant expectations operative and thus to permit both compliance with and deviation from accepted modes of intelligibility' (Culler, 1975, p. 147). Something of the sort was implied in T. S. Eliot's identification of the theme of 'To his coy mistress' as 'one of the great traditional commonplaces of European literature' in a line stretching back through Waller, Herrick and Shakespeare to Lucretius and Catullus; and in Empson's comment on 'Eyes and tears' that 'what is assumed by these verses is a wide acquaintance on the part of the reader with the conceits about tears that have been already made' (Eliot, 1951, p. 295; Empson, 1947, p. 173). One of the great services rendered by J. B. Leishman to the student of Marvell was to assemble between two covers a great many of the inherited materials, not only in the poetry of his English predecessors and contemporaries but also in the literatures of modern Europe and antiquity, which were 'assimilated, re-combined and perfected' in his richly allusive lyrics (Leishman, 1966, p. 70).

The notion of the 'generic horizon' – that the range of literary expectations which can be exploited in a particular age and culture is circumscribed by the available range of genres – is related to the theory of 'intertextuality', which states that any piece of writing 'is intelligible only in terms of a prior body of discourse – other projects and thoughts which it implicitly or explicitly takes up, prolongs, cites, refutes, transforms' (Culler, 1981, p. 101). Modern genre theory directs critical attention to the complex network of connections between a literary text and other texts, whether by explicit allusion or merely by its inescapable participation in a common stock of types and conventions. The peculiar sophistication of Marvell's lyrics – the source at once of delight and perplexity for the modern reader – derives from the *nature* of their participation in the inherited literary tradition. Written at a time when the Court culture that had sustained a particular brand of lyric poetry was being swept away, they have a concentrated and self-conscious allusiveness that gives them an air of detachment from the very themes and modes of expression to which they owed their existence. It is as if Marvell were deliberately 'tidying up and terminating the Caroline tradition, putting the finishing touches on various conventions, giving them one last perfect and unfollowable performance before the shadows of history close on them' (Parry, 1985, p. 222).

Of all the genres within which Marvell orientated his lyric art, that of pastoral supplied him with the richest possibilities. At its centre lies the conception of an idyllic correspondence between man and the universe – a vision of the human creature in simple harmony with his natural surroundings. It is symptomatic of Marvell's individualistic commerce with his literary inheritance, however, that that harmony is almost always disturbed and rarely survives intact in his poetry. 'Clorinda and Damon' enacts the threat to the relationship of a shepherd and shepherdess when one of them adopts the perspectives of Christianity and can no longer look upon the pleasures of the pastoral landscape with eyes unopened to the fact of sin. In 'The nymph complaining for the death of her fawn', the bewildered victim of Sylvio's betrayal and the brutality of the 'wanton troopers' retreats into the 'little wilderness' of her garden and longs to join her dying pet in a 'fair Elysium' beyond the reach of 'false and cruel men'. The four Mower poems embody the pastoral representative's experience of dislodgement from a secure position in the natural order under the influence of his passion for Juliana: 'For she my mind hath so displaced/That I shall never find my home.' Very few of Marvell's lyrics confine themselves so strictly within the pastoral mode as these examples, and it is more common – and another cause of the reader's difficulty in keeping his bearings – for pastoral features to be combined with features from other genres. 'The unfortunate lover', for instance, opens with an evocation of a world of 'fountains cool, and shadows green', inhabited by couples who are blissfully innocent of the destructive forces let loose in the rest of the poem, whereas 'The gallery' closes with a picture of Clora as 'a tender shepherdess', which contrasts tellingly with the sinister and sensuous connotations of earlier portraits. In 'The coronet', the speaker of a devotional lyric in the manner of George Herbert reveals himself to be a converted swain, intent on gathering poetic materials for the praise of his Saviour by 'Dismantling all the fragrant towers/ That once adorned my shepherdess's head'. The little girl in 'The picture of little T.C. in a prospect of flowers' is first seen lying on the green grass and playing with roses, but that golden age of childhood – one of the familiar extensions of the pastoral myth – is soon disrupted by the poet's vision of her future as a 'virtuous enemy of man', resisting the 'wanton Love' or triumphing in her sexual power over her suitors. In 'Bermudas', the cheerful rowers 'in the English boat' regain a pastoral harmony with Nature as Puritan heirs to the art of the Psalmist, singing their Creator's praises in a new world where the 'prelate's rage' cannot harm them.

The Petrarchan love sonnet, with its cruel mistresses and anguished lovers and its conceits, hyperboles and paradoxes, provides many of the details for the violent career of the unfortunate lover and the earlier portraits of Clora in 'The gallery', and makes its contribution to the possible future imagined for little T.C. The 'persuasion to love' reaches its apotheosis in 'To his coy mistress', while 'Young love' is Marvell's subtle variation on the seventeenth-century fusion of the *carpe diem* (seize the day) appeal with a tradition of addresses to very young ladies that goes back to Horace and the Greek Anthology and includes his own 'Picture of little T.C.' Poetic dialogues and debates and definitions of love all supply grist to the mill of Marvell's sophisticated wit; and 'On a drop of dew' and 'The unfortunate lover' both owe a good deal to emblem books and the form of emblematic lyric derived from them.

Most rich and satisfying of all, 'The garden' employs, extends and subverts the conventions of that most characteristic of mid-century genres, the 'retirement poem'. Although it has affinities with pastoral in its celebration of the pleasures of the natural world, there is the essential difference that the speaker in this kind of poem is not a naive shepherd or nymph, but a man or woman of experience and sophistication who has opted to withdraw from the 'busy companies of men' in order to enjoy the sensuous delights or the contemplative solitude of the countryside or a secluded garden. In Marvell's hands, various contradictory tendencies in the genre are resolved: libertine and biblical versions of the 'garden-state' are juxtaposed and merged with Petrarchan conceits, classical metamorphosis myths and elements from Platonic and Christian mysticism in an extraordinarily versatile performance over which a wry intelligence keeps watch.

The awareness of 'a larger consciousness enclosing the naive and innocent speaker' (Creaser, 1970, p. 410) in many of the dramatic lyrics raises the vexed question of the relationship between the historical author and the imagined source from which the words on the page emanate. Most readers have no difficulty in distinguishing between that larger consciousness and such fully realized characters as the nymph and the mower, especially when a narrator's presence is built into the structure of the poem, as it is in stanzas 1 and 10 of 'Damon the mower' or in the paragraphs which frame the song of the oarsmen in 'Bermudas'. In dialogue poems, too, the form itself (whether or not there is a compère, like the one who directs our responses to the Resolved Soul and Created Pleasure) might seem to indicate detachment from the speakers, although this has not prevented considerable argument over which side Marvell was on in the quarrel between the Soul and the Body. This last example illustrates that even in the formally dramatic lyrics and dialogues there is still plenty of room for disagreement about the attitude taken by the 'larger consciousness' towards the enclosed speakers and the ideas they express. Indeed, some would regard the persona in such a poem as 'The mower against gardens' as merely a surrogate – a device for the communication of the author's opinions. If we bring to bear our knowledge of the genre 'from which the original work took its departure', however, and allow 'the relevant expectations' to operate as we read, we must adopt with the author an amused and critical stance towards the pastoral spokesman's distaste for the art of horticulture. For it is one of the fundamental conventions of the pastoral mode that it involves 'the recognition of a contrast, implicit or expressed, between pastoral life and some more complex type of civilization' (Greg, 1906, p. 4). The gap between the sophisticated author and the naive character or speaker may result in nostalgia or satire, a yearning for a lost simplicity or a judgement on the limitations or absurdities of the inexperienced, but to read a poem *as pastoral* is to be conscious above all of the gap itself. By the same convention, the 'I' who once adorned a shepherdess's head with 'fragrant towers' is not to be identified in any simplistic way with Andrew Marvell the seventeenth-century Puritan, but to be seen as a device for exposing the spiritual difficulties that lie in wait for the poet who rashly undertakes to compose a coronet of verse fit for 'the King of Glory'.

How does the principle of placing a work within the 'generic horizon' of its age affect our reading of the kind of dramatic lyric which implies the presence of another 'character' to whom the speaker addresses himself? Are we expected to judge the attitudes or the 'personalities' of the men who invite Clora to 'view my soul', or urge a reluctant mistress to throw discretion to the winds in the pursuit of physical pleasure, or whimsically pay court to a 'little infant'? An alertness to the witty variations that had already been played on the Petrarchan conceit of the beloved's picture engraved in the heart of the lover may encourage us to read 'The gallery' as a virtuoso performance, not only by Marvell but by the sophisticated gallant who displays the tastefully contrived 'furniture' of his soul to an equally sophisticated mistress. Such a reading would lend a poignant (or cynical) irony to the final portrait of Clora in a guise of pastoral simplicity. Similarly, to be aware of previous treatments, like Jonson's, of the appeal to 'prove,/While we may, the sports of love' is to read Marvell's *carpe diem* poems with an eye to the possibility that the speakers who have recourse to this particular set of literary conventions may be the object of moral scrutiny – hence those interpretations which ascribe the voice we hear in 'To his coy mistress' to a clever seducer. On the other hand, if self-conscious irony is detected in allusions to the kind of hyperbole typical of Donne's love poetry and to the extravagant claims that 'powerful rhyme' can outlive 'marble' and resist the sweep of Time's scythe in some of Shakespeare's sonnets, then a more sympathetic response may be evoked by the witty realism of one who seeks to convince his lady that time can only be outmanoeuvred by the desperate expedients proposed in the final paragraph.

A similar inclination to weigh what is said against the apparent limitations or maturity of the speaker may be felt to operate in all Marvell's lyrics, including those like 'The definition of love', 'Eyes and tears', 'Mourning', 'On a drop of dew' and 'The garden' in which the voice addresses the reader directly or seems to be overheard in reverie. Another way of putting it would be to say that their very allusiveness seems to demand the active participation of an educated and sceptical intelligence, ready to enter into a critical examination of the values and attitudes inscribed in various literary genres which are on the point of being rendered obsolete by the revolutionary changes taking place in the poet's culture. Or perhaps, since we have little evidence that they were ever intended for dissemination beyond a few friends, we should see them as essentially private exercises – 'self-contained and self-absorbed to an unusual degree' (Parry, 1985, p. 223) – which, like the letters discussed earlier, present a deceptively straight face to an inquisitive world.

SOCIAL VOICES

The poems that fall into this next category display a similar concern with the expressive possibilities of familiar genres, but an overtly social dimension in their subject matter poses different kinds of problem for the modern reader. Instead of fictional characters and episodes, the persons and situations evoked in these texts belong to the historically verifiable world of seventeenth-century England. Two of them were printed as commendations of other men's volumes of poetry; two were satires on contemporary writers; two were addressed to the poet's employer; and one was written to mark the return of a victorious general. It is usually accepted that many of the lyrics – particularly those with a pastoral emphasis – were the fruits of the two years spent with Fairfax in Yorkshire, but there is little evidence for what Barbara Everett terms the 'mythical chronology', according to which 'Marvell is assumed to have grown out of writing lyric poetry and into writing satire, a more mature even if a distinctly coarser style and vision' (in Brett, 1979, p. 63). Assumptions about the dates of the poems we are about to consider rest on firmer ground. The commendatory poems to *Lucasta* and *Paradise Lost* were published in 1649 and 1674, and from allusions to such events as the licensing of Lovelace's volume for the press and the sequestration of his estate or the adaptation of Milton's epic for the stage by John Dryden, it is possible to fix their time of composition within relatively narrow limits. Marvell's encounter with Richard Flecknoe took place in Rome in March 1646 and Thomas May died on 13 November 1650. It seems reasonable to infer that the satires on these events occupied the poet in the following weeks or months. The dedication of 'Upon the hill and grove at Bilbrough' and 'Upon Appleton House' to Lord Fairfax suggests that they were written during Marvell's two years' residence in the retired general's household from some time late in 1650 or early 1651; and the 'Horatian ode' clearly belongs to the period between Cromwell's recall from Ireland in May 1650 and his march northwards to Scotland in July. So that whereas the problem of 'the adjustment of individual conduct to external conditions and forces' (Hill, 1968, p. 348) is embedded at a thematic level in the lyrics, it becomes the explicit subject of those poems in which Marvell adapts his voice, as we saw him doing in the letters to Cromwell and the Hull Corporation, to the requirements of a more precisely defined social or historical occasion. In place of a nymph or a resolved soul, we listen to a poet addressing himself to the problems of writing and publishing during a period of civil war or a tutor finding ways of complimenting his famous employer on a political decision which has laid him open to public criticism. In place of a pastoral Golden Age, when innocent lovers were 'sorted by pairs' in an idyllic landscape and a mower's mind was 'the true survey/Of all these meadows fresh and gay', we are reminded of 'that candid age' before 1640 when young Richard Lovelace was making his mark at the cultivated Court of King Charles I, and we share the lament of Mary Fairfax's tutor for the days when the 'dear and happy isle' of Great Britain had not yet been torn apart by armed conflict.

One of the consequences of our awareness that we are dealing with texts produced in direct response to a particular historical situation is the tendency to judge them by other than literary criteria. Such poems as 'Tom May's death' and 'An Horatian ode' are often assessed as personal statements or even political gestures and scrutinized for evidence of what Andrew Marvell believed or felt. There is nothing inherently wrong in using a man's poems as materials for his biography – especially the kind of occasional poems we are concerned with here – but there is a strong temptation to accommodate them to some preconceived idea of what the poet might have thought, or even ought to have thought, about a given set of circumstances. This was the chief burden of Douglas Bush's charge against Cleanth Brooks's reading of the 'Ode': 'that, far from making a disinterested inquiry into the evidence provided by the poem, he is forcing the evidence to fit an unspoken assumption – namely, that a sensitive, penetrating, and well-balanced mind like Marvell could not really have admired a crude, single-minded, and ruthless man of action like Cromwell' (Bush, 1952, p. 364). A number of incompatible versions of the Marvell of the years 1648–52 have been deduced from this group of texts (together with elegies on Lord Francis Villiers and Lord Hastings). They range from John Wallace's loyalist supporter of *de facto* authority to R. I. V. Hodge's deeply rooted Royalist painfully coming to terms with political realities (Hodge, 1978, pp. 113–31), and from J. B. Leishman's temperamental Royalist, who could nevertheless contemplate the rise of Cromwell with 'complete detachment and uncommittedness' (Leishman, 1966, p. 13), to Warren Chernaik's 'consistent opponent of arbitrary power and champion of man's rational freedom' (Chernaik, 1983, p. 7). An alternative approach to the apparent contradictions among and ambivalences within these poems is afforded by Ruth Nevo's suggestion that the proper context of the troublesome ode is 'that of contemporary panegyric and the contemporary preoccupation with the problem of history and the hero' (Nevo, 1963, p. 98) and Annabel Patterson's related insight that in the Fairfax and Cromwell poems Marvell 'is constantly testing his resources, most of which are traditional, against the tendency of events to innovate' (Patterson, 1978, p. 53). This method can profitably be applied to all the works in which we attend to the social or public voices of Marvell, changing the focus of critical enquiry from what he *thought* about Tom May or Cromwell and the casting of kingdoms 'into another mould' to his exploration of the adequacy of the available *ways of thinking and writing* about such men and such events.

That Marvell was preoccupied by the question of the conduct and function of the poet both as private person and as citizen is evident in the verses he wrote on four of his contemporaries. The earliest, which is untouched by the ideological issues being fought out in England while he was on his European travels, draws upon the tradition of satires against folly, affectation and vanity which includes Donne's 'Satire IV' and Horace's Satire I. ix. Like his predecessors, he is trapped by an insufferable companion, but unlike Donne's narrator, who makes his distaste obvious by 'all signs of loathing', Marvell's suffers in silence and presents the image of 'a private, reserved character', who 'does the polite, the socially resourceful thing' (Duncan-Jones, 1975, p. 276). As an Englishman in Rome, he has been sought out by Richard Flecknoe and feels 'obliged by frequent visits of this man' to return the compliment. The patience with which he submits to the 'martyrdom' of the poetaster's recitation of his 'hideous verse', and the social skill with which he handles the foppish young aristocrat who joins them and takes offence at the least hint of an insult, provide the yardstick by which we are invited to judge the behaviour of these self-important fools. The amused contempt and cruelly accurate observations which he gives vent to in his role as satirist are in marked contrast to his courteous self-control while the persecution was taking place, just as the letters to William Popple reveal personal opinions and anxieties which were not allowed to surface in the reports to the aldermen of Hull. To that extent, 'Flecknoe' is an intensely private poem. But the fundamental issue raised by this comical experience is not a private one, for satire is a public mode of discourse, and its traditional purpose is to ensure the maintenance of civilized values against the folly and vice that constantly threaten to undermine them. In this instance, the particular danger represented by the vain poet and the ignorant patron – each of whom uses poetry as a means of inflating his own ego – is signalled by a veiled allusion to the lines in which Milton had confronted the same moral dilemma:

> *Fame* is the spur that the clear spirit doth raise
> (That last infirmity of noble mind)
> To scorn delights, and live laborious days.
>
> ('Lycidas' (1637), ll. 70–2)

Marvell's nod in the direction of 'Lycidas' comes in a passage of wry self-mockery describing the torture which his sense of social decorum compels him to undergo:

> Only this frail ambition did remain,
> The last distemper of the sober brain,
> That there had been some present to assure
> The future ages how I did endure. (ll. 27–30)

The reader who picks up the allusion – by the very fact of recognizing its source and understanding the paradoxical moral insight it embodies – identifies himself with Milton's (and by association Marvell's) high estimate of a vocation which has been brought into disrepute by Flecknoe and his foolish admirer; and 'Flecknoe' itself, by asserting its claim to a place within the literary tradition to which Milton, Donne and Horace have contributed, becomes a statement of principle.

In 'To his noble friend Mr Richard Lovelace, upon his poems', written during 1648, Marvell makes a declaration of the same principle in the public medium of commendatory verse. It is not primarily Lovelace the colonel in the Royalist army who wins his praise or the harassment of the man who had presented a Royalist petition to Parliament in 1642 that excites his anger and contempt. The speaker in this poem is above all an elegist for the social and moral values which once governed the fraternity of poets and which have been 'banished out of town' by 'our Civil Wars'. The very genre within which he is writing allies him and his fellow poet with the tradition of 'speaking well' – the tradition that flourished in those better times when 'Who best could praise, had then the greatest praise'. The middle paragraph pours scorn on the alien values of those who have permitted or incited factional interests to invade the ideal world of artistic endeavour and honest admiration. This, rather than political commitment to one side or another in the national conflict, is what is emphasized in the jibes at the 'book-scorpions' and 'barbed censurers' and in the poet's anxiety to dissociate himself from 'the rout' attacked by 'the beauteous ladies' who stand for the elegant civilization that bore fruit in *Lucasta*.

Tom May is consigned to the pillory of satire as a traitor not so much to his king as to his profession. Marvell's chief rhetorical ploy is to introduce the figure of Ben Jonson as spokesman for the conception of the poet's calling which has been endorsed in each of these poems of praise and blame. Jonson's presence not only functions, like the allusion to 'Lycidas', as an indication of the poem's system of values but also distances Marvell from any suspicion of personal rancour. The charges brought against May are felt to bear the weight of a literary tradition which had its roots in Virgil and Horace and in which Jonson was the revered master in the preceding generation. It is important for Marvell to establish an objective stance because, in addition to branding the turncoat poet as a 'servile wit, and mercenary pen', he accuses him of 'malice fixed and understood' caused by jealousy over William Davenant's appointment to the post of poet laureate. Events have moved on since Marvell wrote in praise of Richard Lovelace, however, and it is no longer possible for him to uphold unquestioned the ideal of an artistic community that remains aloof from the world of political strife. The 'chronicler to Spartacus' may be despised as an apostate who has 'prostituted' the 'spotless knowledge and the studies chaste' of the true poets, but lines 64–70 forcefully acknowledge the artist's obligation to enter the arena in time of violent revolution and fight 'forsaken virtue's cause'. Under the pressure of history – 'when the wheel of empire whirleth back' and 'ancient rights' are overborne by 'successful crimes' – the cherished impartiality of 'that candid age' in which Lovelace was a tyro and Jonson ruled in the realm of poetry cannot be maintained.

The method of 'On Mr Milton's *Paradise Lost*' reflects the very different world of Restoration London, in which the great poet and propagandist of militant Puritanism could hope for no more than that his masterpiece would 'fit audience find, though few' (Book VII, l. 31). Instead of proclaiming himself a sympathizer and friend, as he did in the tribute to Lovelace, Marvell begins in the tones of one who has reservations about the 'vast design' of the epic poet and who suspects that this survivor of a defeated cause will allow personal bitterness to contaminate the 'sacred truths' of the Bible: 'The world o'erwhelming to revenge his sight.' His doubts gradually evaporate as he reads, and by the end he stands in awe of 'such a vast expense of mind' and turns the tables on those who had gleefully interpreted Milton's blindness as a divine punishment: 'Just heaven thee, like

Tiresias, to requite,/Rewards with prophecy thy loss of sight.' Taking his cue from the note on blank verse which was added to the second edition of *Paradise Lost*, he weighs Milton's achievement against that of men like Dryden who rely on the superficial appeal of 'tinkling rhyme' – a contrast which carries with it much broader moral and political connotations. As Elsie Duncan-Jones points out, the entire poem is 'topical, circumstantial, useful' and is skilfully directed to 'what will most serve Milton's fame in the London of 1674 with likely readers' (Duncan-Jones, 1975, p. 289). Even the self-deprecatory joke at the end is part of a consistent rhetorical purpose. Forced by the exigencies of his fashionable couplets to 'commend' rather than 'praise' the great poet, Marvell illustrates how the slavery to rhyme can damage the social propriety of his own performance. After all, he implies, 'it is not for the inferior to commend his superior' (Duncan-Jones, 1975, p. 289).

Although not itself a poem for public consumption like those printed in the volumes of Lovelace and Milton, 'An Horatian ode upon Cromwell's return from Ireland' establishes at once an urgent concern with the poet's relation to the contemporary world. Its very title locates it within the tradition of the triumphal ode celebrating the return of a national leader, which took Horace's odes to Caesar Augustus as its classical model and which had been popular in the heyday of the Caroline Court; and its opening gambit sets the contemplative and scholarly ideal of life 'in the shadows' against the imperative to 'appear' on the stage where stirring events are moving towards a climax. Nevertheless, the poem that follows is no straightforward panegyric or partisan intervention in the political scene. Working against the expectations aroused by the title are intertextual links with another classical and contemporary source – Lucan's *Pharsalia* and Thomas May's rendering of it into English couplets. This work deals significantly with the civil wars that led to the overthrow of the Roman republic and begins with an event which suggests a parallel with the situation in England in the early summer of 1650. After his conquest of Gaul, Julius Caesar took the momentous step of crossing the river Rubicon with his army – an act which broke with long-standing tradition and signalled his intention of seizing control in Italy. Marvell's initial account of the career of

England's returning general borrows a number of details from the *Pharsalia*. His 'restless Cromwell' has the 'restless valour' of May's Caesar and the extended simile of Cromwell dividing his 'fiery way' like lightning is developed from a passage describing Caesar's rise to power. But whereas Caesar was presented unequivocally as a man of reckless ambition, bent on destroying the ancient liberties of Rome, Cromwell is transformed into an impersonal force of nature (or of history) operating outside the normal laws of morality: ''Tis madness to resist or blame/The force of angry heaven's flame.' The allusions to the *Pharsalia* seem to invoke a judgement on Cromwell as another Caesar which is then deliberately called into question. No sooner have personal qualities and responsibilities been subordinated to the concept of the inexorable process of history, however, than the poem's voice insists on bringing them back into consideration: 'And, if we would speak true,/Much to the man is due.'

The entire ode can be seen as a structure of tensions between apparently irreconcilable principles and contradictory interpretations: Justice against Fate; 'industrious valour' against 'ancient rights'; the hero who urges 'his active star' against the 'royal actor' who submits gracefully to his destiny, bowing 'his comely head/ Down as upon a bed'; 'helpless right' against 'forced power'; a 'bleeding head' which becomes an omen of future glory; a defeated people which affirms the fitness of its subduer 'for highest trust'; a victorious soldier whose success in Ireland excites the hope of further victories in Scotland – and perhaps even in a Protestant crusade against France and Italy (though the references to Caesar and Hannibal are themselves ambivalent, since the conquest of Gaul was the prelude to dictatorship in Rome and the latter's campaign ended in ultimate failure) – but who is warned that the price of his achievement is eternal vigilance, since 'The same arts that did *gain*/A power must it *maintain*.'

The effect of this technique is not to blur the issues or to create a stance of 'almost inhuman aloofness' (Legouis, 1965, p. 14), still less to undermine apparent praise with irony, but to evince 'an overwhelming sense of the significance of the historical moment' (Nevo, 1963, pp. 98–9). The execution of Charles I was indeed 'a memorable scene', symbolizing a break with the past that could never be completely repaired. It was also the 'memorable hour' that inaugurated a new order in the state. But although Cromwell was credited earlier in the poem with casting the 'kingdoms old/Into another mould', the shape of things to come must have seemed very uncertain as the nation waited to see how this man would use the political power which his military career had brought him. At such a juncture in his country's history, the true poet has a more important task to perform than simply abandoning 'his Muses dear' for active service of the kind implied by oiling 'th' unused armour's rust'. The clear opposition between contemplating and doing is as much an oversimplification of actual experience in a world turned upside down as the desire to find a simple moral resolution to the problem of 'ancient rights' and 'forced power' or to distinguish between the roles played by 'industrious valour' and the 'force of angry heaven's flame' in the unfolding of the plot of history. Rather than exchanging the pen for the sword, or turning 'the chronicler to Spartacus' as Tom May did, the poet who would rise to the occasion and preserve the integrity of his art will mobilize the resources of literature in the service of an honest and realistic appraisal of the situation confronting his nation. In doing so, he may discover that traditional genres and the habits of mind they embody have to be adapted to meet the challenge of new circumstances – a process of breaking through to new ways of thinking which is one of the poet's most valuable cultural functions. The phenomenon of Cromwell and the consequences of beheading a monarch cannot be accommodated within the simple categories of hero and villain or justice and fate that operate in Lucan's verse epic or May's prose chronicle of the Roman and English civil wars; and a straightforward triumphal ode, like those which greeted Charles I's return from patching up a peace in Scotland in 1640, would scarcely be appropriate to the conflict of moral, emotional and political responses – not only among rival factions but within individual minds – engendered by Cromwell's return from Ireland.

It may be the case that the tension slackens after the strenuous effort to come to terms with the recent past and that a note of patriotic enthusiasm for the conqueror of the Irish and the prospective conqueror of the Scots sounds too unequivocally for modern taste, as the poet's voice relaxes into a less demanding mode after its exertions. If so, then the celebrated passage in 'Tom May's death', written six months later when Marvell was about to take up a position as tutor to the daughter of the man who had resigned over the policy of invading Scotland, may reflect a personal reaction against the great poem in which he had been too absorbed by the complexities and possibilities of the historical moment to follow the simpler Jonsonian precept of seeking 'wretched good' and arraigning 'successful crimes'.

The poems addressed to Fairfax are closely related in theme and manner to such lyrics as 'The garden' and 'Bermudas', but their rhetorical strategies are governed by the kind of social discretion required in the letters. For the man under whose roof Marvell lived for some two years posed as many difficulties as Cromwell for the poet. His inactivity during the period of the king's trial – made conspicuous by his wife's disruption of the proceedings from the gallery – and his eventual retreat into private life in June 1650 confirmed, in some quarters, a reputation for political ineptitude and led to the suspicion that Lady Fairfax was the more decisive character. In 'Upon the hill and grove at Bilbrough', Marvell has recourse to a poetic convention which idealizes the influence of wife over husband by designating her grandly 'Vera the Nymph that him inspired'; and in 'Upon Appleton House', he accords them equal status as the 'Governor' and 'Governess' of the flower gardens (stanza 38), whose pedigrees are locked in a firm union (stanza 62) and who preside mutually over the 'domestic heaven' where young Mary Fairfax is being prepared for life under the 'discipline severe' of a model Puritan household. In both poems, he employs the popular mid-century technique of reading the qualities of human beings into the features of a landscape or the architectural style of a country house. A favourable gloss is placed on Fairfax's retirement from public life by the contrast between the regular contours of the Bilbrough hillside and the 'hook-shouldered height' of mountains which 'to abrupter greatness thrust': 'Learn here those humble steps to tread,/Which to securer glory lead.' It is tempting to discern a glance here at the restless energy of Fairfax's successor, who 'could not cease/In the inglorious arts of peace'. An inversion of the same rhyme words in a couplet from 'Upon Appleton House' makes it even more likely that the 'Horatian ode' is part of the conscious context of these later poems. The gardens at Nun Appleton, laid out in the figure of a fort, are said to be the handiwork of a member of the Fairfax family, possibly Marvell's employer, 'Who, when retired here to peace,/His warlike studies could not cease'. The repeated rhymes function as a point of reference, built into the text like the allusions to the *Pharsalia* in the 'Ode' itself, though whether anyone but Marvell was expected to be aware of them is an interesting matter for speculation. Certainly the careers of the two men are presented as mirror images of each other: Cromwell leaving his 'private gardens' for 'advent'rous war', and Fairfax withdrawing from 'groves of pikes' to stand 'in unenvied greatness' like his favourite hill-top retreat and enjoy the privacy of its clump of oak trees. The only hint of overt criticism of Fairfax in the Bilbrough poem is expressed by these very trees, in one of Marvell's most ingenious and audacious pieces of ventriloquism: '"Much other groves," say they, "than these/And other hills him once did please."' The implication is that in denying himself the chance to win 'civic garlands' and the 'trophies' of war, he has also abrogated his public responsibilities. But the poet tactfully breaks in to warn them – 'if you his favour prize' – against offending the modesty of one who flies his 'own praises'.

Personal modesty and social unpretentiousness are among the qualities celebrated in the seventeenth-century genre of the country-house poem and Marvell exploits its conventions to the full in his most elaborate compliment to the family that employed him. The house at Nun Appleton is commended in the first ten stanzas for reflecting its owner's sobriety and humility, but not without touches of humour and playful wit which turn the edge of any charge of obsequiousness on the part of the poet or of oversolemnity on the part of the patron. The account of the founding of the family fortunes in the sixteenth century in stanzas 11–35 mingles romance and mock heroic, while at the same time honouring the strong Protestant pedigree of the former leader of the Puritan armies. In stanzas 36–46, the well-tended gardens provide an opportunity for the subject of Fairfax's retirement to be broached and Marvell negotiates its potential awkwardness with great aplomb. Without disguising his regret that 'there walks one on the sod' who might have played his part in restoring the garden of England from the ravages of civil war, he concedes that Fairfax was the best judge of where his destiny lay – 'had it pleased him and God' – and pays unreserved homage to the integrity with which he followed the promptings of conscience rather than ambition.

Panegyric gives way to the lyric mode as the tutor-poet develops his persona of witty observer of the pageant of the meadows and rapt interpreter of Nature's mysteries in the woodland sanctuary. Self-mockery is never far away, however, and when 'the young Maria' discovers the 'easy philosopher' idly fishing – ''Twere shame that such judicious eyes/Should with such toys a man surprise' (ll. 653–4) – the poem reverts to the mode of panegyric for its graceful closing tribute to Fairfax's daughter.

The whole work is conducted with a charming mixture of deference and familiarity, which contrives to set off the secluded lives of the retired man of achievement and the young woman who is making herself ready to fulfil her dynastic duty against examples of more dubious forms of retirement: the 'holy leisure' advocated for sinister purposes by the 'subtle nuns' and the narrator's own dream of escaping from the rigours of the world of sex and politics – 'How safe, methinks, and strong, behind/These trees have I encamped my mind.' But although the Fairfaxes were morally justified in cultivating the 'lesser world' of Nun Appleton, Marvell himself evidently became convinced of the need to face the realities of that greater world which had been 'negligently overthrown' in the turmoil of the 1640s, and early in 1653 was applying, through the good offices of John Milton, for the vacant post of assistant Latin secretary to the Council of State.

PUBLIC VOICES

His application did not meet with immediate success, and the private motive of self-advancement may have played its part in the genesis of the poem which he wrote two years later and published (presumably with official approval) to celebrate the first anniversary of Cromwell's Protectorate. Nevertheless, as a literary artefact it speaks with a public voice more clearly than even the poems written to commend *Lucasta* and *Paradise Lost* to prospective readers. It is rooted in a view of literature which has had little currency in Western culture since the advent of Romanticism in the late eighteenth century. As a recent historical survey of the role of the reader in critical theory points out, the Renaissance and Augustan periods inherited from the classical tradition of Plato, Aristotle and Horace ideological assumptions which conceived of language 'as a force acting on the world, rather than as a series of signs to be deciphered' and which emphasized the role of literature as 'the instrument of a social transaction' (Tompkins, 1980, pp. 203, 211). Marvell's Commonwealth panegyrics and Restoration satires belong with that body of late seventeenth- and early eighteenth-century poetry which 'traffics in power both in the broad sense of exerting influence on personal behaviour and public opinion, and in the narrower sense of dealing explicitly with political issues', and consequently the reader needs to recognize that they are 'embedded in the historical setting, engendered by it, and responsive to it in detail' (Tompkins, 1980, pp. 213, 212).

The historical setting of 'The first anniversary' was one of crisis for the new constitution that had been established by the Instrument of Government in December 1653. Cromwell, as Lord Protector, had summoned his first Parliament on 3 September 1654 but relations between them had quickly become strained. Composed while there was still hope that the system of checks and balances between Protector, Council of State and representatives of the people could be made to work, Marvell's poem supports Cromwell unreservedly, but its wider ideological perspective has been open to interpretation. It has been read 'as an argument that Cromwell should accept the English crown and institute a new dynasty of kings' (Wallace, 1968, p. 108); elements of confusion have been detected in its commitment to Cromwell the man, which suggest that politically Marvell 'is still reluctant to acknowledge what that commitment entails' (Hodge, 1978, p. 112); and it has been regarded as an attempt 'to convince others of the legitimacy of the Protectorate government' (Chernaik,

1983, p. 43). The fact that these divergences of opinion exist indicates that, whatever else it may be, 'The first anniversary' is not a simple panegyric in the manner of Caroline tributes to members of the Stuart family. If the intelligibility of any statement is dependent upon its relation to 'a prior body of discourse' (Culler, 1981, p. 101), one way of approaching Marvell's text is to see it as the result of what Isabel Rivers calls 'the need to fit wherever possible Cromwell's originality to old patterns of thought' (Rivers, 1973, p. 113). In specifically literary terms, the source of the difficulty – for the poet and the reader – can be located in the obsolescence of the available generic models.

Capitalizing on the occasion of an anniversary, Marvell appropriates the symbolism familiar in idealizations of kingship to express 'sun-like' Cromwell's superiority to 'heavy monarchs', who are more tardy and 'malignant' in effecting their policies than Saturn. The hereditary principle, which was one of the cornerstones of Royalist theory, is mocked in the contrast between what the Protector has achieved 'in one year' and the unfinished projects passed on from father to son: 'For one thing never was by one king done.' In the long passage likening Cromwell, who 'tuned the ruling Instrument', to Amphion, Marvell takes a lead from a poem by Edmund Waller in praise of the repairs to St Paul's cathedral carried out by Charles I. Waller had used the analogy of the mythical founder of the city of Thebes and had ended with the reflection that it 'is easier to destroy than build'. Marvell's vision of Cromwell as the architect of a new order in the state – built out of 'the minds of stubborn men' – alludes both to Waller's remark and to his own earlier image of the man who had been responsible for ruining 'the great work of time'.

Having subverted the conventions of Royalist panegyric to serve his own purposes, Marvell turns to the Bible, finding in the figure of Gideon a crucial distinction between Old Testament judge and king. Indeed, scriptural history 'provides a vocabulary and system of analogies charged with political and spiritual meaning for his readership' (Zwicker, 1974, p. 3), from the Fall to the 'latter days' leading up to the Last Judgement, and from Elijah and Noah to the Whore of Babylon, the Beast of the Apocalypse and the plague of locusts sent by Apollyon. It is from this network of allusions that Cromwell emerges as the Protestant hero, thwarted in his task of ushering in the millennium by the 'regal sloth' of neighbouring princes, a nation which remains 'all unconcerned, or unprepared', and the 'frantic army' of Fifth Monarchists, Ranters and Quakers which seeks to repudiate his rule.

The coaching accident in the previous September in which Cromwell had narrowly escaped death furnishes the occasion for one of Marvell's most remarkable manipulations of literary convention. Sensitive to the moral stigma that might attach to an art form associated with a sycophantic Court culture, he self-consciously parries any accusation of flattery in his homage to the Protector by transforming panegyric into elegy: 'So with more modesty we may be true,/And speak as of the dead the praises due.' In a similarly daring rhetorical ploy, he adopts Waller's conceit of the wonder with which 'our neighbour kings' watched Charles I effect the restoration of St Paul's. The closing account of Cromwell's success in building up the navy and winning respect for Britain overseas is thus put into the mouth of a foreign monarch. The reluctant admiration expressed by this hostile observer is a rebuke to those at home whose support for the Protectorate is less than wholehearted.

The elegy which Marvell composed four years later contains much that is merely conventional – the symbolic storm that marks the passing of the great man, the assessments of his military prowess, his piety, his patriotism, his statesmanship – but it also forces an adjustment of perspective by giving unexpected prominence to the domestic qualities of the man whose public service entailed a sacrifice of the peaceful life he might have preferred. Expiring quietly of grief for his favourite daughter, rather than satisfying the crude taste of 'spectators vain' with a more dramatic climax to his career, Cromwell in death as in life cannot be fitted comfortably into the stereotypes of literature. The problem of knowing what or how to think about such a revolutionary figure is itself the subject of one of the poem's sharpest insights. Comparing him to 'the sacred oak', hung with trophies and at last laid low by the lightning which 'angry Jove' darts at a sinful people, Marvell concludes: 'The tree erewhile foreshortened to our view,/When fall'n shows taller yet than as it grew.' It is always difficult to measure objectively the stature of a human being while he is at the centre of the historical process. In this instance, his true worth can only begin to be appreciated when the community confronts the task of filling the gap left by his departure from the political scene; and although Marvell asserts that Richard will be equal to the responsibility thrust upon him by Oliver's death – 'A Cromwell in an hour a prince will grow' – the forlorn sense of political loss and foreboding cannot quite be expelled from the closing lines.

The poet of the Cromwell poems was a private citizen and (at the time of the elegy) a civil servant. When Marvell took up his pen to write of contemporary affairs after the restoration of the monarchy, he had been engaged for some years in the practical business of politics as an MP. His major verse satire, 'The last instructions to a painter', was part of a concerted opposition campaign inside and outside Westminster to discredit the Chancellor, Clarendon, and to lay the blame for the naval humiliation by the Dutch in June 1667 squarely at the door of the Cabal of leading Court ministers. It has been suggested that Marvell may have been 'at the innovative centre' (Patterson, 1978, p. 167) of a group of writers working together on the series of advice-to-a-painter satires; and a similar claim has been made that *An Account of the Growth of Popery* a decade later was 'to some extent a collaborative enterprise', which was probably produced 'in direct consultation with Shaftesbury and other Country Party leaders' (Chernaik, 1983, p. 96). Whether or not these post-Restoration texts were public in quite this way, it is evident that the old ideal of 'speaking well' and singly fighting 'forsaken virtue's cause' was of little practical use in a world dominated by 'drunkards, pimps, and fools', and satire takes over from panegyric as the staple mode of Marvell's interventions as a writer. He did not abandon his concern for the principles at stake when a poet assumes a public voice, however, and the works in verse and prose that earned him his reputation as a champion of liberty never lost touch with the theoretical and moral issues of 'the relationship between partisanship and objectivity, and the interdependence of aesthetic and political values' (Patterson, 1978, p. 112).

'Last instructions', though itself written in controlled and hard-edged couplets, exploits the advice-to-a-painter motif to suggest that artistic decorum would be well served if the portrait of 'our Lady State', in an age characterized by 'great debauch and little skill', were daubed in the style of an inn sign or obscene graffiti; and in the concluding address to the king, the poet is anxious to defend the integrity of an art which he has been obliged to harness to such uncongenial purposes: 'Blame not the Muse that brought those spots to sight'. It may well be that the metrical crudity of such later stanzaic satires as 'Upon Sir Robert Viner's setting up the King's statue in Wool-church Market' was a deliberate device to match form to content – a poetic equivalent of daubing or sketching rough caricatures on an 'alley-roof'.

One of the prime charges levelled at Samuel Parker in the first part of *The Rehearsal Transpros'd* is that he has conducted his argument against religious toleration with a marked lack of 'prudence and civility'. With regard to his own practice, Marvell explicitly raises the question of 'the nature of *Animadversions*' and apologizes for importing an element of knockabout humour into the genre. But just as it would be inexcusable to 'speak of serious things ridiculously', so it would be inappropriate to 'discourse of ridiculous things seriously'. In the present work, therefore, he will endeavour to apply the principle that he recommended to the painter in 'Last instructions' and 'so far as possible, observe decorum, and, whatever I talk of, not commit such an absurdity as to be grave with a buffoon'. But if he has no qualms about making Parker the butt of his comic wit, he is more uneasy about being 'drawn in' by the character of the matters under discussion 'to mention kings and princes', lest he 'trip in a word, or fail in the mannerliness of an expression'. He returns at the end to the problem of maintaining decorum in public controversy, with the hope that his readers will have learned from the way he has managed this work 'that it is not impossible to be merry and angry as long time as I have been writing, without profaning and violating those things which are and ought to be most sacred'.

In the second part, Marvell analyses at considerable length the motives and the behaviour of those 'that take upon themselves to be writers' and warns of the pitfalls that lie in their path. By the very act of publishing, an author 'does either make a treat, or send a challenge to all readers', and so exposes his abilities as entertainer or controversialist to public judgement. Thus far, his aim has been largely to emphasize his opponent's singular lack of qualifications for success in this 'envious and dangerous employment'. But when he comes to the kind of work in which he is himself currently engaged as 'the author of an invective', he earnestly undertakes the moral justification of commenting in print 'upon the blemishes and imperfections of some particular person'. In theory, the activity of 'privateering upon reputation' fills him with repugnance; but in practice, as he skilfully argues, to write satirically – 'even against a clergyman' – may in certain circumstances 'be not only excusable but necessary'. At the centre of his justification for entering the lists against Parker is the fact that his adversary – like Tom May in an earlier generation – had committed his obnoxious and socially divisive ideas to permanent and public form: 'he that hath once printed an ill book has thereby condensed his words on purpose lest they should be carried away by the wind.' In such a case, it is the duty of someone like Marvell to stand up as spokesman for the community and 'hunt him through the woods with hounds and horn home to his harbour'.

He was drawn into print again in 1676 by what he regarded as another abuse of the press. Francis Turner not only was deficient in the positive qualities needed 'to sustain the dignity of the Church's jester', but had launched his attack on the spirit of moderation shown by the Bishop of Hereford with a 'virulence' that did little credit to himself or his ecclesiastical masters, ignoring 'the ordinary rules of civility' and 'the sober way of arguing controversy', and subjecting his victim to 'the utmost extremity of jeer, disdain, and indignation'. Throughout *Mr Smirke; Or, the Divine in Mode*, Marvell shows increasing signs of impatience at having to play contentious clergymen at their own game, and eventually breaks off the point-by-point refutation of Turner's *Animadversions* to offer his own views on the freedom of individual conscience in matters of religion.

The methods of satire give way entirely to 'a naked narrative' of recent history in his last major prose work, *An Account of the Growth of Popery, and Arbitrary Government in England*. Responding not to some particular example of intolerance or injustice but to the general threat to ancient liberties in church and state, he is at pains to appear objective in his presentation of facts which speak for themselves, and refuses to name names on the grounds that he has 'only a public enmity, no private animosity' towards the men at the heart of 'the conspiracy'. This stance is reinforced by the studied impersonality with which he refers to himself as 'the relator' or merges himself with his countrymen as 'we' or resorts to the passive voice to insist that 'this book . . . was written with no other intent than of mere fidelity and service to His Majesty'. Indeed, as we might expect, the careful projection of a persona appropriate to the occasion is a feature of all Marvell's works of public satire and controversy.

In 'Last instructions', the speaker is very much the professional man of letters, advising his fellow artist on the best way to handle his subject matter; joking about the ease with which the title of the 'Plenipotentiary ambassadors' – '(verse the name abhors)' – fits after all into the pattern of the iambic pentameter; and turning to his own advantage the well-tried modes of Restoration poetic flattery – portraits of courtiers and royal mistresses done 'to the life' rather than idealized; mock-heroic for the parliamentary battle over Excise between the troops of 'Court and Country', with allusions to the allegory of Satan, Sin and Death in Milton's recently published epic; mythological idyll for the Dutch fleet's incursion up the Thames and Medway, with De Ruyter surveying 'their crystal streams and banks so green' and disconcerting 'the bashful nymphs' among the sedges; allegorical dream for Charles II's tardy recognition of the sad plight of 'England or the Peace'. Using Waller's heroic treatment of the Duke of York's naval victory over the Dutch as a literary point of reference, he not only satirizes the self-seeking and inept politicians who were responsible for the disaster at Chatham, but at the same time exposes the sham mythology which transformed the Court ladies into goddesses and the Duke of York into a colossus bestriding the ocean. The genuine heroism of Captain Douglas stands out in poignant relief against the 'confusion, folly, treach'ry, fear, neglect' that surrounds his lonely gesture, just as the 'gross of English gentry, nobly born' earlier emerged as a precious bastion of integrity against the horde of 'wittols', 'procurers', 'privateers' and 'drunkards' that assembled for the Excise debate.

This subtle manipulation of literary resources is eschewed by the popular rhymster of the verses on the king's statue, whose idiom is perfectly geared to broad jests at the expense of a monarch who is rumoured to be 'bought too and sold' and to the back-handed compliment of the last line: 'Yet we'd better by far have him than his brother.' The voice we hear in *The Rehearsal Transpros'd*, by contrast, is that of 'a neutral, fair-minded observer, a wit rather than a zealot' (Chernaik, 1983, p. 122), who has pondered the causes of the hostility towards Puritans in the 1620s 'with my greatest and earnest impartiality' and 'cannot upon my best judgement believe' that a man like Archbishop Laud intended to reintroduce 'the Roman religion' into England. It is this voice that utters the famous verdict that the 'Good Old Cause' of reformation 'was too good to have been fought for' and that 'the world will not go the faster for our driving'. These may be Andrew Marvell's considered opinions on the history of his own times, but primarily the judicious tones are part of an overall rhetorical strategy designed to enlist the support of moderate men and women of all persuasions against the fanaticism with which Samuel Parker was promoting the cause of conformity to the established church and persecuting the ironically named 'Fanatics'. When reading the works of the man who, in 1672, could speak of the 'happy conjuncture of his Majesty's Restoration' and also declare that ''tis such a king as no chisel can mend', and who rounded off one of his teasingly elusive lyrics with the remark 'I yet my silent judgement keep', it is perhaps wiser to be content to admire the brilliance with which voice is adapted to occasion than to seek for the face behind the mask.

Reading list

ABBREVIATIONS

The following abbreviations are used in the reading list and notes.

CQ	*Critical Quarterly*
CR	*Critical Review*
Crit	*Criticism*
EA	*Etudes Anglaises*
EC	*Essays in Criticism*
ELR	*English Literary Renaissance*
Leishman	J. B. Leishman, *The Art of Marvell's Poetry* (London, Hutchinson, 1966)
MLN	*Modern Language Notes*
MLR	*Modern Language Review*
MP	*Modern Philology*
N&Q	*Notes and Queries*
PBA	*Proceedings of the British Academy*
PMLA	*Publications of the Modern Language Association*
PQ	*Philological Quarterly*
RenN	*Renaissance News*
RenQ	*Renaissance Quarterly*
RES	*Review of English Studies*
SEL	*Studies in English Literature*

SewR	*Sewanee Review*
SR	*Studies in the Renaissance*
TLS	*Times Literary Supplement*

Belsey, C. (1980) *Critical Practice*, London and New York, Methuen.

Berthoff, A. E. (1970) *The Resolved Soul: A Study of Marvell's Major Poems*, Princeton, Princeton University Press.

Bradbrook, M. C. and Lloyd Thomas, M. G. (1940) *Andrew Marvell*, Cambridge, Cambridge University Press.

Brett, R. L. (ed.) (1979) *Andrew Marvell: Essays on the Tercentenary of His Death*, Oxford, Oxford University Press.

Brooks, C. (1946) 'Marvell's "Horatian ode"', *English Institute Essays*, New York, Columbia University Press, pp. 127–58.

—— (1953) 'A note on the limits of "History" and the limits of "Criticism"', *SewR*, 61, pp. 129–35.

Bush, D. (1952) 'Marvell's "Horatian ode"', *SewR*, 60, pp. 363–76.

Chernaik, W. L. (1983) *The Poet's Time: Politics and Religion in the Work of Andrew Marvell*, Cambridge, Cambridge University Press.

Colie, R. L. (1970) *'My Ecchoing Song': Andrew Marvell's Poetry of Criticism*, Princeton, Princeton University Press.

Collins, D. S. (1981) *Andrew Marvell: A Reference Guide*, Boston, G. K. Hall.

Craze, M. (1979) *The Life and Lyrics of Andrew Marvell*, London, Macmillan.

Creaser, J. (1970) 'Marvell's effortless superiority', *EC*, 20, pp. 403–23.

Culler, J. (1975) *Structuralist Poetics: Structuralism, Linguistics and the Study of Literature*, London, Routledge & Kegan Paul.

—— (1981) *The Pursuit of Signs: Semiotics, Literature, Deconstruction*, London and Melbourne, Routledge & Kegan Paul.

Donno, E. S. (1978) *Andrew Marvell: The Critical Heritage*, London and Boston, Routledge & Kegan Paul.

Duncan-Jones, E. E. (1975) 'Marvell: a great master of words', *PBA*, 61, pp. 267–90.

Eliot, T. S. (1951) *Selected Essays*, 3rd edn, London, Faber & Faber.

Empson, W. (1935) *Some Versions of Pastoral*, London, Chatto & Windus.

—— (1947) *Seven Types of Ambiguity*, 2nd edn, London, Chatto & Windus.

Fowler, A. (1982) *Kinds of Literature: An Introduction to the Theory of Genres and Modes*, Oxford, Clarendon Press.

Friedman, D. M. (1970) *Marvell's Pastoral Art*, London, Routledge & Kegan Paul.

Greg, W. W. (1906) *Pastoral Poetry and Pastoral Drama*, London, A. H. Bullen.

Grove, R. (1981) 'Poetry and reader: Marvell's Triumphs of the Hay', *CR*, 23, pp. 34–48.

Hill, C. (1968) *Puritanism and Revolution*, London, Panther.

Hodge, R. I. V. (1978) *Foreshortened Time: Andrew Marvell and Seventeenth Century Revolutions*, Cambridge, D. S. Brewer.

Hunt, J. D. (1978) *Andrew Marvell: His Life and Writings*, London, Paul Elek.

Kelliher, H. (1978) *Andrew Marvell: Poet and Politician 1621–78*, London, British Library.

King, B. (1977) *Marvell's Allegorical Poetry*, New York and Cambridge, Oleander Press.

Klause, J. (1983) *The Unfortunate Fall: Theodicy and the Moral Imagination of Andrew Marvell*, Hamden, Connecticut, Archon Books.

Legouis, P. (1928) *André Marvell: Poète, Puritain, Patriote*, Paris, Henri Didier (*Andrew Marvell: Poet, Puritan, Patriot*, Oxford, Clarendon Press, 1965).

Leishman, J. B. (1966) *The Art of Marvell's Poetry*, London, Hutchinson.

Long, M. (1984) *Marvell, Nabokov: Childhood and Arcadia*, Oxford, Clarendon Press.

Nevo, R. (1963) *The Dial of Virtue: A Study of Poems on Affairs of State in the Seventeenth Century*, Princeton, Princeton University Press.

Parry, G. (1985) *Seventeenth-Century Poetry: the Social Context*, London, Hutchinson.

Patrides, C. A. (ed.) (1978) *Approaches to Marvell: The York Tercentenary Lectures*, London and Boston, Routledge & Kegan Paul.

Patterson, A. M. (1975) 'Against polarization: literature and politics in Marvell's Cromwell poems', *ELR*, 5, pp. 251–72.
—— (1978) *Marvell and the Civic Crown*, Princeton, Princeton University Press.
Rivers, I. (1973) *The Poetry of Conservatism: A Study of Poets and Public Affairs from Jonson to Pope*, Cambridge, Rivers Press.
Stocker, M. (1986) *Apocalyptic Marvell: The Second Coming in Seventeenth Century Poetry*, Brighton, Harvester Press.
Toliver, H. E. (1965) *Marvell's Ironic Vision*, New Haven and London, Yale University Press.
Tompkins, J. P. (1980) 'The reader in history: the changing shape of literary response', in Tompkins, J. (ed.) *Reader-Response Criticism: From Formalism to Post-Structuralism*, Baltimore, Johns Hopkins University Press, pp. 201–32.
Tupper, F. S. (1938) 'Mary Palmer, alias Mrs Andrew Marvell', *PMLA*, 53, pp. 367–92.
Wallace, J. M. (1968) *Destiny His Choice: The Loyalism of Andrew Marvell*, Cambridge, Cambridge University Press.
Wilcher, R. (1985) *Andrew Marvell*, Cambridge, Cambridge University Press.
Zwicker, S. N. (1974) 'Models of governance in Marvell's "The first anniversary"', *Crit*, 16, pp. 1–12.

Notes

A DIALOGUE BETWEEN THE SOUL AND BODY

In the annotated copy of the 1681 folio in the Bodleian Library, the last four lines of this poem have been crossed out and the words '*Desunt multa*' written below. It is not known whether ll. 41–4, which break the pattern of the ten-line stanzas, belong to a missing continuation of the poem, or whether they constitute a deliberately asymmetrical effect designed to signal the conclusion of the argument.

There was a revival in the seventeenth century of a medieval tradition of poetic debates, which dramatized the antagonism between body and soul expressed in St Paul's Epistle to the Galatians 5: 17: 'For the flesh lusteth against the Spirit, and the Spirit against the flesh: and these are contrary the one to the other: so that ye cannot do the things that ye would.' Particular resemblances have been noted between Marvell's poem and James Howell's *The Vision: or a Dialogue between the Soul and Body* (1651–2). For further information about the literary context, see Leishman, pp. 209–14; Kitty Scoular Datta, 'New light on Marvell's "A dialogue between the Soul and Body"', *RenQ*, 22 (1969), 242–55; and Rosalie Osmond, 'Body and soul dialogues in the seventeenth century', *ELR*, 4 (1974), 364–403. Marvell is somewhat unusual in the way he avoids favouring one side in the dispute or resolving the problem of the mutual incompatibility of the participants.

4 *manacled* a play on the Latin root (*manus* = hand). The hands themselves constitute manacles for the immaterial Soul, just as the feet constitute fetters in the similar word-play of the preceding line.

10 *double heart* The heart is literally 'double', with its two ventricles, and figuratively guilty of duplicity.

11–12 *O, who . . . tyrannic soul* a witty adaptation by the Body of the Epistle to the Romans 7: 24: 'O wretched man that I am! who shall deliver me from the body of this death?'

14 *mine own precipice I go* It is by virtue of the indwelling soul that mankind alone among the creatures walks erect; but this privilege is attended by the constant danger of falling.

15 *needless* not subject to want until animated by the Soul.

21–2 *What magic . . . to pine* Picking up the Body's reference to possession by a demon in l. 20, the Soul imagines itself suffering the common fate of such familiar spirits as Ariel in *The Tempest*, whom the witch Sycorax 'did confine . . ./ Into a cloven pine' (I. ii. 274–7).

23–4 *whatsoever it complain . . . the pain* whatever the Body suffers is communicated paradoxically to the immaterial Soul.

28 *the cure* i.e. being restored to health, so that the longed-for release from the Body is postponed.

29 *the port* death.

34 *the palsy shakes of fear* The verb ('shakes') is placed unusually between the two parts of the nominal group ('the palsy of fear').

41–4 *What but . . . forest grew* These last two couplets broaden the basis of the dispute from the different kinds of torment inflicted upon each other by the two halves of human nature to issues of theological and philosophical significance: is the sinfulness of mankind to be laid at the door of the flesh or the spirit? and is the unspoiled natural world to be preferred to the achievements of civilization?

ON A DROP OF DEW

A Latin version of this poem, entitled *Ros*, was printed alongside the

English version in the 1681 folio. Which was the original and which the translation has not been determined. For the arguments on each side of the case, see Carl E. Bain, 'The Latin poetry of Andrew Marvell', *PQ*, 38 (1959), 436–49; and *The Latin Poetry of Andrew Marvell*, edited by William A. McQueen and Kiffin A. Rockwell, Chapel Hill, University of North Carolina Press, 1964.

The poem is written in the manner of an emblem, and is carefully balanced: the first eighteen lines, governed by the injunction to 'See', describe the physical characteristics of the dew on the rose; the next eighteen lines apply these details systematically to the situation of the soul in the body; a four-line coda relates both the dew and the soul to the biblical story of the manna in the desert.

1 *orient* pearl-like, but also associated with the east where the sun rises.

5 *For* because of. The punctuation of the 1681 folio retained here makes l. 5 relate forward to l. 6. Some editors establish syntactical identity between the English and Latin versions by omitting the semicolon at the end of l. 4, and reading l. 5 as an explanation of l. 4.

6 *incloses* closes in, an intransitive verb.

8 *as it can* so far as it is able.

native element the sky, the 'clear region' from which the dew falls to earth.

14 *the sphere* the particular sphere in the heavens of the Ptolemaic universe from which it descended.

24 *recollecting* collecting again, and perhaps also remembering.

25–6 *Does, in its pure . . . an heaven less* The little sphere of moisture is like a model of the spheres of the heavens.

29 *So the world excluding round* thus shutting out the surrounding world.

34 *girt* prepared for action.

37–40 *manna's sacred dew . . . almighty sun* an allusion to the miraculous food that sustained the Israelites in the wilderness, which fell with the dew by night and melted in the heat of the sun by day. See Exodus 16: 11–21.

EYES AND TEARS

There is a copy of this poem in a manuscript in the Bodleian Library (Tanner 306), which omits stanza 9 and contains a few insignificant variants. 'Tear' poetry was widespread in the Renaissance, but Marvell may have developed his conceits from Richard Crashaw's 'The weeper' (1646), which – like stanza 8 of 'Eyes and tears' (translated by Marvell himself into Latin verses at the end of the poem) – celebrates the tears of Mary Magdalen.

3 *having viewed . . . vain* cf. Ecclesiastes 1: 14: 'I have seen all the works that are done under the sun; and, behold, all is vanity and vexation of spirit.'

11 *poise* balance.

29 *Magdalen* a disciple of Christ named Mary, commonly regarded as a repentant harlot and identified with the woman in Luke 7: 37–8: 'And, behold, a woman in the city, which was a sinner, when she knew that Jesus sat at meat in the Pharisee's house, brought an alabaster box of ointment, And stood at his feet behind him weeping, and began to wash his feet with tears, and did wipe them with the hairs of her head, and kissed his feet, and anointed them with the ointment.'

35 *Cynthia teeming* the full moon.

57–60 *Magdala . . . pedes* So, when Magdalen sent away her wanton lovers, and dissolved her burning eyes into chaste waters; Christ stood fettered in a stream of tears, and a moist chain held his sacred feet.

A DIALOGUE, BETWEEN THE RESOLVED SOUL AND CREATED PLEASURE

A version of this poem in a seventeenth-century manuscript (Bodleian MS Rawlinson A176) omits ll. 15–16 and bears the title 'A combat between the Soul and Sense'. The exchanges between Pleasure and the Soul do, indeed, have more the air of a tournament than a debate, as a series of temptations are triumphantly thrust aside rather than a train of arguments refuted.

2–4 *immortal shield . . . the fight* The Soul's armour derives from St Paul's Epistle to the Ephesians 6: 16–17: 'the shield of faith . . . the helmet of salvation . . . the sword of the Spirit'.

7 *that thing divine* i.e. a *resolved* soul.

9 *wants* lacks.

18 *bait* pause for refreshment.

21–2 *On these . . . should strain* an allusion to the story of the Sybarite who complained of discomfort because the rose petals on which he was lying were crumpled. See Seneca, *De Ira* II. xxv. 2.

plain evenly.

23 *rest* both repose and support.

36 *but* merely.

39 *the posting winds recall* call back the hastening winds.

44 *chordage* a pun on 'cord' and 'chord'. Compare Marvell's conceit in 'The fair singer': 'Whose subtle art invisibly can wreathe/My fetters of the very air I breathe.'

46 *fence* ward off.

49 *persevere* another glance at Ephesians 6: 18: 'watching thereunto with all perseverance.'

60 *want* lack.

61 *Were't not a price* if it had not recognized monetary worth.

69 *each hidden cause* the origins of natural phenomena.

71 *the centre* i.e. of the earth, which was itself at the centre of the Ptolemaic universe.

73 *degree* both step of a ladder and academic qualification.

74 *humility* i.e. by the degree of humility.

THE CORONET

The conceit of weaving a garland of verses in honour of Christ is found in Donne's linked sequence of seven sonnets, 'La corona', and George Herbert's 'A wreath'. Marvell's poem imitates the formal inventiveness of Herbert's brand of religious lyric.

7 *towers* tall head-dresses.

11 *chaplet* coronet.

14 *twining in* entwining.
16 *wreaths* coils.
19 *thou* i.e. Christ, who alone has the power to defeat Satan.
22 *curious frame* ingeniously structured coronet of poetic flowers, i.e. the poem itself.
23 *these* i.e. the flowers.

THE DEFINITION OF LOVE

This poem has been related to the long line of definitions of love reaching back to Ralegh's 'Now what is Love, I pray thee tell' and Greene's 'Ah, what is love?' (See Rosemond Tuve, *Elizabethan and Metaphysical Imagery*, Chicago, University of Chicago Press, 1947, p. 302.) It also has much in common with seventeenth-century treatments of the theme of parting and separation. Two of these appear to have contributed directly to Marvell's poem: Donne's 'A valediction: forbidding mourning' and Lovelace's 'To Lucasta, going beyond the seas', which contains the following stanza:

> Though seas and land betwixt us both,
> Our faith and troth,
> Like separated souls,
> All time and place controls:
> Above the highest sphere we meet
> Unseen, unknown, and greet as angels greet.

10 *Where my . . . is fixed* The soul reaches out towards the object of its yearning. Marvell may have in mind Donne's conceit of the united souls of the parted lovers expanding like beaten gold and the lady as the 'fixed foot' of the compasses, which controls the movements of the absent lover, in 'A valediction: forbidding mourning'.
14 *close* unite.
15–16 *Their union . . . depose* Since these lovers are 'star-crossed' (see l. 32), their union would undermine the authority of Fate.
18 *distant poles* the poles of the earth, or the poles of the Ptolemaic universe.

19 *Though love's . . . doth wheel* a glance at the hyperbolical claims made in such poems as Donne's 'The sun rising': 'This bed thy centre is, these walls, thy sphere.'

20 *by themselves* i.e. by each other.

24 *planisphere* a flat projection of the spherical earth or heavens, in which the poles are compressed together.

25–7 *oblique . . . parallel* like lines of longitude, which form angles where they converge at the poles, and lines of latitude, which run parallel to the equator.

31–2 *conjunction . . . the stars* Marvell uses astrological terms to restate the hostility of Fate to the lovers' union.
conjunction the point of maximum proximity of two heavenly bodies.
opposition the point of maximum distance between two heavenly bodies.

THE NYMPH COMPLAINING FOR THE DEATH OF HER FAWN

In this poem Marvell brings together the lament for the death of a girl's pet (a literary topic dating back to Catullus' poem on Lesbia's sparrow and Ovid's on Corinna's parrot (*Amores* II. 6)) and the pastoral complaint of a forsaken shepherd or betrayed 'nymph'. In classical mythology, a nymph was a semi-divine being inhabiting fountains, rivers or trees; in Renaissance poetry, the term frequently meant no more than a beautiful young woman, and carried with it overtones of pastoral simplicity.

1 *troopers* The word first occurred in print in 1640 with reference to the invading army of the Scottish Covenanters, but it soon became associated with the Parliamentarian troops of mounted soldiers.

13 *so* unavenged by heaven, i.e. in spite of my prayers to the contrary.

17 *deodands* beasts which were forfeit to the Crown for pious uses because they had caused the death of a human being. The nymph suggests that a similar law should be applied to men who unjustly take the life of a beast.

32 *dear* a well-worn pun on 'deer' in pastoral poetry.

36 *heart* a similar pun on 'hart'.

99–100 *brotherless Heliades ... these* The daughters of Helios, weeping for the death of their brother, Phaethon, were turned into poplar trees and the tears which oozed from their bark hardened into beads of amber.

104 *Diana's shrine* because Diana was patroness of both virginity and hunting.

106 *turtles* turtledoves.

107 *Elysium* the shepherds' heaven in Renaissance pastoral.

116 *weep ... stone* i.e. like Niobe, who, though turned to marble, continued to weep for her dead family.

CLORINDA AND DAMON

In this dialogue the familiar features of the pastoral landscape offered as seductive pleasures by the pagan Clorinda are reinterpreted as Christian symbols by the newly converted shepherd.

1–2 *come drive ... astray* Behind these lines are the words of the Prayer Book: 'we have erred and strayed from thy ways, like lost sheep.'
too late too recently.

3–4 *grassy scutcheon ... pride* a meadow serving as the shield on which the goddess of flowers displays her coat of arms.

7 *Grass ... fade* see Isaiah 40: 8: 'the grass withereth, the flower fadeth.'

8 *vade* pass away.

20 *Pan* a rural deity in ancient Greece, but often used in later pastoral poetry to refer to Christ.

23 *oat* an oaten straw on which shepherds piped their pastoral music.

THE MOWER AGAINST GARDENS

The four Mower poems appeared in the 1681 edition in the same order in which they are printed here, and many critics base their interpretations on the assumption that they were intended to be read as a sequence.

This first poem is in the same unusual pattern of alternating ten- and eight-syllable lines rhymed in couplets as two epodes in praise of a country life by Ben Jonson: 'To Sir Robert Wroth' and a translation of Horace's Second Epode. The same verse form had also been used by Thomas Randolph in 'Upon love fondly refused for conscience' sake', which contains allusions to the kinds of horticultural practices that Marvell exploits to witty effect in ll. 21–30. For further information about the ancient debate on Art and Nature to which Marvell's and Randolph's poems contribute, see Frank Kermode, *N&Q*, 197 (1952), 136–8; and for discussions of the horticultural allusions, see Nicholas A. Salerno, 'Andrew Marvell and the grafter's art', *EA*, 21 (1968), 125–32, and Robert Wilcher, 'Marvell's cherry', *EA*, 23 (1970), 406–9.

1 *Luxurious* lecherous, voluptuous.
bring . . . in use spread his vice to the rest of the created world.

5 *garden's square* i.e. the confines of a square garden, perhaps implying that such geometrical shapes are unnatural.

6 *dead . . . air* Air enclosed by the walls of a garden stagnates like water in a pond.

15–16 *onion root . . . sold* During the tulip mania of the 1630s extravagant sums were paid for bulbs.

18 *Marvel of Peru* *Mirabilis Jalapa*, a tropical plant found in the New World.

21 *dealt between* performed the function of pander.

22 *Forbidden mixtures* Pliny, in his *Natural History*, had disapproved of taking grafting and other interferences with natural processes too far. See Leishman, pp. 134–6.

27 *seraglio* enclosure, harem.

29–30 *And in . . . a sex* The precise meaning of these lines has been much debated. The following glosses result in a reading which makes sense in the context of ll. 27–8: 'vex' can mean 'trouble, exercise, or embarrass in respect of a solution' (*OED*, 3. c); 'procreate' can be an intransitive verb meaning 'produce offspring' (*OED*, b); 'without a sex' may allude to the *stoneless* cherry, since 'stone' had the common meaning 'testicle' in the seventeenth century (*OED*, *sb.* 11). The lines can then be paraphrased: 'By producing a stoneless cherry, which cannot procreate naturally, man poses an insoluble problem for Nature.'

DAMON THE MOWER

Marvell's chief source for this complaint by a lovesick rustic was Virgil's second eclogue, but such details as the cool cave and fountain of stanza 4, the catalogue of presents in stanza 5, and the rejected suitor's comic boastfulness and examination of his own reflection in stanzas 7 and 8 were widespread in the pastoral literature of antiquity and the Renaissance. See Theocritus' *Idylls* VI and XI, Ovid's *Metamorphoses* XIII and Marlowe's 'The passionate shepherd to his love'; and for further information, see Leishman, pp. 137–41.

12 *hamstringed* crippled (the tendons of the legs being affected by the heat).

18 *Dog Star* Sirius, which was associated with the excessive heat of the dog days at the height of summer.

22 *Phaëton* son of Phoebus, who scorched the earth when he lost control of the chariot of the sun.

28 *gelid* chilly.

48 *cowslip-water* used as a skin lotion by ladies.

51 *discovers wide* uncovers widely.

53 *golden fleece* The mower compares his hay to the object of Jason's mythical quest.

54 *closes* enclosed fields.

83–4 *With shepherd's-purse . . . I seal* The plants shepherd's-purse and clown's-all-heal were used to stop bleeding and cure wounds. In the 1633 edition of Gerard's *Herball*, pp. 1004–5, there is an account of a man who applied 'Clownes Wound wort or All-heale' to his leg after a mowing accident similar to Damon's.

THE MOWER TO THE GLOW-WORMS

A number of the details in this poem were probably suggested to Marvell by Philemon Holland's translation of Pliny's *Natural History*. See Leishman, pp. 151–3.

5–8 *country comets . . . grass's fall* Marvell wittily combines the belief that comets were signs of impending disaster and Pliny's observation that the season in which the glow-worms shine coincides with the time of year when the grass is mown.

9 *officious* efficacious, zealous.

12 *foolish fires* *ignis fatuus*, a phosphorescent light that hovers over marshy ground, and hence figuratively something which deludes or misleads.

THE MOWER'S SONG

1 *survey* a coloured estate map.

3–4 *in the greenness . . . a glass* Green was the colour symbolic of hope.

26 *more green* more natural, or more inexperienced.

27 *heraldry* a heraldic device, suitably symbolic of the mower's occupation and fate.

THE GALLERY

Marvell's conceit may be derived from *La galeria* (1619), Marino's collection of poems based on real and imaginary paintings and sculptures, although it may owe a more general debt to the familiar idea of the beloved's image engraved in the lover's heart. Margoliouth suggests that if 'were' in l. 48 is read as past tense not as subjunctive, it may date the poem's composition or revision later than July 1650, when Charles I's collection of paintings at Whitehall was sold and dispersed. For further information about the poem's literary and pictorial connections, see Jean H. Hagstrum, *The Sister Arts*, Chicago, University of Chicago Press, 1958, pp. 114–17, and

Charles H. Hinnant, 'Marvell's gallery of art', *RQ*, 24 (1971), 26–37.

5 *arras-hangings* tapestries.
6 *various faces* i.e. of former mistresses.
11 *Examining* testing.
13 *Engines* instruments (of torture).
14 *cabinet* private room or picture gallery.
18 *Aurora* goddess of morning.
27 *light obscure* a witty glance at the technical term (*chiaroscuro*) for the disposition of brighter and darker masses in a picture.
34 *Venus . . . boat* Venus, goddess of beauty, sprang from the foam of the sea and is depicted in Renaissance paintings seated in a conch shell on a calm ocean.
35 *halcyons* birds believed to nest on the ocean and to calm the wind and waves during the nesting season.
38 *ambergris* a fragrant secretion of the sperm whale.
47–8 *a collection . . . Mantua's were* See head-note. Charles I had acquired the paintings in the Duke of Mantua's cabinet in 1627–8.
50 *likes me best* is most pleasing to me.

MOURNING

1–2 *You, that . . . the skies* i.e. astrologers who cast horoscopes.
3 *infants* i.e. tears.
9 *moulding . . . spheres* taking their shape from the moist spheres (of her eyes).
20 *Danaë* a girl upon whom Jove made an amorous assault by transforming himself into a shower of golden rain.
27 *donatives* largesse.
29 *wide* i.e. wide of the mark.
29–30 *Indian slaves . . . profound* Marvell's conceit may owe something to George Herbert's 'Mary Magdalen': 'Though we could dive/In tears like seas, our sins are piled/Deeper than they.'

sink This word is corrected to 'dive' in the Bodleian copy of the 1681 folio, but the printed reading is retained here because, in combination with the phrase 'seas profound', it expresses the dreamlike mystery of Chlora's tears more effectively than the purposeful action of diving.

TO HIS COY MISTRESS

This poem draws upon the long tradition of lyric persuasions to enjoy love before it is too late, which goes back to classical times and includes Herrick's 'Gather ye rose-buds while ye may' and Jonson's song from *Volpone*: 'Come my Celia, let us prove,/While we may, the sports of love.' There is a shorter version copied into a manuscript miscellany by Sir William Haward in 1672 (Bod. MS. Don. b. 8). For a discussion of its relation to the 1681 folio text, see W. Hilton Kelliher, *N&Q*, 215 (1970), 254–6.

8 *the flood* an image for the physical consummation of their relationship, with a witty allusion to the Flood of the Old Testament.

10 *conversion of the Jews* an event which was expected to precede the final destruction of the world on the Day of Judgement.

11 *vegetable* plantlike, perhaps more specifically treelike, in its slow but steady growth.

29 *quaint honour* Both words contain punning references to the female genital organs.

33–4 *youthful glew . . . morning dew* The Bodleian copy of the 1681 folio amends 'hew' to 'glew' in l. 33 and 'glew' to 'dew' in l. 34. Cooke made the emendation to 'dew' independently in the first collected edition of 1726 and has been followed by most subsequent editors. The rhyme word of l. 33 remains a problem. Margoliouth, Macdonald and Lord retain 'hew' from the folio; Kermode modernizes 'hew' to 'hue'; Donno accepts the emendation in the Bodleian copy, but modernizes it to 'glue'. In the Haward

MS (see head-note), the couplet reads thus: 'Now then whil'st ye youthfull Glue/Stickes on your Cheeke, like Morning Dew.' From its presence in the three earliest texts (the Haward MS, the 1681 folio and the Bodleian MS), it looks as if the word 'glew' or 'glue' figured in Marvell's poem at some stage of its composition. In this edition, the force of the agreement between the Haward MS and the emended text in the Bodleian MS is acknowledged, and the spelling 'glew' is retained since it makes apparent the possibility that Marvell, a Yorkshireman, had in mind not only the modern meaning of 'glue', but also a homophonic northern dialect form of 'glow' current in fourteenth- and fifteenth-century texts. (See under *gle* n. 4 = shining brightness, splendour, and *glouen* v. 1 = to glow, radiate heat, in vols 5–6 of *Middle English Dictionary*, ed. Sherman M. Kuhn and John Reidy, Ann Arbor, University of Michigan Press, 1963.)

40 *slow-chapped power* the power of his slowly devouring jaws.

44 *Thorough* through.

gates This is the reading of the 1681 text. Some modern editors adopt the emendation to 'grates' found in the Bodleian copy of the folio, but the phrase 'iron gates of life', an unexpected variation on the commoner image of the 'gates of death', has the ring of Marvellian wit.

45–6 *though we . . . run* Sources for this conceit have been found in the classical myth of Phaëton, who let the chariot of the sun run out of control (see Frederick L. Gwynn, *The Explicator*, 11 (1953), Item 49), and in the contrast between the story of the sun standing still at the behest of an Israelite hero (Joshua 10: 12) and the image of the sun rejoicing 'as a strong man to run a race' (Psalms 19: 5). Closer to the subject matter and ambience of Marvell's poem are numerous passages in Renaissance amatory verse, such as Donne's injunction to the sun to stay its course over the lovers' bed in 'The sun rising', and Herrick's reminders that 'our days run/As fast away as does the sun' ('Corinna's going a-Maying') and that the higher the sun climbs in the sky,

'The sooner will his race be run' ('To the Virgins to make much of Time').

THE UNFORTUNATE LOVER

This hyperbolical account of the pains and misfortunes attendant upon the birth, life and death of a lover owes something to the visual and spectacular arts of the Renaissance (see 'masque' in l. 26, 'spectacle' in l. 42 and the heraldic terms in ll. 63–4), and may be related specifically to the series of emblems depicting the experience of love in Otto van Veen's *Amorum Emblemata* (1608) and Crispin de Passe's *Thronus Cupidinis* (1618). More generally, the images of the poem are exaggerated variations on the conceits and paradoxes associated with Petrarchan love poetry.

5–8 *But soon . . . time* Meteors were thought to burn out when they reached the sphere of fire, never ascending as far as the timeless and incorruptible region beyond the moon.
impression both an attack and a physical or mental mark left by pressure. The word could also mean a 'meteor' in the seventeenth century.

36 *bill* peck.

43–4 *to play . . . sharp* to fence with unbated weapons.

46 *winged artillery* Cupid's arrows.

48 *Ajax* the son of Oileus, who was shipwrecked and destroyed by the gods after he had taken refuge on a rock (see Virgil, *Aeneid* I. 41–5).

55–6 *And all . . . relish best* Some commentators take the last line and a half to be the words spoken by the Lover. Donno glosses 'says' as a shortened form of 'assays'. Less violence is done to the text by taking 'all he says' as the object of 'relish'; the couplet can then be paraphrased: 'A lover covered in his own blood can best appreciate everything that this unfortunate lover says.'
dressed clothed, but also garnished (looking forward to 'relish' in the next line).

57 *banneret* a knight dubbed on the field of battle for acts of bravery. King Charles had revived this honour at the battle of Edgehill in 1642.

64 *a field . . . gules* in the language of heraldry, a red lover on a black ground. Love's 'only banneret' – 'ragg'd with wounds' against a stormy sky – finds a fitting memorial in this emblematic coat of arms.

THE PICTURE OF LITTLE T.C. IN A PROSPECT OF FLOWERS

For an account of the tradition of addresses to young girls to which this poem and the following one, 'Young love', belong, see Leishman, pp. 165–89. Margoliouth has suggested that the initials 'T.C.' stand for Theophila Cornewall, the daughter of friends of the Marvell family, who was baptized in September 1644 (*MLR*, 17 (1922), 351–61).

5 *gives them names* traditionally the prerogative of Eve in the Garden of Eden.

10 *darling of the gods* Theophila means 'dear to the gods'.

12 *The wanton Love* i.e. Cupid.

17 *compound* come to terms.

22 *but* only.

36 *Flora* Roman goddess of flowers.

40 *Nip . . . and thee* The year before Theophila Cornewall was born, her parents had lost a previous daughter, also named Theophila, in early infancy.

YOUNG LOVE

2–4 *While thine . . . jealousy and fears* In adult invitations to love, the lovers had to circumvent the suspicions of parent or husband. Such unpleasantness does not attend the playful courtship of this 'little infant'.

9 *stay fifteen* wait until they are fifteen.

23 *antedate* enjoy before its appointed time.

24 *Or, if ill . . . prevent* or, if misfortune is to be our lot, at least enjoy some good beforehand.
prevent act in advance of.

THE GARDEN

Hortus, a Latin version of this poem printed in the 1681 folio, contains no equivalent to stanzas 5–8.

James Shirley, Joseph Beaumont and Abraham Cowley all wrote poems entitled 'The garden', and the themes of rural retirement and contemplative solitude were widespread in the literature of the seventeenth century. See George Williamson, 'The context of Marvell's "Hortus" and "Garden"', *MLN*, 76 (1961), 590–8; Herbert G. Wright, 'The theme of solitude and retirement in seventeenth century literature', *EA*, 7 (1954), 22–35; and Stanley Stewart, *The Enclosed Garden*, Madison, University of Wisconsin Press, 1966.

2 *the palm . . . or bays* honours awarded for military, civic or literary achievements.
7 *close* come together.
13 *if here below* if they are to be found on earth.
15 *rude* uncivil or uncivilized.
17 *white nor red* the colours of female beauty.
19 *Fond* doting.
25 *heat* both ardour and race.
28 *Still* always.
29–32 *Apollo . . . a reed* Daphne and Syrinx avoided rape by turning into plants. Marvell wittily suggests that this was the desired goal of the pursuing gods.
37 *curious* exquisite.
41 *from pleasures less* from inferior delights (i.e. those offered to the senses in stanza 5).
43--4 *that ocean . . . find* an allusion to the belief that the sea contained counterparts to every creature found on dry land.
45–6 *it creates . . . other seas* The imaginative faculty of the mind creates another world which greatly surpasses that of nature.

47 *Annihilating . . . To* reducing the whole of creation to the insubstantiality of.

51 *vest* vesture.

54 *whets* preens.

56 *various light* In Neoplatonic symbolism, the various colours of the natural world spring from the one divine light of eternity.

57 *garden-state* i.e. paradise.

60 *What other . . . meet* Eve was created as 'an help meet' – a suitable companion – for Adam (Genesis 2: 18).

68 *fragrant zodiac* the 'flowers and herbs' planted in the form of a sundial.

70 *time* A pun on 'thyme' is sanctioned by the parallel passage in *Hortus*.

BERMUDAS

Some of the details in this poem derive from Edmund Waller's *Battle of the Summer Islands* (1645). For information about the wider poetic tradition of earthly paradises, see Leishman, pp. 278–82; and for Marvell's familiarity with accounts of the English colonies in the New World, see Rosalie L. Colie, 'Marvell's "Bermudas" and the Puritan Paradise', *RenN*, 10 (1957), 75–9.

8 *kinder* both more benign and more natural.

9 *sea-monsters* Stranded whales figure in Waller's poem (see head-note).

12 *prelate's rage* The Puritan John Oxenbridge, with whom Marvell lodged as tutor to William Dutton in 1653, had served as minister in the Bermudas after Archbishop Laud had deprived him of his Oxford fellowship in 1634.

20 *Ormus* Hormuz, on the Persian Gulf.

23 *plants* a transitive verb with 'apples' as its object.

28 *ambergris* a fragrant secretion of the sperm whale.

36 *beyond the Mexique Bay* i.e. into pagan or Roman Catholic territories.

FLECKNOE, AN ENGLISH PRIEST AT ROME

The encounter that provided the material for this satire occurred in March 1646, during Marvell's four years abroad after leaving Cambridge. (See P. H. Burdon, 'Andrew Marvell and Richard Flecknoe in Rome', *N&Q*, 217 (1972), 16–18.) Richard Flecknoe was a Roman Catholic priest and minor writer, who was later to be the butt of Dryden's wit in his poem *MacFlecknoe*. Marvell's comic account of the predicament and behaviour of the starving poetaster owes something to the ingenious hyperbolical style of Cleveland and something to the tradition of verse satire that reaches back through Donne to the Roman poet, Horace.

3 *Melchizadek* His roles of prophet, priest and king (Genesis 15: 18–20) may have suggested the link with Flecknoe, 'priest, poet, and musician'.

4 *Though . . . Lord Brooke* It is not known whether Flecknoe had any right to claim descent from Fulke Greville, first Lord Brooke, the poet and courtier, who died in 1628. Marvell's phrasing suggests otherwise.

6–7 *Sad Pelican . . . poetry* The Pelican was an emblem of Christ, hence a 'subject divine'.

8 *triple property* i.e. as 'priest, poet, and musician'.

12 *nor ceiling . . . sheet* neither wainscoting (or black hangings), nor a bed-sheet (or winding-sheet). Marvell pursues the witty comparison of the room to a coffin.

13–14 *door. . . room* The door supplied the missing wainscot along one half of the wall against which it opened.

18 *stanzas* The Italian word *stanza* means either verse or room.

appartament suite of rooms.

28 *The last . . . brain* a mocking echo of Milton's description of Fame in 'Lycidas': 'That last infirmity of noble mind.'

46 *Lent* a time of abstinence for Roman Catholics.

48 *this of gen'rous* this aspect or degree of generosity.

53 *he was sick* and therefore not obliged to abstain.

54 *th' Ordinance* i.e. against eating meat during Lent.

56 *at once* at the same time.

61 *Host* Communion wafer.

63 *basso relievo* bas-relief, a carving with very little depth.

64–6 *a camel . . . rich* an allusion to Matthew 19: 24: 'It is easier for a camel to go through the eye of a needle, than for a rich man to enter into the kingdom of God.'

69 *circumscribes* surrounds himself with writing (i.e. wraps himself in paper).

71 *buff* leather.

72 *third dimension* i.e. his thickness, since he has chiefly length and breadth, like a bas-relief.

74 *sottana* cassock.

75–8 *antique cloak . . . redeemed* Marvell is mocking both the condition of Flecknoe's clothes and the authority of traditions over scripture and the veneration of relics in the Roman church. The first Council of Antioch was in AD 264.

85 *complimenting doubt* i.e. over who should be given precedence.

98 *Delightful* delighted.

99 *penetration* occupation of the same space by two bodies simultaneously.

100–1 *nor can . . . one substance* i.e. as in the Trinity.

126 *Nero's poem* No one was allowed to leave the theatre while Nero was singing.

127–8 *the pelican . . . young* The pelican pierces its own breast to nourish its young on its blood.

130 *foul copies* rough drafts.

137 *chancres and poulains* sores caused by venereal disease.

152 *Perillus* the first victim of a bronze bull which he had contrived himself for roasting people alive.

156 *is no lie* i.e. it is no occasion for a challenge.

170 *for a vow* as a votive offering in gratitude for his deliverance.

TO HIS NOBLE FRIEND MR RICHARD LOVELACE, UPON HIS POEMS

This poem was printed, along with sixteen other commendatory pieces, in Richard Lovelace's *Lucasta* (1649), and not included in the 1681 folio. The volume was licensed for publication on 4 February 1648, but not entered in the Stationers' Register till 14 May 1649, and probably published in June. The delay was apparently due to the poet's detention in the Peterhouse Prison between 9 June 1648 and 10 April 1649. Lines 21–4 seem to imply that *Lucasta* had not yet been licensed when Marvell was writing, but see the note on l. 29 below.

Lovelace was one of the Cavalier poets. Educated at Oxford 1634–6, he spent a few months at Cambridge in 1637, when Marvell presumably made his acquaintance, and later became popular at Court for his good looks and skill as a poet.

1–2 *Our times . . . fortune chose* The present contrasts with the situation ten years earlier, when Lovelace first made his mark as a poet and courtier.

5 *candid* frank and impartial, but also suggesting 'innocent' (from Latin root *candidus*, white).

8 *the bays* a garland of bay leaves awarded for poetry.

12 *civic crown* a garland of oak leaves awarded for saving the life of a citizen in battle.

19–20 *Word-peckers . . . unfashioned sons* party hacks engendered like maggots from the corruption of wit.

21 *barbed censurers* Censorship had been reimposed by the Printing Ordinance, 1643.

22 *grim consistory* Court of Presbyters, part of the system of ecclesiastical government by elders rather than ordained bishops.

24 *young Presbytery* The episcopacy had been replaced in 1643.

28 *wronged . . . House's privilege* by daring to assume the right of free speech which was one of the privileges of the House of Commons.

29 *under sequestration are* The sequestration, or confiscation, of Lovelace's estate was ordered by the Commons on 28 November 1648 because of his open support for the Royalist cause. The allusion to this event means that, even if Marvell began work on the poem before 4 February 1648

as ll. 21–4 imply, he revised it at a date nearer its publication, at least to the extent of adding ll. 29–30.

30 *when going to the war* an allusion to Lovelace's song, 'To Lucasta, going to the wars'.

31–2 *because Kent . . . sent* Lovelace had been imprisoned by Parliament in 1642 for presenting a Kentish petition, in which the legal rights of the king and the use of the Book of Common Prayer were defended.

45–50 '*O no . . . with you love*' There are no quotation marks in *Lucasta* (1649). Some editors close them at the end of l. 46.

AN HORATIAN ODE UPON CROMWELL'S RETURN FROM IRELAND

Cancelled in most copies of the 1681 folio (though surviving in British Museum C. 59. i. 8 and Huntington 79660), this ode was reprinted in Thompson's collected edition of 1776. The version included in Bodleian MS Eng. poet. d. 49 accords with the 1776 text in its minor variants from the folio.

Cromwell was recalled from Ireland at the end of May 1650 to take part in a campaign against the Scots. When Lord Fairfax resigned his command of the army in protest against a pre-emptive attack on Scotland, Cromwell was appointed in his place on 26 June and marched across the border on 22 July. It can be assumed, therefore, that Marvell's poem was composed during June and July 1650.

For Marvell's debt to Horace's *Odes* and Lucan's *Pharsalia* (both in the original Latin and in the translation by Thomas May), see R. H. Syfret, 'Marvell's "Horatian ode"', *RES*, N.S. 12 (1961), 160–72, and John S. Coolidge, 'Marvell and Horace', *MP*, 63 (1965), 111–20; for a general account of the classical ambience of the poem, see A. J. N. Wilson, 'Andrew Marvell', *CQ*, 11 (1969), 325–41; for a discussion of the stanza form and its possible derivation from a poem by Sir Richard Fanshawe, see William Simeone, *N&Q*, 197 (1952), 316–18, and Barbara Everett, in *Andrew Marvell: Essays on the Tercentenary of his Death*, ed. R. L. Brett, Oxford, Oxford University Press, 1979, pp. 74–7.

1 *appear* make himself known in the public world.

3 *in the shadows* associated with reprehensible idleness in Roman poetry.

9 *cease* remain inactive, an intransitive verb.

15–16 *Did thorough ... way divide* Cromwell emerged as the dominant figure among the leaders of the anti-Royalist forces during the later 1640s.

17–18 *'tis all one ... or enemy* a man of spirit makes no distinction between rivals in his own party and opponents on the other side.

19–20 *with such ... to oppose* such a man finds competition more irksome than opposition.

23–4 *Caesar's head ... laurels blast* an allusion to the beheading of Charles I, whose crown could not protect him from the destructive force of Cromwell. Roman emperors wore a laurel wreath and laurels were believed to be proof against lightning.

32 *bergamot* a variety of pear known as the 'pear of kings'.

38 *ancient rights* i.e. of monarchy.

41–2 *Nature ... penetration less* Nature abhors a vacuum, and has an even stricter law against two bodies occupying the same space simultaneously.

47–52 *And Hampton ... narrow case* Cromwell was believed to have served his own ends by conniving at the king's flight from Hampton Court to Carisbrooke Castle on the Isle of Wight in November 1647.

case cage (where Charles I found himself a prisoner).

59–60 *But with ... did try* a play on the Latin word *acies*, which can refer to both sharpness of sight and the sharp edge of a blade.

66 *forced* gained by force.

67–72 *So when ... happy fate* Livy (*Annals* I. 55) relates that a human head discovered during the digging of the foundations of the temple of Jupiter Capitolium was taken to be an omen of the future greatness of Rome.

74 *in one year* Cromwell's campaign in Ireland began in August 1649.

87 *what he may* so far as he can.

95 *lure* in the terminology of falconry, to recall the hawk from free flight.

101–2 *A Caesar . . . an Hannibal* Julius Caesar conquered Gaul, and returned to make himself master of Rome; Hannibal reduced much of Italy under his power but was ultimately defeated. Marvell has in mind the possibility of a Protestant crusade against the Catholic states of Europe.

104 *climacteric* critical or fatal.

105–8 *The Pict . . . the plaid* a pun on the derivation of Pict from Latin *picti* (painted) is taken up in the references to the 'parti-coloured mind' of the untrustworthy Scots and the tartan pattern on the plaid, a garment worn by Highlanders.

107 *sad* steadfast.

110 *mistake* fail to notice, because of his camouflage.

117–18 *the force . . . shady night* According to classical authorities (Homer, *Odyssey* XI. 48, and Virgil, *Aeneid* VI. 260) the spirits of the dead fear the drawn sword (E. E. Duncan-Jones, *EA*, 15 (1962), 172–4). Many spirits, including that of the executed king, might be expected to haunt Cromwell, as they did Shakespeare's Richard III.

TOM MAY'S DEATH

Occasioned by the death of Thomas May on 13 November 1650, this poem was first published in the 1681 folio. Its omission from the Bodleian MS Eng. poet. d. 49 has led Lord to question its authenticity.

Thomas May made his reputation at the Court of Charles I as playwright, poet and translator of Lucan, but later defected to the anti-Royalist cause and wrote a partisan history of the Long Parliament. For the bearing of Marvell's attitude to May on the problem of his own political allegiance in late 1650, see Gerard Reedy, S. J., '"An Horatian ode" and "Tom May's death"', *SEL*, 20 (1980), 137–51.

1–2 *As one . . . not know't* In Aubrey's *Brief Lives*, May is said to have died 'after drinking with his chin tied with his cap (being fat); suffocated'.

6 *Stephen's Alley* the street in Westminster where May lived, well known for its taverns.

10 *Ares* presumably the name of a tavern-keeper.

13 *Ben* i.e. Ben Jonson, who boasts of his 'mountain belly' in 'My picture, left in Scotland'.

14 *laid* lay.

17–18 *But how . . . people's cheats* Brutus and Cassius were consigned to perpetual torment in Dante's *Inferno* as treacherous assassins of Julius Caesar.

21–4 *'Cups more . . . conquering health'* a parody of the opening lines of May's translation of Lucan's *Pharsalia*:

> Wars more than civil on Emathian plains
> We sing; rage licensed; where great Rome distains
> In her own bowels her victorious swords.

26 *translated* i.e. by death and by Jonson.

27 *as stumbling as his tongue* May suffered from a speech defect.

29–30 *knew not . . . do pretend* permitted neither enmity nor friendship to influence his judgement on those who claimed a place 'among the learned throng'.

37–8 *whipped him . . . masque* an allusion to an incident in which the Earl of Pembroke had broken his staff across May's shoulders at a court masque in 1634.

41 *Polydore . . . Goth* Polydore Virgil, an Italian whose *Historia anglica*, written at the courts of Henry VII and Henry VIII, offended the national pride of Englishmen; Lucan, the historian of the Roman civil wars; Alan, Vandal, Goth, three barbarian tribes. All are offered as examples of servile or mercenary behaviour.

47–9 *bestow . . . your talk* May's *History of the Parliament of England* contains many parallels between English and Roman history.

50 *Bethlem's . . . walk* the house of the Virgin miraculously transported from the Holy Land to Loreto.

54 *Those but . . . continue May* an allusion to May's *Continuation of Lucan's Historical Poem till the Death of Julius Caesar.*

57–8 *Because some one . . . these tears* May had hoped to succeed Jonson as poet laureate in 1637, but the honour went to Davenant.

60 *gazette writer* hack journalist.

61–2 *must we . . . Ghib'llines be* must we embrace political causes for mercenary ends?

As for the basket from Latin *sportula*, a basket in which patrons distributed gifts to their clients, hence a gratuity.

Guelphs and Ghib'llines rival factions in Italian politics.

73 *Apostatizing . . . and us* i.e. deserting the fellowship of true poets.

74 *chronicler to Spartacus* historian of the rebellious Parliament. Spartacus led a slaves' revolt against Rome in 73 BC.

76 *Before thou . . . relate* May's second volume on the Civil Wars stopped short of the trial and execution of the king.

78 *surviving Davenant* William Davenant, his successful rival for the laureateship in 1637, was in the Tower awaiting trial on a charge of treason at the same time that May was being honoured with a monument in Westminster Abbey.

82 *thy last . . . pay* £100 was voted by the Council of State for May's burial.

88 *th'eagle's plumes . . . divide* Eagle feathers were believed to have the property of consuming the feathers of other birds.

90 *Phlegethon* a river of Hades.

91 *Cerberus* the three-headed hell-hound.

92 *Megaera* a serpent-haired Fury.

93 *Ixion's wheel* the fiery wheel upon which Ixion revolved forever in Hades.

94 *perpetual vulture feel* like Prometheus, whose liver was endlessly torn and consumed by vultures.

UPON THE HILL AND GROVE AT BILBROUGH: TO THE LORD FAIRFAX

Lord Fairfax, who withdrew to his Yorkshire estates after resigning his command of the army in June 1650, owned property at Bilbrough, which is about 5 miles north-west of his house at Nun

Appleton. Marvell was employed as tutor in the Fairfax household for about two years (1651–3), and presumably wrote this and a companion poem in Latin ('*Epigramma in duos montes Amosclivium et Bilboreum*') during that time.

4 *like* even.

5 *pencil* paintbrush.

7 *a model* i.e. for the construction of the spherical earth.

13 *For* on account of.

14 *Nature . . . centre find* the spherical perfection of the earth is distorted by such irregularities.

28 *Tenerife* a volcanic peak in the Canary Islands, 12,192 feet high, compared to Bilbrough's 145 feet.

34 *plume* The 1681 folio reads 'plum'. Margoliouth conjectured 'plump', meaning 'troop' or 'clump', but the emendation adopted here, first proposed by Cooke, seems to fit the image of a plumed helmet implicit in the words 'crest' and 'wave'.

38 *great Master's terror* fear of the great soldier who owns it.

43 *Vera the Nymph* Fairfax's wife was the daughter of Sir Horace Vere.

52 *genius* guardian spirit.

56 *this* i.e. this particular head of the house.

74 *oracles in oak* an allusion to the sacred grove at Dodona.

UPON APPLETON HOUSE: TO MY LORD FAIRFAX

Upon Appleton House belongs to a line of poems in praise of well-managed country houses and estates, and thus indirectly of the moral and social qualities of their owners, which began with Ben Jonson's 'To Penshurst' and 'To Sir Robert Wroth'. (See G. R. Hibbard, 'The country house poem of the seventeenth century', *Journal of the Warburg and Courtauld Institutes*, 19 (1956), 159–74; and, for the classical tradition which lies behind this English development, Leishman, pp. 253–60.) It is also related to the mid-century fashion for prospective poems, strongly influenced by Sir John Denham's *Cooper's Hill* (1642), which read aesthetic, moral and political significances into the topographical features of a stretch of landscape. (See

James Turner, *The Politics of Landscape*, Oxford, Blackwell, 1979, pp. 49–84.) Marvell's poem was presumably written during the period of his employment as tutor to Lord Fairfax's daughter, Mary, in the early 1650s.

There is some debate about precisely which building Marvell had in mind in the opening stanzas. Thomas Lord Fairfax is known to have pulled down the old house at Nun Appleton and erected a more imposing brick mansion. His nineteenth-century biographer, C. R. Markham, says that the rebuilding, begun in 1637, was completed at about the time of the Lord General's retirement in 1650, but there is no independent evidence for this dating, and it seems more likely, as John Newman has argued, that Marvell was referring to the 'modest house cobbled up out of part of the nunnery, next to the ruined church' (*TLS*, 28 January 1972, p. 99). This view has been supported by A. A. Tait, who has found a mention in the Fairfax papers of stone being taken from 'my quarry at Towston Moor' in 1652 (*TLS*, 11 February 1972, p. 157). The Nun Appleton estate came into the possession of the Fairfax family following the dissolution of the monasteries in the 1540s, but there appears to be no evidence (apart from Markham's *Life of the Great Lord Fairfax* (1870), which derives its information from Marvell's poem) for the story of Sir William Fairfax's dramatic rescue of his bride related in stanzas 12–35. (See Lee Erickson, 'Marvell's *Upon Appleton House* and the Fairfax family', *ELR*, 9 (1979), 158–68.)

5–6 *Who . . . vault his brain* whose skull expanded under the pressure of his ambitious conception till it became itself a model for the arched roof.

12 *equal* adequate for their size.

24 *first builders* i.e. of the Tower of Babel (Genesis 11: 1–9).

30 *loop* opening.

36 *Vere* Anne Vere, Fairfax's wife.

40 *Romulus . . . cell* the thatched hut in which the founder of Rome lived.

45–6 *Let others . . . quadrature* an allusion to the unsolved problem in mathematics of transforming a circle into a square of the same area.

47 *holy mathematics* ‘holy’ because the square and the circle were symbolic of human and divine perfection.

48 *In every . . . man* According to Vitruvius a circle imposed upon a square gave the perfect proportions of a human body.

60 *clownishly* in an uncouth manner.

64 *invent* find out.

65 *frontispiece of poor* the poor expecting alms decorate the entrance.

73–4 *Bishop's Hill . . . Denton . . . Bilbrough* other houses belonging to Fairfax.

90 *blooming virgin Thwaites* Sir William Fairfax of Steeton had married the heiress Isabel Thwaites in 1518.

105 *armour white* the colour of the Cistercian habit.

107–8 *chaste lamps . . . them dim* an allusion to the parable of the wise and foolish virgins (Matthew 25: 1–12).

122 *Legend* a saint's life.

123 *paint* i.e. embroider.

152 *devoto* devoted worshipper.

169 *nice* fastidious.

173–6 *So through . . . clear and full* A parallel is drawn between spiritual purification and the process of preserving fruit.

180 *sea-born amber* i.e. ambergris, a fragrant, wax-like secretion of the sperm whale, often found floating in tropical seas.

181 *grieved* wounded.

pastes pasties or pâtés.

183–4 *unless . . . confess* unless we should regard these pleasures as sinful and need to confess them to a priest.

187–8 *Whom if . . . behind* See note to ll. 107–8.

197–9 *seek her . . . does begin* claim her promise of marriage, which has been annulled by the religious life she has just entered.

221 *'state* property.

232 *First from . . . bred* an allusion to his father and maternal grandfather.

233 *the storm* i.e. storming the priory.

241–4 *offspring fierce . . . Germany* His son, grandson and great-grandson all distinguished themselves in continental wars.

245–6 *Till one . . . ride?* an allusion to the present Lord Fairfax, the general of the victorious parliamentary army.

248 *the great . . . intercept* would prevent the founding of this great line.

274 *escheat* the legal process by which an estate reverted to the lord of the manor if a tenant died heirless.

281–2 *the hero . . . does fame* probably Sir Thomas Fairfax, son of Sir William and Isabel.

292 *dian* reveille.

295 *pan* part of the musket lock.

296 *flask* i.e. in which the musketeer kept his powder.

301 *the virgin Nymph* i.e. Marvell's pupil, Mary Fairfax.

303 *compare* comparable.

326 *flaming sword* set by God to keep intruders out of paradise (Genesis 3: 24).

336 *Switzers* The Swiss guard in the Vatican wore striped uniforms.

349 *Cinque Ports* As a member of the Council of State until his resignation, Fairfax held joint responsibility for these five ancient Channel ports.

351 *spanned* confined.

358 *that which . . . touch* an allusion to the sensitive plant.

363 *Cawood Castle* formerly a seat of the Archbishop of York.

365 *quarrelled* found fault with.

368 *graze* The 1681 text reads 'gaze', but the emendation in Bodleian MS Eng. poet. d. 49 is adopted here because the conceit of the eyes grazing upon the meadows like cattle seems more in keeping with the wit of the poem than the folio's less imaginative choice of verb.

371–2 *Where men . . . giants there* 'And there we saw the giants . . . and we were in our own sight as grasshoppers' (Numbers 13: 33).

380 *or go* or move forwards.

382 *the ground* the seabed.

385 *engines strange* machinery for effecting scene changes in court masques.

402 *cates* provisions.
405 *quick* alive.
408 *Rails rain . . . dew* an allusion to the experience of the Israelites in the wilderness (Exodus 16: 11–15).
416 *sourdine* device for muting a trumpet.
419 *traverse* stage curtain on which a scene was depicted.
426 *hay* country dance (as well as mown grass).
428 *Alexander's sweat* reputed to have been sweet-smelling.
435–6 *We wond'ring . . . steer* Distance deceives the eye and makes the boats on the river beyond the meadows appear to pass between the piles of hay.
439 *Roman camps* burial mounds (now known to be of British origin).
444 *cloths* canvases.
Lely the painter Sir Peter Lely.
446 *table rase* i.e. *tabula rasa*, a blank tablet.
447 *toril* bullring.
448 *Madril* Madrid.
450 *Levellers* egalitarian movement of the 1640s.
take pattern at use as a model.
455–6 *Such . . . universal herd* an allusion to a description of a painting of the Creation in William Davenant's *Gondibert* (II. vi), an epic published in 1651.
458 *landskip . . . looking-glass* a landscape painted on plateglass (because the grass shines as if it were polished to make it reflect).
461–2 *Such fleas . . . lie* So fleas lie between the glass plates of an early microscope, before raised to the eye to effect magnification.
466 *Denton* a Fairfax estate on the River Wharfe 30 miles above Nun Appleton.
475–6 *How horses . . . leeches quick* Horse-hairs were believed to turn into eels or leeches in water.
480 *pound* enclosure for animals.
486 *pressed* commandeered.
491 *pedigrees* family trees (united by wedlock).
493 *fell in war* i.e. to provide timber for military purposes.

499 *neighbourhood* proximity.

502 *fifth element* i.e. different from the usual four – earth, air, fire and water.

508 *Corinthian porticoes* airy colonnades in the lightest style of Greek architecture.

530 *gelid* cold.

532 *throstle* thrush.

535 *stork-like* Storks were thought to leave young ones behind for owners of houses on which they nested.

537 *hewel* green woodpecker.

538 *holtfelster* woodcutter.

563 *wants* is lacking.

568 *inverted tree* For the long history of the commonplace that man is like an inverted tree, see A. B. Chambers, *SR*, 8 (1961), 291–9.

577 *Sibyl's leaves* The Sibyl of Cumae recorded her oracular sayings on dead leaves.

580 *Mexique paintings* pictures made out of feathers.

582 *light mosaic* the patterns formed by light dappling through the leaves (in witty contrast to the more serious wisdom of the Old Testament books attributed to Moses).

586 *with . . . hit* supply a masquing costume appropriate to my studies.

591 *antic cope* grotesque (and antique) ecclesiastical vestment.

599 *shed* separate.

607 *play* shoot.

608 *gall* harass.

629–30 *No serpent . . . Nile* an allusion to the belief that these creatures were bred of Nile mud.

631 *itself* i.e. the river.

636 *slick* sleek.

639 *shade* reflected image.

640 *Narcissus-like* Narcissus fell in love with his own reflection.

649 *quills* floats.

650 *angles* rods and lines.

651 *Maria* i.e. Mary Fairfax.

657 *loose* lax.

659 *whisht* hushed.

660 *Starts . . . bonne mine* puts on its best appearance.

668 *eben shuts* ebony (black) shutters.

669 *halcyon* kingfisher.

671 *horror* reverent awe.

675 *compacts* solidifies.

677 *stupid* stupefied.

679 *assist* attend.

686 *exhale* Meteors were believed to be vapours rising from the earth.

688 *vitrified* turned to glass (like the pure crystalline sphere of the fixed stars).

713–14 *prevent . . . meant* anticipate the artillery trained upon you by young men.

727–8 *goodness . . . a male* Since Mary was an only child, the Fairfax virtues will be bequeathed to her. (Marvell may also be alluding to the legal arrangements Fairfax made to ensure that she would inherit the Nun Appleton estate.)

729 *fond* foolish.

734 *black-bag* mask.

738 *Supplies . . . the line* Although she is a female, the Fairfax lineage will descend through her.

744 *make . . . choice* i.e. accept their lack of a son without regret.

753 *Thessalian Tempe* a valley in Thessaly celebrated for its beauty.

755–6 *Aranjuez . . . Bel-Retiro* royal residences in Spain, noted for their gardens.

757 *Idalian grove* Cyprus, the island of Venus.

765 *Your lesser world* i.e. the estate at Nun Appleton.

770 *leathern boats* coracles.

771 *Antipodes* men from the opposite side of the globe.

774 *rational amphibii* creatures equally at home on land or in water, but also (unlike turtles) endowed with reason.

This poem was first printed in the second edition of *Paradise Lost* (1674), just before a note by Milton on the superiority of blank verse to rhyme. The relationship between the two poets went back at least to 1653, when Milton recommended Marvell for a government post. Marvell had spoken on Milton's behalf at the Restoration and was to defend him against slanders by Samuel Parker in the second part of *The Rehearsal Transpros'd* (1673). (See the extract on pp. 153–60.)

5 *argument* subject.

6 *misdoubting* having misgivings about.

9–10 *So Samson . . . his sight* an allusion to Judges 16: 29–30 and to Milton's tragedy *Samson Agonistes* (1671).

18–22 *some less . . . a play* John Dryden had adapted Milton's epic for the stage and licensed it on 17 April 1674, though he delayed publication until 1677.

25–6 *none will dare . . . a share* a reference to the fact that Dryden apparently halted plans to publish or perform his adaptation, *The State of Innocence*.

39–40 *The bird . . . on wing* It was believed that the bird of paradise had no feet and spent its life in flight.

43 *Tiresias* the blind prophet of Thebes.

46 *tinkling rhyme* Milton scorned 'the jingling sound of like endings' in his prefatory note.

47 *Town-Bays* Buckingham had presented Dryden under the name of Bayes in his comedy, *The Rehearsal* (1672).

49 *bushy points* tasselled fastening for hose.

50 *tag* add rhyme to blank verse.

51 *transported by the mode* carried away by the fashion.

52 *And while . . . must commend* the rhyme demands the weaker of the two italicized verbs.

54 *number . . . measure* an allusion to Wisdom 11: 20: 'thou hast ordered all things in measure, and number, and weight.'

THE FIRST ANNIVERSARY OF THE GOVERNMENT UNDER HIS HIGHNESS THE LORD PROTECTOR

This poem was first published anonymously in a quarto pamphlet in January 1655 by Thomas Newcomb, the government printer. It was one of the poems cancelled from the 1681 folio and subsequently printed among the addenda to the third volume of Thompson's edition. Although Waller's name was attached to it in a seventeenth-century manuscript in the Bodleian Library (Eng. poet. e. 4), and also in volume IV of *Poems on Affairs of State* (1707) and *Poems on Several Occasions* (1717), Marvell's authorship is confirmed by its original inclusion in the folio and its appearance among the manuscript additions to the Bodleian copy (Eng. poet. d. 49). The version in Bod. MS Eng. poet. e. 4 omits ll. 33–6, 65–6 and 145–8 and contains a good many variants, only one of which has been adopted in preference to the 1655 and folio readings.

Marvell wrote the poem towards the end of 1654 to celebrate the achievements of the first year of the Protectorate, which had been instituted on 16 December 1653. At the time he was still employed by Cromwell as tutor to William Dutton. Since it was printed by Newcomb and advertised in a government journal, *Mercurius Politicus* (no. 240, 11–18 January 1655), it was evidently issued with official sanction as a propaganda piece for the regime.

12 *jewel . . . ring* i.e. as the sun is the brightest of the heavenly bodies in the zodiac.

16 *Longer . . . Saturn* Saturn had the longest orbit of any planet known to Marvell and its astrological influence was unpropitious.

17 *Platonic years* A Platonic year, estimated at between 26,000 and 36,000 solar years, was the time it took the planets and constellations to complete a cycle and return to their original positions.

20 *China clay* Chinese porcelain was believed to be prepared by burying the clay for long periods.

23 *some* i.e. some king (singular).

30 *This common enemy* i.e. their own subjects.

33–4 *neither build . . . raise* David was instructed by God to leave the building of the temple in Jerusalem to his son Solomon. See 1 Chronicles 28.

41–2 *(image-like) . . . hourly bell* i.e. like mechanical figures on a clock.

43–4 *Nor more . . . viol's strings* they make no more practical contribution to the business of life than the decorative head of an instrument to the music produced by the strings.

47–8 *Learning . . . higher sphere* Cromwell's commerce with heavenly things taught him to achieve a harmony in the state comparable to that of the music of the spheres.

49 *Amphion* The walls of Thebes rose in response to his music.

50 *the god* Hermes, who gave Amphion a golden lyre.

58 *stops* positions on the strings.

68 *ruling Instrument* Cromwell was made Protector by an Instrument of Government.

69–70 *While tedious . . . went back* an allusion to the failure to devise a workable constitution to replace the monarchy.
hack to break a note in music.

89–90 *crossest spirits . . . thwart* those most antagonistic to each other contribute to the tension of opposing forces which sustains the structure.
contignation joining together of beams.

97 *senate free* parliament.

98 *roof's protecting weight* i.e. the authority of the Protector.

99–100 *When . . . him round* an allusion to Archimedes' remark that he could move the earth if he had somewhere to place his foot.

101 *aspects* astrological influences, for good or ill.

106 *Kiss . . . angry Son* See Psalms 2: 11: 'Kiss the son, lest he be angry.'

108 *holy oracles* biblical prophecies. Lines 105–58 contain various allusions to the apocalyptic prophecies in Daniel 7–8 and Revelations 12–20 about the days preceding the Last Judgement.

110 *latter days* the days leading up to the Last Judgement. See Daniel 10: 14.

113 *the Whore* the Whore of Babylon (Revelations 17: 5),

interpreted by Protestants as the Roman Church.

123 *prevents the east* anticipates daybreak.

128 *the Monster* the Beast of the Apocalypse. See Daniel 7: 19 and Revelations 17: 3.

140 *the latest day* the Day of Judgement.

151–2 *stars still . . . horrid flail* an allusion to Revelations 12: 3–4.

153 *suspend* i.e. at the time of the Flood.

156 *th' elected* men chosen by God.

161–2 *mother . . . pedigree* Cromwell's mother was in her ninety-fourth year when she died in November 1654.

171–2 *conspiracies . . . prophecies* There were several plots against Cromwell's life by Levellers and Fifth Monarchists.

178 *Hurried . . . thee* an allusion to an accident in September 1654 when a coach being driven by Cromwell overturned in Hyde Park.

182 *yearly* anniversary.

184 *purling ore* gold or silver thread used for embroidery.

191 *poor beasts* i.e. the coach-horses.

203 *panic* i.e. from the natural surroundings (the word is derived from Pan, the god of Nature).

205–6 *It seemed . . . the sphere* an allusion to Ptolemaic astronomy, which placed the earth at the centre of a system of concentric spheres, one of which carried the sun.

215–20 *thee triumphant . . . rent* an allusion to Elijah's translation to heaven and his son Elisha's rending of his garments. See 2 Kings 2: 11–13.

233–8 *Till . . . wet for King* an allusion to the rain which Elijah obtained for Israel in the time of King Ahab. See 1 Kings 18: 43–5.

249–56 *When Gideon . . . his son* Cromwell's career parallels that of Gideon, who delivered Israel from an invasion led by two kings, punished those who refused him aid by destroying the tower at Penuel and scourging the elders of Succoth with briars, and declined the offer of hereditary kingship. See Judges 8: 1–23.

257–62 *Thou with . . . cedar's top* an allusion to Jotham's story of how the olive, the fig and the vine refused the crown and the bramble accepted it with a warning, 'let fire come out of the bramble, and devour the cedars of Lebanon'. See Judges 9: 7–15.

262 *Had quickly . . . top* an allusion to the egalitarian policies of the Levellers.

263–4 *Therefore . . . didst awe* Cromwell used his personal power to put down the Levellers and other extremist groups.

269 *Tritons* sea gods.

270 *corposants* balls of fire sometimes seen about the masts of ships during a storm.

281 *bounders* limits.

283 *like Noah's eight* Cromwell, with his wife and six children, is compared to Noah's family.

286–8 *thou but . . . its wine* i.e. unlike Noah, whose misuse of wine is recorded in Genesis 9: 20–1.

291–2 *such as . . . nakedness* When he was drunk Noah revealed his nakedness to his son Ham. See Genesis 9: 21–3.

293 *Yet such . . . rage* Ham's descendants were cursed by Noah (Genesis 9: 24–5), and Marvell likens them to the extremist sects of his own day.

297 *fifth sceptre* an allusion to the Fifth Monarchists, who looked to the establishment of a kingdom of the saints that would succeed the four kingdoms prophesied in Daniel 7: 17–18.

298 *quake* a glance at the Quakers.

302–4 *their religion . . . reign* Sectarians claiming inspiration are likened to Mahomet, whose revelations occurred during epileptic fits.

305 *Feake and Simpson* Fifth Monarchists who were imprisoned in 1654 for preaching sedition.

307 *rant* a glance at another sect, the Ranters.

308 *Were't . . . unmoved tulipant* if only because you (like the Quakers) refused to uncover your head.
tulipant turban.

310 *Alcoraned* turned into a holy book (like the Koran).

311–12 *Accursed locusts . . . pit* an allusion to the locusts sent by Apollyon from the 'bottomless pit' to plague men not sealed by God. See Revelations 9: 1–11.

313 *Munser's rest* the remnant of the Anabaptist movement, founded by Thomas Münzer.

316 *points* for fastening hose.

319 *act . . . Eve* go naked, like the Adamists.

331 *blacks* black drapes to indicate mourning.

350 *both wars* the Civil War and the First Dutch War of 1652–4.

352 *their state* This reading has been adopted from Bodleian MS Eng. poet. e. 4 in preference to the reading 'our state' found in both the 1655 text and the 1681 folio. The allusion is obviously to the constitutional changes in England under Cromwell.

355–6 *proceed . . . breed* Solan geese were thought to be generated from leaves falling into water.

362 *brazen hurricanes* bronze cannons.

366 *wat'ry leaguers* forces besieging by sea.

381 *enchased* inlaid.

384 *falchion* sword.

our knots unties an allusion to Alexander's cutting of the Gordian knot, which made him master of Asia.

398 *So that . . . our end* provided that my failure in praise is matched by the failure of the foreign king's hope to see Cromwell dead.

401–2 *as the Angel . . . heal* Cromwell's interventions in politics are likened to the periodic troubling of the waters in the pool of Bethesda, which gave them curative powers. See John 5: 2–4.

A POEM UPON THE DEATH OF HIS LATE HIGHNESS THE LORD PROTECTOR

This poem was cancelled from all known copies of the 1681 folio except the one in the British Library, which contains only ll. 1–184. It was printed among the addenda to the third volume of Thompson's edition. The present text is based on the manuscript version added to the Bodleian copy of the folio, which is substantially the same as Thompson's text.

Cromwell died on 3 September 1658, and his embalmed body was displayed in state for some time. Marvell, as one of the Latin secretaries to the Council of State, took part in the funeral procession on 23 November, along with John Milton and John Dryden. (See W. Arthur Turner, 'Milton, Marvell and "Dradon" at Cromwell's funeral', *PQ*, 28 (1949), 320–3.) On 20 January 1659, a book which was to contain verse tributes to Cromwell by Marvell, Dryden and Sprat was entered in the Stationers' Register, but when it eventually appeared, an elegy by Waller was substituted for Marvell's poem.

4 *seen the period* foreseen the completion.

18 *what he least affected* i.e. his success as a soldier.

21 *fatal writ* death warrant.

30 *Eliza* Elizabeth Claypole, Cromwell's second daughter, who died on 6 August 1658.

31 *taken with* enchanted by.

45 *not knowing* not by rational knowledge.

53–4 *A silent fire . . . racks* Cromwell suffers to see Eliza, an image of himself, burning with fever. The allusion is to the practice in witchcraft of melting a wax effigy of an intended victim.

62 *feigns* disguises.

63 *their skills* what they know.

67–8 *Eliza's purple . . . worn* an adaptation of the story of Scylla, who killed her father Nisus by cutting off the lock of hair on which his life depended.

79–80 *mournful swans . . . pelicans* Swans were believed to sing as they approached death, halcyons to calm the winter seas, and pelicans to feed their young with their own blood.

96 *humour* fluid.

112 *what pangs . . . cost* There was a great storm on the day before Cromwell died.

124 *hecatomb* public sacrifice.

127 *Numbers . . . pains unknown* There was a fever epidemic in the spring and summer of 1658.

128 *not to* i.e. in order not to.

130 *so exactly mixed* i.e. in Cromwell, the perfectly balanced man.

139 *cast* calculated (an astrological term).

144 *Twice . . . crowned* He died on the anniversary of his victories at Dunbar in 1650 and at Worcester in 1651.

146 *through . . . ending war* He crossed the Severn to defeat the Scottish army and so end Charles's attempt to claim his father's throne.

154 *Gave chase . . . coast* A Spanish force led by the Prince de Ligne was defeated in Flanders by an Anglo-French army in September 1658.

156 *laurel* symbol of victory.

162 *those of Moses . . . eyes* The site of Moses' burial was unknown. See Deuteronomy 34: 6.

169 *supplies* i.e. of salt water.

173–4 *Who planted . . . Indian ore* Dunkirk was captured from the Spaniards in 1658 and Jamaica in 1655.

177 *Arthur's deeds* King Arthur was one of the Nine Worthies.

178 *Confessor* i.e. King Edward the Confessor.

180 *manned* brought to manhood.

187 *Preston's field* where Cromwell defeated the Scots in 1648.

188 *impregnable Clonmel* Cromwell had failed to take this Irish stronghold in 1650.

189–90 *where . . . sea between* Lt-Col. Roger Fenwick was mortally wounded at the battle of the Dunes in the campaign to take Dunkirk.

190 *yet hence . . . prevailed* The battle took place on a day of public prayer called by Cromwell and the Council of State.

192 *Since . . . stayed* an allusion to God's granting of Joshua's request. See Joshua 10: 12–14.

202 *The first . . . name* His great grandfather, Richard Williams, had adopted the family surname out of love for his maternal uncle, Thomas Cromwell, Earl of Essex.

203–4 *But within . . . unto all* but whereas friendship is narrowly personal, his affection extended to all mankind.

213 *nature's tribute* i.e. death.

215 *cast* diagnosed.

226 *And you . . . task* and only Heaven has the power to keep you in order (since you resist human laws, l. 222). In ll. 221–6, Marvell is criticizing those who were too self-righteous to accept Cromwell's authority.

234 *It seemed . . . gate* He seemed like the god of war himself bursting open the gates of the temple of Janus to signify battle.

242 *ungirt David . . . dance* an allusion to David's expression of his zeal for God. See 2 Samuel 6: 14–22.

245 *Francisca* Frances, Cromwell's youngest daughter.

259 *feign* imagine.

264 *honoured wreaths* A garland of oak leaves was the award for civic achievement.

275–6 *But when . . . how great* Being blinded by envy, we acknowledge the true stature of great men only when they are dead.

282 *Cynthia* the moon.

287 *pitch* height.

305 *Richard* Richard Cromwell was proclaimed Protector in succession to his father, but resigned in April 1659.

317 *enchased* adorned.

THE LAST INSTRUCTIONS TO A PAINTER

This poem was probably first printed in *The Third Part of the Collection of Poems on Affairs of State* (1689) as 'Marvell's further instructions to a painter', although a version published in the form of a pamphlet, which survives in a single copy lacking a title-page in the Free Library of Philadelphia, may date from as early as 1669 (Legouis). It was reprinted in the 1697 edition of *Poems on Affairs of State*, with the omission of ll. 649–96, which constitute the nucleus of 'The loyal Scot', another poem attributed to Marvell. A seventeenth-century manuscript copy of the poem survives in the Osborne Collection at Yale. The present text is based on the manuscript version added to the Bodleian copy of the folio. This supplies the proper names indicated only by initial and final letters in the 1689 text and appends the date 'September 4th 1667' to the title.

The purpose of the poem is to expose to critical scrutiny the parliamentary proceedings of 1666–7 and the mismanagement of the war against Holland, which had culminated in the humiliating destruction and capture of English warships during an audacious raid up the Thames and Medway by a Dutch fleet in June 1667. It was part of a campaign conducted inside and outside Parliament against the Court party and in particular the administration of the Earl of Clarendon. Charles II bowed to mounting pressure and Clarendon was dismissed from his office as Lord Chancellor on 30 August; the House of Commons impeached him on 10 October; and he fled to France on 29 November. Since Marvell refers only to the first of these events, the poem was presumably completed during September 1667, as the Bodleian MS indicates.

'The last instructions to a painter' is one of a series of satires prompted by Edmund Waller's panegyric on the Duke of York, 'Instructions to a painter, for the drawing of the posture and progress of His Majesty's Forces at sea, under the command of His Highness-Royal: together with the battle and victory obtained over the Dutch, June 3, 1665'. A 'Second advice to a painter, for drawing the history of our naval business' had appeared in December 1666, and three more satirical developments of Waller's conceit were added in the course of 1667. Marvell's name has been associated with all of them, and Lord claims the second and third 'Advices' as authentic attributions on the grounds of their inclusion among the manuscript additions to the Bodleian copy of the folio. Margoliouth and Legouis, however, accept only 'The last instructions' as undoubtedly the work of Marvell. Further information about the genre can be found in Mary Tom Osborne's *Advice-to-a-Painter Poems, 1633–1856: An Annotated Finding List* (Austin, University of Texas, 1949) and Earl Miner's 'The "Poetic Picture, Painted Poetry" of *The Last Instructions to a Painter*', *MP*, 63 (1966), 288–94.

1–2 *After two . . . wait* A subject usually sat three times for a portrait.

6 *without a fleet* The fleet had been laid up in May 1667.

7 *sign-post* i.e. an inn sign.

9 *antique* with a play on the word 'antic', meaning grotesque.

10 *alley-roof* the ceiling of a bowling-alley at a tavern.

11 *tools* male generative organs. Lines 9–11 refer to obscene graffiti.

14 *in plumes* an allusion to feather-pictures made in the Americas.

15 *score out* mark out, sketch.

compendious tiny.

16–18 *With Hooke . . . staff* a complex allusion to Robert Hooke's drawing of a louse climbing along a human hair in his volume of microscopic studies, *Micrographia* (1665), which is likened to the recently appointed Comptroller of the Household, Lord Clifford, carrying his white staff of office.

19 *pencil* brush.

21 *painter* i.e. Protogenes. The story that follows derives from Pliny's *Natural History* XXXV. 10 (36).

cloth canvas.

29 *St Albans* Henry Jermyn, Earl of St Albans, who was ambassador at the French court.

32 *salt* lecherous.

33 *drayman* man who drives a brewer's cart.

34 *chine* spine or back.

36 *Bacon* Francis Bacon, author of *The Advancement of Learning*, became Viscount St Albans in 1621.

38 *play . . . treat* Jermyn was a notorious gambler and was Charles II's agent in negotiating the Treaty of Breda, which brought the Dutch war to a close in July 1667.

39–40 *no commission . . . supply* Marvell implies that the purpose of St Albans' mission was not publicly acknowledged because Charles wanted a further supply of money to be voted by Parliament for the continuation of the war.

41 *St James's lease* Jermyn obtained a grant of land in Pall Mall in 1664 and planned St James's Square.

42–4 *Whose breeches ... plenipotence* Although he lacks an official commission, he will be able to produce ample evidence of his authority from his breeches. A gross insult is intended, whether this is an allusion to Jermyn's supposed affair with Queen Henrietta Maria (Lord and Donno) or to the size of his bottom (Legouis).

45 *the Most Christian* i.e. Louis XIV.

46 *St Germain, St Alban* a play on Jermyn's name and title, and possibly the quarter of Paris in which he stayed.

49 *Her Highness* Anne Hyde, daughter of Clarendon and wife of the Duke of York.

50 *Newcastle's wife* Margaret Cavendish, Duchess of Newcastle, who published a number of works on natural philosophy.

52 *an experiment . . . crown* Since Charles II had no heir, Anne Hyde's children by the Duke of York would be directly in line for the throne.

53 *engine* device.

55–6 *And found . . . endured* She gave birth to a son two months after her marriage to the Duke of York in 1660.

57–8 *Crowther . . . Royal Society* Dr Joseph Crowther had performed the marriage ceremony, and the Duke of York was a charter member of the newly formed Royal Society.

60 *glassen Dukes* the two fragile sons of this marriage, who died in infancy.

61 *breath of fame* i.e. with distended cheeks, like allegorical pictures of Fame blowing a trumpet.

62 *that 'sparagus . . . proclaim* i.e. like a street-seller of asparagus crying her wares.

65–8 *Express her . . . cacao* an allusion to the recent death of Lady Denham, the Duke of York's mistress, allegedly brought about by poison administered in a cup of chocolate. It was believed that china vessels would not endure contact with poison.

72 *fawns* the young of an animal.

75 *Sidney's disgrace* Henry Sidney, the Duchess's Master of

the Horse, had been dismissed by the Duke of York in a fit of jealousy.

79 *Castlemaine* Barbara Villiers, Countess of Castlemaine, one of Charles II's mistresses.

98 *fob* pocket.

101 *Porter's Den* the Porter's lodge, where servants were chastised.

102 *Jermyn* a nephew of St Albans, one of the Countess's lovers.

103–4 *Alexander . . . Apelles, give* Alexander gave Campaspe to Apelles, who had fallen in love with her while painting her portrait.

105 *tables* a folding board on which backgammon was played.

106 *the men* i.e. the backgammon pieces.

109 *tric-trac* a variety of backgammon.

114 *Turner* Sir Edward Turner, Speaker of the House of Commons.

116 *strike the die* throw the dice fraudulently.

120 *recreate* refresh. The painter Rubens was more than once employed on diplomatic business.

121 *the close Cabal* a committee drawn from members of the Privy Council.

123–4 *secretly . . . squeeze* See note to ll. 39–40.

126 *Goodrick . . . Paston* Sir John Goodrick and Sir Robert Paston, supporters of the court in the House of Commons.

129 *Bennet* Henry Bennet, Baron Arlington.

130 *Excise* an unpopular tax on commodities. During October 1666, the House of Commons was divided over the means of raising the large sum it had voted to prosecute the war against Holland. While some favoured a land tax, the Court party tried to impose an excise on domestic goods. The attempt was abandoned on 8 November. Marvell's account of the protracted debate in ll. 147–306 is compressed in the interests of drama.

136 *cassowar* the cassowary, an ostrich-like bird remarkable for its capacity to devour anything.

138 *indented* both serrated (with teeth) and authorized by a

legal agreement (as farmers of excise were).

142–6 *Her . . . mongrel beast* Marvell's mock-heroic account of the generation of Excise derives from the description of Satan, Sin and Death in Book II of Milton's *Paradise Lost*, which was published in 1667.

143 *Black Birch* John Birch, who was Auditor after the Restoration, had been an excise official under the Commonwealth.

151 *wittols* complacent cuckolds.

154 *Denham* husband of the woman referred to in the note to ll. 65–8.

156 *Ashburnham* John Ashburnham, believed to have betrayed Charles I to the Governor of the Isle of Wight when he fled from Hampton Court in 1647.

160 *Stew'rd* Probably Sir Nicholas Steward, one of the two Chamberlains of the Exchequer.

162 *Wood . . . Cane* Sir Henry Wood, Clerk of the Spicery to Charles I (see l. 166), and as Clerk Comptroller of the Board of the Green Cloth now responsible for examining the accounts and for keeping order in the palace, hence the appropriate armorial bearings of horn and cane, symbolic of plenty and discipline.

167 *Headless St Denys* patron saint of France, often depicted carrying his severed head in his hands. The allusion is prompted by Wood's 'posture strange' described in ll. 163–6.

168 *French martyrs* implying that Wood was a victim of syphilis (the 'French disease').

169 *as used* as was customary.

170 *Fox* Sir Stephen Fox, Paymaster-General.

173–5 *Progers . . . Love's squire* Edward Progers and Henry Brouncker, procurers respectively for the king and the Duke of York.

178 *to teal . . . bull* a play on the name of John Bulteel, secretary to Clarendon. The phrase implies that they are gluttons.

180 *Wren* Matthew Wren, secretary to Clarendon.

181–2 *Charlton . . . Mitre troop* Sir Job Charlton, Chief Justice of

Chester and the King's Sergeant, whose coif, or white lawyer's cap, might strike fear into either frequenters of the Mitre (a tavern) or members of the Mitre Court, formerly one of the Inns of Court.

186 *Finch* Sir Heneage Finch, Solicitor-General.

Thurland Sir Edward Thurland, solicitor to the Duke of York.

187 *troop of privilege* those who evade punishment for debt by claiming parliamentary privilege.

188 *Trelawny* Sir Jonathan Trelawny, employed in the Prize Office.

193 *For chimney's . . . Sir Pool* Sir Courtenay Pool was associated with the unpopular tax (Chimney Money) of two shillings on every hearth, imposed in 1662.

195 *privateers* here applied to those MPs who served their own interests by presenting private bills.

197–8 *Higgons . . . Act* Sir Thomas Higgons had recently introduced a bill to recover a large sum of money from the estate of his dead wife, the widow of the Earl of Essex.

199 *Sir Frederick and Sir Solomon* supporters of the Court party, probably Sir Frederick Hyde and Sir Solomon Swale.

200 *politics* i.e. politicians.

203 *Carteret* Sir George Carteret, Treasurer of the Navy.

206 *Talbot* There were three Talbots in the Commons.

207 *Duncombe* Sir John Duncombe, Commissioner of the Ordnance.

projectors speculators.

208 *Fitz-harding . . . Beef* Sir Charles Berkeley, Viscount Fitzharding, Treasurer of the Household with responsibility for the Yeomen of the Guard (i.e. the Beefeaters).

212 *Apsley and Brod'rick* Sir Allen Apsley and Sir Allen Broderick, Treasurer to the Duke of York and agent of Clarendon respectively, heavy drinkers and boon companions.

213 *Powell . . . not ride* Sir Richard Powell, Gentleman of the Horse to the Duchess of York.

214 *welt'ring* reeling.

218 *Cornb'ry* Henry Hyde, Lord Cornbury, eldest son of Clarendon.

220 *Tothill Field* where troops were drilled.

221–4 *Not the first . . . disperse* George Monck, Duke of Albemarle, had narrowly avoided losing his ship in a naval engagement with the Dutch, 'the sea-cod', in June 1666. Sir Thomas Tomkins had opposed the maintenance of the standing army that had been raised in the spring of 1667 to meet the threat from Holland. The fashionable footwear and head-gear of the gallants of the standing army are glanced at contemptuously in the references to 'cork' and 'feather-men'.

225–8 *the two Coventrys . . . Will the Wit* Henry and Sir William Coventry, sons of the Lord Keeper. The first had 'nought to lose' because he had just returned from an embassy to Sweden and had no public office; the second 'had much' to lose because he was Commissioner of the Treasury and of the Navy, both lucrative posts.

233–4 *They, that . . . invade* When the Dutch sailed up the Thames in June 1667, much of the English fleet was laid up in the expectation of peace, which Henry Coventry was helping to negotiate at Breda.

236 *The Speaker* Sir Edward Turner.

245 *Strangeways* Sir John Strangeways, who several times acted as teller against the government in divisions on financial matters.

249 *Cocles* Publius Horatius Cocles, the Roman hero who defended a bridge single-handed.

255–6 *Temple . . . Solicitor* Sir Richard Temple, a leader of the Country party, who had successfully opposed the importation of Irish cattle and bested the Solicitor-General in the debate.

257–8 *Seymour . . . the field* Edward Seymour, who was instrumental in recalling the monopolistic patent granted to the Corporation of the Canary Company.

259–60 *Whorwood . . . giant Mordaunt* Brome Whorwood had been active in the impeachment of John, Viscount Mordaunt, for illegally imprisoning the father of a girl who would not yield to him.

261 *Williams* probably Colonel Henry Williams, who spoke on financial matters.

262 *Lovelace ... the cane* John Lovelace had opposed the Hearth Tax.

263–4 *Waller ... naval fight* Edmund Waller, the panegyrist whose poem on the Duke of York's victory had given rise to the advice-to-a-painter satires.

265–6 *How'rd ... Montezumes* Sir Robert Howard, who collaborated with Dryden in writing a heroic play about Montezuma, *The Indian-Queen* (1664).

275–6 *Orlando ... his lance* The hero of Ariosto's poem, *Orlando Furioso*, once speared six enemies at a time.

280 *toback* i.e. tobacco.

281 *recruit* reinforcements.

287 *A gross ... gentry* the Country party, who proposed a land tax rather than the general excise.

298–9 *Garway ... Lee* William Garway, Sir Thomas Littleton and Sir Thomas Lee all supported the land tax.

301–2 *Sandys ... Satan's nose* Colonel Samuel Sandys represented Worcestershire in Parliament, and St Dunstan, who is often depicted gripping the devil's nose with a pair of pincers, was once Bishop of Worcester.

313 *seamen's clamour* Seamen rioted over arrears of pay in December 1666.

328 *beg in public* Charles II appealed to Parliament for funds in January 1667.

336 *The House prorogued* on 8 February 1667.

337 *Aeson* the father of Jason, whose youth was renewed by Medea's magic brew.

342 *mortal chocolate* See note to ll. 65–8.

345 *the sad tree* the night jasmine of India, which loses its brightness during the day.

349 *within ... tower* Mordaunt was Constable of Windsor Castle. See note to ll. 259–60.

356 *fulminant* thundering.

357–8 *First Buckingham . . . fell* George Villiers, Duke of Buckingham, a leading opponent of Clarendon, was charged with treasonable practices in February 1667.

359 *the twelve Commons* Twelve of the commissioners appointed in March to manage the finances of the war were drawn from the House of Commons.

360 *roll . . . stone* perform an unending task, like that imposed on Sisyphus of rolling a huge stone up a hill.

361 *braved* vaunted.

367 *The Count* i.e. St Albans.

369 *two ambassadors* Henry Coventry and Denzil Holles were sent to Breda in May to negotiate with the Dutch.

371 *Cyclops* one-eyed giants who forged thunderbolts for Jove.

375–86 *From Greenwich . . . hooting by* Marvell describes a folk custom, known as a 'Skimmington ride', in which browbeaten husbands and their 'brawny' wives were publicly ridiculed. One took place at Greenwich on 10 June 1667.

391 *quick* living.

395–6 *So Holland . . . ride* Holland is likened to the wife, and England to the husband, riding in humiliation before their neighbours.

398 *Isle of Candy* Canvey Island, in the Thames estuary.

399 *Bab May* Baptist May, Keeper of the Privy Purse.
Arlington i.e. the Bennet of l. 129.

401–2 *Modern geographers . . . fought* May and Arlington confuse 'Candy' with Candia (Crete), which the Venetians had been defending against the Turks since 1645.

403–4 *While the . . . we've none* In 1665 the English fleet failed to press home its success; in 1666 it was split between Albemarle and Rupert; and in 1667 most of it was out of commission.

406 *Pilgrim Palmer* Roger, husband of the Countess of Castlemaine, went abroad after his wife became the king's mistress – hence the reference to 'the bull's horn'.

408 *Pasiphae* mother by a bull of the Minotaur of Crete.

409 *Morice* Sir William Morice, joint Secretary of State with Arlington.

by the post Arlington was Postmaster-General.

418 *theirs* i.e. their money, which was safe overseas in the event of a Dutch invasion.

420 *mure up* wall up.

422 *Mordaunt, new obliged* Proceedings against him were dropped when Parliament was prorogued.

424 *London's flame* the Great Fire of 1666.

425 *The Bloodworth-Chancellor* Sir Thomas Bloodworth was the ineffectual Lord Mayor of London during the Great Fire. Clarendon's behaviour now is similarly indecisive.

431 *Dolman's disobedient* Colonel Thomas Dolman, English commander of the Dutch land-troops, had ignored a parliamentary order to give himself up in 1665.

435 *prove* try.

437 *De Witt* first minister of the United Provinces.

Ruyter Dutch admiral.

441 *near relation* an allusion to St Albans' rumoured marriage to Queen Henrietta Maria, Louis XIV's aunt.

442 *character* credentials.

443 *gravelled* perplexed.

448 *Seneque* i.e. Seneca, the Roman moral philosopher.

450 *Harry Excellent* i.e. Henry Coventry, one of the English negotiators.

454 *as the look adultery* an allusion to Matthew 5: 28: 'Whosoever looketh on a woman to lust after her hath committed adultery with her already in his heart.'

460 *infecta re* with the business uncompleted.

463–4 *The Dutch . . . commandment* This couplet is in the 1689 edition, but is omitted from the version in the Bodleian MS.

shent reproached.

eleventh commandment i.e. as set out in ll. 453–4.

467–8 *So Spain . . . a Queen* an allusion to Clarendon's part in the negotiations that led to Charles II's marriage to Catherine of Braganza.

471 *banned* cursed.

480 *To raise . . . defence* Twelve infantry regiments were mustered, but many feared the prospect of a standing army, which could be used to enforce the government's will as well as for defence.

488 *Myrmidons* according to legend, a warlike race created from ants. In Marvell's day the term was applied to hired ruffians.

493 *a proclamation* issued on 18 June 1667 to support credit.

494 *banquiers banquerouts* i.e. bankrupt bankers, who had lent money to the king.

495–7 *minion imps . . . vein* Witches were believed to give suck to the devil by means of teats in secret parts of their bodies.

499 *kingdom's farm* i.e. farming of taxes.

503 *scrip* a scrap of paper or a small bag.

510 *Monck* i.e. Albemarle.

513 *ashen wood* the versatile wood of the ash tree.

514 *Herb John* a tasteless herb.

521–2 *Soon then . . . dispose* These lines appear to mean that if Albemarle were removed, Clarendon would have a free hand in establishing a standing army under his own control.

539 *red flags* displayed by the Dutch in time of battle.

547 *Aeolus* ruler of the winds.

549 *Tritons* sea deities.

550 *Sheppey Isle* at the mouth of the Thames.

560 *at Sheerness . . . sides* The Dutch fleet bombarded Sheerness on 10 June.

561 *Spragge* Vice-Admiral Sir Edward Spragge, in command at Sheerness.

564 *not tenantable* because of its poor condition.

572 *Chatham* the navy's main arsenal.

586 *frail chain* a protective boom across the river.

603–4 *their fellows . . . clutch* English seamen were among the crews of the Dutch ships.

605 *Legge* William Legge, Lieutenant-General of the Ordnance.

607 *Upnor Castle* 2 miles below Chatham, but inadequately supplied with munitions.

611 *Royal Charles* the ship in which Charles II had returned to England in 1660 and the largest vessel in the English fleet.

616 *Crowned ... name* Formerly the *Naseby*, it had been renamed after the Restoration.

631 *Daniel* Sir Thomas Daniel, whose company of Foot Guards should have defended one of the ships that was destroyed.

636 *lac* crimson pigment.

642 *Daniel . . . lion's den* an allusion to the story of the biblical Daniel. See Daniel 6: 10–23.

647–8 *Three children . . . Abednego* an allusion to the companions of Daniel who survived a fiery furnace. See Daniel 3: 13–27.

649 *Douglas* Archibald Douglas, who commanded a company of a Scottish regiment charged with the defence of the *Royal Oak*.

655 *Seine* He had served in France with his regiment.

666 *birding* shooting.

678 *tries . . . sheets* Douglas was, in fact, married.

695 *Oeta and Alcides* Alcides (Hercules) was burnt on Mount Oeta.

698 *Loyal London ... burns* The man-of-war, *London*, was blown up in 1665; the city of London was burnt in 1666; now the *Loyal London* follows its namesakes.

702 *the ships ... to dive* Some ships were scuttled to prevent them from being fired.

712 *merchant-men . . . drown* Ships had been sunk in the Thames to block the passage up to London.

715 *howl* This is the reading of the 1689 edition and the Bodleian MS, which Margoliouth glosses as a north-country form of 'hollow'. It was emended to 'hole' in the 1697 edition. Lord and Donno gloss it as 'hold'.

722 *lest navigable* i.e. lest it should be navigable.

735–6 *feared Hebrew . . . scorn* an allusion to Samson. See Judges 16: 25.

761–4 *Court . . . Ruyter those* Frances Stuart, who had married the Duke of Richmond, was the model for Britannia on coins.

The motto *Quattuor maria vindico* (I defend the four seas) appeared on farthings of the period.

765 *relish discontent* gratify the discontented.

767 *Pett* Peter Pett, Commissioner of the Navy at Chatham, the chosen scapegoat for the disaster.

772 *treated . . . at Bergen* An opportunity to attack a Dutch fleet at Bergen in 1665 was lost while the English commander negotiated with the Danes.

775 *prevented* anticipated.

784 *Fanatic* i.e. sectarian, a term of abuse applied to Pett because he had served under the Commonwealth.

789 *one boat . . . sent* i.e. with his own household goods in.

793–4 *Southampton dead . . . share* Sir John Duncombe was a member of the commission put in charge of the Treasury when the Earl of Southampton, Lord High Treasurer, died in May 1667.

797 *petre* i.e. saltpetre, a reference to his association with the Ordnance.

799 *a corn* a grain of gunpowder.

801 *no chimneys* an allusion to the Hearth Tax.

805–6 *brother May . . . obey* Baptist May, Keeper of the Privy Purse, was his brother-in-law.

811 *Sheldon* Gilbert Sheldon, Archbishop of Canterbury.

813 *With Boynton . . . sweet* Katherine Boynton and Jane Middleton were Court beauties. Marvell alludes to the Archbishop's scandalous reputation.

816 *Convocation* ecclesiastical assembly.

820 *Harry came post* i.e. Henry Coventry, from Breda.

826 *Let them . . . again* Parliament met and was rapidly prorogued again at the end of July.

828 *vest* a garment designed by the king to assert England's independence of Paris in fashion.

833 *adust* scorched.

837 *Turner* the Speaker.

840 *adjourn* until 29 July.

846 *Hereford* Tomkins was a Herefordshire MP.

854 *Expects* awaits.

855 *Ayton* Sir John Ayton, Gentleman Usher of the Black Rod.

866 *mace's brain* an allusion to the symbol of authority placed before the Speaker in the House.

870–2 *But all . . . apron look* The Speaker derived large fees from private bills, and so is imagined sweating like a cook as he watches their progress. The text of the poll bill by which part of the supply was raised was presumably spattered like a cook's apron with amendments.

876 *Court-mushrumps* upstarts.

882 *Norfolk* James Norfolk, Sergeant-at-Arms.

883–4 *Chanticleer . . . Pertelotte* an allusion to Chaucer's tale of the cock and hen.

906 *England or the Peace* i.e. embodied in the allegorical form of a naked woman.

907 *startling* starting.

913 *secure* overconfident (i.e. in its trust of Louis XIV).

918–22 *grandsire Harry . . . does show* His grandfather, Henry IV of France, had been assassinated; his father, Charles I, had been beheaded.

927–8 *At his first . . . designed* Lady Castlemaine, Bennet and Sir William Coventry were Clarendon's chief enemies at Court.

933 *Bristol* George Digby, Earl of Bristol, in whose service Arlington (Bennet) had once been.

935 *Who to . . . betray* Coventry had resigned from his position as secretary to Charles II's brother, the Duke of York.

942 *the Pett* i.e. a scapegoat.

949 *tube* telescope.

953 *trunk* nerve.

959–60 *Kings . . . the way* an allusion to Charles's escape in disguise after the defeat at Worcester in 1651.

968 *to isle . . . isle* i.e. to isolate the king from his people.

UPON SIR ROBERT VINER'S SETTING UP THE KING'S STATUE IN WOOL-CHURCH MARKET

This satire was first printed in *Poems on Affairs of State* (1689) and reprinted in subsequent editions. There are also a number of extant copies in manuscript. It was not attributed to Marvell until Thompson included it in the preface to the first volume of his edition, but its claims to authenticity are strengthened by its presence among the manuscript additions to the Bodleian copy of the 1681 folio. The present text is based on the Bodleian version.

The statue which occasioned the poem was erected on 29 May 1672 by Sir Robert Viner, a city financier. It had originally represented John Sobieski, King of Poland, trampling a Turk beneath the feet of his horse. Viner had the figures altered to the likenesses of Charles II and Cromwell, but the adaptation was so poorly executed that he had the statue covered up for further work to be carried out. Marvell was responsible for a pair of related satires on the bronze equestrian statue of Charles I in Charing Cross and on an imaginary dialogue between the horses of the two monarchs.

3 *advanced* erected.

4 *banker defeated . . . broken* The Exchequer was closed in 1672, and repayments on loans made to the state by the bankers of Lombard Street, including Viner, were not honoured.

8 *He that . . . a wrack* a promise may be repudiated when the circumstances under which it was made no longer exist.

17 *herb-women* their produce was sold in the Wool-church or Stocks Market.

20 *Sir William Peak* Lord Mayor of London in 1667.

24 *Say his Majesty . . . sold* a hint at the payments made to Charles II by Louis XIV under the secret Treaty of Dover.

26 *Dutch . . . War* Abusive pictures were among the reasons given for the declaration of war against Holland in 1672.

32 *in gold* Viner was a goldsmith.

37 *Blood* Colonel Thomas Blood, who attempted to steal the crown jewels in 1671.

38 *to Clayton's . . . masquerade* Sir Robert Clayton, Sheriff of London, entertained the king at his house in 1672.

40 *Counter* a debtors' prison.

42 *jackpudding* mountebank's buffoon.

44 *clouts* rags.

47–8 *To express . . . born* The *Royal James* blew up at a naval battle on 28 May 1672, an event reported on the following day, which was the anniversary of Charles's birth and restoration and also the day on which the statue was unveiled.

50 *spankers* gold coins.

51 *the Indies . . . enrich* An attack on the Dutch Smyrna fleet in March 1672, before the declaration of war, had failed to secure the rich prizes hoped for.

THE REHEARSAL TRANSPROS'D: THE FIRST PART

The first part of *The Rehearsal Transpros'd* was printed without licence and with a comic title-page: 'THE / REHEARSAL / TRANSPROS'D: / Or, / Animadversions / Upon a late Book, Intituled, / A PREFACE / SHEWING / *What Grounds there are / of Fears and Jealousies / of* Popery. / / *LONDON*, Printed by *A.B.* for the / Assigns of *John Calvin* and *Theodore / Beza*, at the sign of the Kings Indul- / gence, on the South-side of the *Lake / Leman*. 1672.' A less provocative title-page was substituted in a second issue of the first edition. In the course of 1672, there appeared a pirated edition, claiming to be 'The Second Edition, Corrected', and a genuine second edition, 'The Second Impression, with Additions and Amendments', which contains authoritative variants. Another pirated edition, deriving from the text of the first edition, bears the date 1673. The text of the present extracts is based on a comparison of the first edition and the 'Second Impression'.

Sales of the book were stopped after the clandestine first issue had been distributed, but the king intervened in its favour and the 'Second Impression' came out with the approval of Sir Roger L'Estrange, Surveyor of the Press, although it was never officially entered in the Stationers' Register.

Marvell wrote *The Rehearsal Transpros'd* in direct reply to a work by Samuel Parker entitled *A Preface shewing what grounds there are of Fears and Jealousies of Popery*, which was prefixed to Bishop Bramhall's *Vindication of himself and the Episcopal Clergy from the Presbyterian Charge of Popery* (1672). The author, a former Dissenter, was now an ambitious Anglican clergyman, who had been energetically advancing his career with a series of attacks on the principle of freedom of conscience in religious matters. Although it was the *Preface* which finally provoked Marvell into print, he took the opportunity to expose the doctrine of intolerance presented in two of his opponent's earlier publications: *A Discourse of Ecclesiastical Politie, wherein the authority of the Civil Magistrate over the Consciences of Subjects in matters of Religion is asserted; the Mischiefs and Inconveniences of Toleration are represented, and all Pretences pleaded in behalf of Liberty of Conscience are fully answered* (1669) and *A Defence and Continuation of the Ecclesiastical Politie* (1671). Unfortunately for Parker, Charles II had issued a Declaration of Indulgence on 15 March 1672 which suspended all penal laws against Dissenters and Roman Catholics alike, so that Marvell was able to adopt the role of defender of the king's own policy of toleration against the narrow fanaticism of the spokesman for the Anglican establishment.

Marvell took his title from *The Rehearsal*, a farce by the Duke of Buckingham first performed in December 1671. John Dryden, the author principally satirized in the character of Bayes, had described how his works were derived from other men's books: 'if it be prose put it into verse (but that takes some time); if it be verse, put it into prose.' Another character had retorted: 'Methinks, Mr Bayes, that putting verse into prose should be called transprosing.'

3 *motion* proposal.

4 *Mr Bayes* a character in *The Rehearsal* (see head-note).

10 *distaste* offend his taste.

12 *symbolize* agree in belief and practice.

16–17 *players . . . divisions* probably a reference to the quarrels between the two theatre companies of Restoration London, the King's and the Duke of York's.

18 *personating* representing.

22 *Roscius* Quintus Roscius (*c.* 134–*c.* 62 BC), a Roman comic actor and friend of the great orator, Cicero.

Lacy John Lacy, dramatist and comedian, had played the part of Bayes in *The Rehearsal*.

25 *Caitiff* despicable wretch.

tuant cutting or biting.

26 *irrefragable Doctor* Alexander of Hales (d. 1245), a medieval theologian. Marvell assumes a mock scholarship in citing him as an authority for giving Parker a new name.

32 *whether* whichever.

37 *square-cap* academic cap or mortar-board.

38 *quadrangle* i.e. of a college.

40 *quadrature of the circle* the proverbially difficult problem in mathematics of converting a circle into a square of equal area.

46 *auditory* audience.

48 *a nobleman* Gilbert Sheldon, Archbishop of Canterbury, to whom Parker became chaplain in 1667.

52 *drolling upon* making fun of.

53 *take* be popular.

57 *family* household (Sheldon was unmarried).

64 *complexion* temperament.

70 *Canonical hours* set times of day for prayers.

72 *tippet* a band of silk worn round the neck by ecclesiastics.

76 *shifted himself* changed his garments.

82 *bishop . . . altar* a painting of a bishop of Winchester by Isaac Fuller (1606–72), the altar-piece in the chapel of Magdalen College, Oxford.

82–3 *Maudlin de la Croix* a sixteenth-century abbess of Cordova, supposed to be in league with the devil and noted for her ability to levitate.

90 *speculate . . . baby* contemplate the reflection of his own image.

96 *Animadversions* books of reproof or censure.

102 *observe decorum* keep to the rules for composition.

110 *quality* profession.

114 *the ass . . . fable* i.e. the twenty-fourth fable of Aesop.

116 *ramp* raise the forepaws in the air.
117 *copy* pattern, example.
118 *large* lengthy.
120 *pretended* professed.
126 *Jure Divino* i.e. by divine right.
127 *Jure Regio* i.e. by royal right.
128 *propriety* right of ownership.
129 *Letters of Reprisal* official warrant authorizing the exaction of forcible reparation.
131 *temporalities* material possessions.
136 *Jack Gentleman* a play on several proverbial expressions, suggesting that social distinctions were being challenged.
141 *Dissolution* i.e. of the monasteries.
143 *ecclesiastical loan* The clergy supported Charles I's exaction of a forced loan from his subjects in 1626.
146 *magnificate* increase the status.
147 *three ceremonies . . . law* the three services of Mattins, Evensong and Holy Communion authorized by the Book of Common Prayer.
150 *a second service* i.e. the celebration of Holy Communion after Mattins in a more elaborate manner than that set out in the Prayer Book.
155 *remembrancer* someone appointed to remind another, technically the title of an official of the Court of Exchequer.
156 *uncouth* unattractive.
180 *Arminianism* the teachings of Jacob Arminius, a Dutch theologian who opposed Calvin's doctrine of predestination.
181 *King James* James I of England, who supported the attack on Arminius at the Synod of Dort in 1618.
182 *Barneveldt* Johan van Olden Barneveldt, Grand Pensionary of Holland, was arrested and executed following the Synod of Dort.
193 *shibboleth* a formula for distinguishing those to be accepted or excluded.
Calvinists followers of the teaching of John Calvin, i.e. the Puritan faction within the Church of England.

97 *Montague's Arminian book* Richard Montague's *Appello Caesarem* was at the centre of dissension within the Church of England over Arminianism in the 1620s. The author was appointed to the bishopric of Chichester in 1628.

200 *Manwaring* Roger Manwaring (1590–1653), who rose to be Bishop of St David's in 1635 in spite of being censured by the Lords in Parliament in 1628 for preaching absolutism.

207 *in those days* i.e. in the early years of Charles I's reign.

212 *Sibthorpianism* the anti-Puritan and absolutist opinions of Robert Sibthorpe, vicar of Brackley in Northamptonshire during the 1620s.

213 *conversation* behaviour.

214–15 *dis-Ghibelline . . . from* dissociate themselves from the narrow opinions of. (The Guelphs and Ghibellines of Italy were by-words for factional strife.)

222–3 *propriety* rights of ownership.

229–30 *Bishop Laud . . . Canterbury* William Laud, Bishop of London, became Archbishop of Canterbury in 1633.

251 *the best prince* i.e. Charles I.

268–9 *sent thither . . . upon them* There was a riot when an attempt was made to read services from the English Prayer Book at St Giles's, in Edinburgh, in 1637.

274 *the Cause* the 'good old cause' of Puritan reform of the Church of England.

276–7 *The arms . . . and tears* This saying had been cited in *Eikon Basilike*, the book of meditations supposed to be by Charles I, which was on sale within a few days of his execution in 1649.

285 *that rebellion* i.e. the Civil Wars of the 1640s.

286 *sea-marks* conspicuous objects which serve to warn or guide sailors in navigation.

294 *Independents* forerunners of the Congregationalists.

297 *bead-roll* catalogue (originally a list of persons to be prayed for).

304–5 *Grub Street* a street near Moorfields in London associated with literary hackwork.

306 *Feasts of Love* Marvell is being ironical in the light of the

outcome of these meetings.

309 *Declaration* i.e. the Declaration of Breda, 1660, in which Charles II promised liberty of conscience to his subjects in matters of religion.

311–12 *a conference* the Savoy Conference of 1661, in which a panel of bishops and Puritan divines was commissioned to review the Book of Common Prayer.

322–3 *ingrateful and stigmatical* disagreeable and ignominious.

325 *period* rhetorically constructed sentence.

334 *one memorable day* The Act of Uniformity came into operation on St Bartholomew's Day, 24 August 1662, and resulted in some 2000 dissenting clergymen being removed from their church livings.

341–2 *because all . . . patronage* from Parker's *Preface*, p. C7^{r}.

347 *lease* i.e. of church lands which had been sold during the Commonwealth.

351 *take their places* i.e. in the House of Lords.

352 *new liturgy* i.e. the revised Prayer Book of 1662.

cumulate crown.

353 *Fanatics* Nonconformists. Marvell pointedly adopts the pejorative term used by those whose intolerance he is condemning.

THE REHEARSAL TRANSPROS'D: THE SECOND PART

There were two editions of the second part of *The Rehearsal Transpros'd*, published in 1673 and 1674 with Marvell's name on the title-page. Although it was not entered in the Stationers' Register, there was no attempt to interfere with its publication or sale.

The first part had been answered by a number of hostile pamphlets, but it was *A Reproof to the Rehearsal Transpros'd* by his original antagonist, Samuel Parker, that stung Marvell into entering the arena again. He was also responding, as the title-page informs us, to a letter left for him at a friend's house, signed with the initials J.G. and dated 3 November 1673, which concluded with a threat: 'If thou darest to print or publish any lie or libel against Doctor Parker, by the Eternal God I will cut thy throat.'

5 *envious* open to the envy of others.

27–30 *if his Book . . . own reward* Parker's *Preface*, p. A4^{r}.

32–3 *he must . . . understanding* *Preface*, p. A4^{v}.

38 *credit* reputation.

39–43 *that the . . . under security* This echoes Thomas Hobbes's view, propounded in *Leviathan* (1651), that men banded themselves into societies and developed political institutions for mutual protection.

48 *deodands* chattels confiscated for causing death. See note to l. 17 of 'The nymph complaining for the death of her fawn'.

68 *satyrs* woodland creatures, half-beast and half-man, associated by false etymology with satire.

72–3 *aftermath . . . first herbage* the second crop of grass which grows after the mowing of early summer is never so abundant.

75 *divertisement* amusement.

84 *privateering* A privateer was a private vessel authorized to attack the shipping of a hostile nation.

87 *free-booter* pirate.

92 *rencounter* duel.

108 *vacated* rendered invalid.

110 *conversation* conduct.

115 *wrings* pinches.

116 *billet* wood cut for fuel.

126–7 *their maintenance . . . labour* an allusion to the tithes paid by the laity for the upkeep of the clergy.

130–1 *let the eye . . . connivance* i.e. by winking at it.

148 *expect* wait for.

diocesan bishop in charge of a diocese.

150 *wholesome usage* healthy custom.

158 *praedicari* literally 'to be proclaimed', here with the implication of being declared competent.

circumspection vigilant and cautious observation.

159 *oversight* supervision.

166 *blown* tainted.

171 *upon their omission* because those with authority in the church have failed to do their duty.

173 *with bell . . . candle* i.e. cursed with excommunication.

177–8 *do contribute . . . separation* i.e. increase the disaffection of those who refuse to conform to the Church of England and drive others into the separatist sects.

184 *condensed* given solid form to.

187 *recollection* calling back.

195 *degrades himself* divests himself of all claim to reverence (i.e. by removing the garments which are the only evidence of his priestly calling).

197 *footing* footprints.

200 *harbour* den.

201 *three times* i.e. on pp. 125, 191, 212.

202 *Transproser Rehears'd* by Richard Leigh.

203 *J.M.* i.e. John Milton, the poet and apologist for regicide.

210 *my consequences* i.e. the consequences for me.

212 *Common Places* *A Common-Place-Book Out of the Rehearsal Transpros'd* (1673). (Passages were recorded in commonplace books for future reference.)

222 *his answer to Salmasius* Milton's *First Defence of the English People* (1651), written in reply to Salmasius's defence of Charles I.

228 *flagrante bello* in the heat of war.

books of Divorce Milton's *The Doctrine and Discipline of Divorce* (1643), *The Judgement of Martin Bucer Concerning Divorce* (1644), *Tetrachordon* (1645) and *Colasterion* (1645).

230–1 *that which . . . own father* i.e. John Parker's *The Government of the People of England* (1650), written in support of the oath of engagement to the Commonwealth.

235 *his High . . . Justice* John Parker was a judge who prospered under Cromwell.

239 *his house* Milton lived in Jewin Street near Moorfields from 1661 to 1664.

244 *astrologizing upon* calculating.

249 *Scaramuccios* a topical allusion to the visit of an Italian troupe to London in 1673, led by Tiberio Fiorilli, who adopted the name of his principal characterization, Scaramouche', the boastful poltroon of the *commedia dell'arte*.

Marvell is referring to the other writers who sided with Parker in attacking the first part of *The Rehearsal Transpros'd*.

250 *a school-master* Milton ran a small private academy during the 1640s.

259 *trepan* ensnare.

HIS MAJESTY'S MOST GRACIOUS SPEECH TO BOTH HOUSES OF PARLIAMENT

This parody of the speech with which Charles II opened the thirteenth session of the Cavalier Parliament on 13 April 1675 exists in variant forms in a number of contemporary manuscripts. It was first attributed to Marvell in Part 3 of the 1704 edition of *Poems on Affairs of State* and from there was reprinted by Cooke and then by Thompson. The present text is based on the version in Cooke's edition. Another version, from British Library MS Add. 34362, is reprinted in M. C. Bradbrook and M. G. Lloyd Thomas, *Andrew Marvell* (Cambridge, Cambridge University Press, 1961), pp. 125–7.

Marvell sent a straightforward account of the king's actual speech and its reception in a letter to the Hull Corporation (reprinted on pp. 177–8). A shortened version of what Charles said can be found in Arthur Bryant's *Letters, Speeches and Declarations of King Charles II* (London, Cassell, 1935), pp. 280–1.

2 *our last meeting* Charles II had prorogued the previous session of Parliament on 24 February 1674.

3 *my Lord Treasurer* Thomas Osborne, Earl of Danby, Charles's leading minister.

4–5 *subsidies* Charles was financially dependent on grants of money voted by Parliament.

18 *reformado* a military term, referring to officers who had not yet been appointed to a company in the army, but were waiting for vacancies at their respective ranks.

22–3 *next year's . . . swaddling-clothes* Charles II had a large number of illegitimate children.

23–4 *What . . . ships, then?* Charles had summoned Parliament chiefly to ask for a supply for a much needed naval building programme.

25–6 *I lived . . . without* i.e. between 1651 and 1660, when he was in exile.

37–8 *do those things . . . liberty* Charles had actually spoken of 'what you think may be yet wanting to the securing of religion and property' (Bryant, *Letters . . . of Charles II*). Marvell's addition of the pronoun – '*your* religion' – implies that Charles, who was suspected of being a secret Roman Catholic, dissociates himself from the Church of England.

41–2 *lie at your doors* be your own responsibility.

45 *my proclamation* i.e. against Roman Catholics and Dissenters.

56 *my Lord Lauderdale* John Maitland, Earl of Lauderdale, the High Commissioner for Scotland.

60 *natural* illegitimate.

63 *George* Born in 1665, George was the third and youngest of Charles II's sons by the Duchess of Cleveland. He was made Earl of Northumberland in 1674.

68 *Carwel* i.e. Louise de Kéroualle, who had become Charles II's mistress in 1670.

69 *her sister* Henriette de Kéroualle, married to Philip Herbert, seventh Earl of Pembroke, on 17 December 1674.

70 *my Lord Inchiquin* William O'Brien, second Earl of Inchiquin, succeeded to the title on his father's death in September 1674 and became a member of the Privy Council. Early in 1674 he had been appointed Captain-General of His Majesty's forces in Africa and Governor of the royal citadel of Tangier.

Barbary countries along the north coast of Africa.

72 *Crewe* Nathaniel Crew, Bishop of Oxford, solemnized the marriage between Charles II's brother, James, Duke of York, and the Catholic princess, Mary of Modena, in 1673, and in 1674 he was made Bishop of Durham.

74 *Prideaux* a mistake for Ralph Brideoak, appointed Chaplain to the King in 1660, Dean of Salisbury in 1667 and

Bishop of Chichester in March 1675.

78 *My behaviour . . . bankers* The Exchequer had been closed, preventing repayment of loans made to the state, in December 1674.

79 *proceedings . . . Sutton* an allusion to a scandal involving the Lord Treasurer, which Marvell reported in letters to the Hull Corporation on 24 and 29 April 1675. Bridget Hyde, the 12-year-old stepdaughter of Sir Robert Viner, had been secretly married to one Mr Emerton while Danby was negotiating a match between her and his son, Lord Dunblane. Danby was subsequently accused of putting pressure on the clergyman in the case to deny that he had officiated at the clandestine marriage.

MR SMIRKE; OR, THE DIVINE IN MODE

Mr Smirke; Or, the Divine in Mode appeared in 1676 with the name Andreus Rivetus, Junior, on the title-page. It was occasioned by Francis Turner's *Animadversions Upon a Late Pamphlet Intituled The Naked Truth*, which had been published earlier in the same year. Turner's purpose was to ridicule the spirit of reconciliation and moderate reform in the appeal made to the Lords and Commons by Herbert Croft, Bishop of Hereford, in *The Naked Truth. Or, the True State of the Primitive Church*. Croft's work, like Turner's, had been printed anonymously.

The title of Marvell's pamphlet in defence of the author of *The Naked Truth* is an allusion to a popular comedy of the day, *The Man of Mode* by George Etherege. Repeating the satiric device of *The Rehearsal Transpros'd*, he likens his opponent to a minor character in the play, one Mr Smirke, chaplain to Lady Biggot.

4 *divertisement* amusement.

10 *their own Faculty* i.e. Divinity.

13 *pregnant* quick-witted, promising.

18 *discussed* driven away, dispersed.

25 *complexion* temperament.

29 *arcanum* profound secret.

38–9 *of apostolical right* deriving authority by direct descent from the Apostles.

42 *complacency for* satisfaction with.

50 *stick* hesitate, scruple.

57 *effluvium* exhalation.

58 *residentiary* a canon living in a cathedral close.

60 *dubbing or creating of wits* on the analogy of conferring knighthood.

66 *collating* bestowing.

71 *exquisite* careful.

74 *droll* buffoon.

76–7 *omne . . . spirituale* each and every aspect of his nature, as much temporal as spiritual.

83 *Visitation* visit of inspection by a bishop.

87 *ingenious* talented.

89–90 *do the greatest execution* have the greatest effect.

94 *uncanonical* ill-suited to the clergy.

98 *Gazette* official government journal.

101 *The Naked Truth* See head-note.

103 *evidence . . . Spirit* i.e. it bears the marks of holy inspiration.

122–3 *a true son . . . England* a faithful member of the laity, if not himself a priest, of the established church.

126 *the Animadverter* i.e. Francis Turner.

129 *our mother of England* i.e. the Anglican church.

131 *itinerated* travelled from place to place.

132 *the morning . . . chaplains* clergymen retained by households to say morning and evening prayers.

134 *whoever he were* Marvell claims to be ignorant of the anonymous author's identity.

142–3 *Shrove Tuesday . . . cock* One of the traditional sports of Shrove Tuesday, the apprentices' holiday, was to pelt a cock with stones.

144 *coffee-farthings* tokens issued by the coffee shops.

145 *Easter-pence* parishioners' Easter offering to their parson.

146 *close* secretive.

147 *Preferment* promotion.

149 *sufficiency* capacity or qualification.
161–2 *sum himself up* bring himself to perfection.
162 *the whole . . . function* all his ecclesiastical finery.
165 *fluster* pomp.
166 *out-boniface* a nonce-word, probably implying both out-face and outdo in splendour.
167 *Moderator* a minister in the Presbyterian church. Croft had styled himself 'an humble moderator' in *The Naked Truth*.
168 *Dorimant* a fashionable rake in Etherege's *The Man of Mode*.
169 *Sir Fopling Flutter* a fop in the same play.
170 *tiring-room* dressing-room of a theatre.
173–4 *the first . . . concerned* because on the first day his play might be damned and on the third day he shared in the profits.
174–5 *like men . . . purpose* Audiences were often packed in order to secure the success of a new play.

AN ACCOUNT OF THE GROWTH OF POPERY, AND ARBITRARY GOVERNMENT IN ENGLAND

This tract was first published anonymously towards the end of 1677. A folio edition, with Marvell's name on the title-page, appeared after his death in 1678.

Unlike Marvell's other prose works, it is not satirical in method, but sets out the political history of the previous decade and particularly of the fifteenth session of the Cavalier Parliament which opened on 15 February 1677. It reflects the growing concern of the Country party at the ineffectiveness of a Parliament grown complacent and corrupt over the years since it had been elected in 1661 and at the influence of the French king, Louis XIV, which is traced to a long-standing conspiracy of crypto-Catholics to undermine the political and religious freedoms of the English people.

9 *address* skill, adroitness.
20 *propriety* individuality.
24 *prerogative* sovereign right.

25 *Broad Seal* the stamp used to authenticate documents issued in the name of the sovereign.

27 *particular* personal, as distinct from official.

37 *inviolable* to be kept from assault.

44 *competence* adequate income.

47 *pretended* presented, claimed.

60 *abridged* debarred.

77 *tenures* conditions.

88 *commonwealth* republic.

96 *incapacity* legal disqualification from holding office.

98 *incapable* i.e. disqualified under the Acts of Parliament referred to in the previous sentence.

101 *penal* punishable.

104 *Cavaliers* i.e. supporters of Charles I.

107 *balsam* healing ointment.

108 *weapon-salve* magical remedy for wounds.

109–10 *this Long Parliament also* Marvell mischievously compares the current Parliament, which had been elected in 1661, with the Long Parliament of the 1640s which defeated Charles I in the Civil Wars.

116 *impression* belief.

129–30 *under . . . Protestants* an allusion to the belief that there were crypto-Catholics in high places.

134–5 *passages* events.

146 *redundant* plentiful.
deduce trace the course of.

149 *fourth act* i.e. just before the catastrophe or dénouement of the fifth and final act of the drama.

156 *draw . . . deeper* encourage him to bet more heavily.

158–9 *sweep the table* win wholesale.

160 *the relator* i.e. the author of the present work.

161 *heads* points, topics.

173 *woodman* huntsman.

183 *discharges . . . ministers* transfers culpability from the sovereign to his advisers.

186 *entitle . . . crimes* involve him in the responsibility for their crimes.

189 *objecting* exposing.

202 *healing touch* an allusion to the belief that scrofula could be cured by the touch of the monarch, a practice continued until the eighteenth century.

205 *Caesar's wife* an allusion to the saying that Caesar's wife must be above suspicion.

207 *our . . . devotions* i.e. in the Book of Common Prayer.

207–8 *From all . . . deliver us* a quotation from the Litany, from which Marvell pointedly omits, among others, the words 'and rebellion'.

FOR HIS EXCELLENCY, THE LORD GENERAL CROMWELL

This letter was first printed in volume 7 of *A General Dictionary, Historical and Critical* (1738) and reprinted in the preface to Thompson's edition.

5–6 *the work . . . about* i.e. as tutor to William Dutton.

9 *Mr Dutton* Marvell's pupil, son and heir of Sir Ralph Dutton of Gloucestershire, who had died in 1646. His legal guardian was John Dutton of Sherborne, a personal friend of Cromwell.

10 *Oxenbridge* John Oxenbridge, Fellow of Eton College, with whom Marvell and Dutton lodged.

10–11 *tell over* count.

19 *waxen* i.e. upon which an impression may be made, as on wax.

33 *Mrs Oxenbridge* formerly Jane Butler. Marvell wrote a Latin epitaph for her in 1658.

TO WILLIAM POPPLE

This letter was first printed in Cooke's edition. William Popple was the son of Marvell's second sister, Mary, and Edmund Popple, a Hull merchant. William, Marvell's favourite nephew and himself a merchant, had recently settled in Bordeaux.

5 *Mr Nelthorpe* a banker distantly related to Marvell.

8 *Lauderdale* the High Commiss[illegible]land, one of Charles II's chief ministers.

12 *Duke of York* i.e. the king's brother, later James II.

16 *be covered* put their hats on (which they had removed as a mark of respect).

23 *Conventicle Bill* a bill to renew the Conventicles Act, 1664, which made religious meetings of Nonconformists illegal.

24 *the Lord Ross's* a bill to enable Lord Ross to marry again after obtaining a divorce. Its significance becomes clear later in the reported rumours about a possible replacement for Charles II's queen. Marvell refers to the bill in a letter to the Hull Corporation on 26 March 1670.

27 *weigh up* turn the scales against.

38 *voices* votes.

43 *the Conquest* i.e. the Norman Conquest, regarded by opponents of royal power as the event which deprived Englishmen of their liberty.

48 *this Interval* the parliamentary session had ended on 11 April.

50 *Cabal* secret council, applied in Charles II's reign to a small group of influential ministers originally consisting of *C*lifford, *A*rlington, *B*uckingham, *A*shley and *L*auderdale.

Buckingham George Villiers, second Duke of Buckingham, husband of Mary Fairfax.

Lauderdale John Maitland, first Duke of Lauderdale.

51 *Ashley* Anthony Ashley Cooper, first Earl of Shaftesbury, a strong supporter of the Ross Bill.

Orrery Roger Boyle, first Earl of Orrery.

Trevor Sir John Trevor, appointed a secretary of state in 1668.

the other Cabal i.e. the king's sister and others involved in the 'family counsels'.

52 *Madame . . . sister* Henrietta, Charles's youngest and favourite sister, wife to the Duke of Orléans, younger brother of Louis XIV. She was in England from 24 May to 12 June as intermediary between the French and English kings in negotiating the secret Treaty of Dover.

53 *King of France* Louis XIV.

58–9 *he knew not . . . barrenness* Charles's queen, Catherine of Braganza, bore him no children, but he did not in the event divorce her.

59 *Lord Barclay* i.e. George Berkeley, ninth baron of Berkeley, one of the Commissioners deputed to proceed to the Hague and invite Charles II to return in 1660.

60 *Newmarket* a favourite haunt of Charles II, where he retired to enjoy the horseracing.

TO MAYOR HOARE

This letter, from the collection preserved at the Guildhall, Hull, was first printed by Thompson. It is one of the regular reports which Marvell sent to the Mayor and Aldermen of the city which he represented as MP and contains a factual account of the occasion which he burlesqued in 'His Majesty's most gracious speech to both Houses of Parliament' (reprinted on pp. 160–3). Daniel Hoare was Mayor of Hull, 1674–5.

11 *signalized* distinguished.

19 *Keeper* Lord Keeper of the Great Seal, who presided over debates in the House of Lords.

33–4 *proportionable* correspondingly agreeable.

TO WILLIAM POPPLE

First printed in Cooke's edition, this is the last surviving letter of Marvell to his nephew.

3 *their oppressions* an allusion to the persecution of dissenting Presbyterians in Scotland during 1677–8.

5 *field conventicles* meetings for prayer and preaching held on the open hillsides.

8 *a large book* Marvell is referring impishly to his own *Account of the Growth of Popery, and Arbitrary Government in England*, published anonymously in 1677.